Rediscovering Institutions

The Organizational Basis of Politics

JAMES G. MARCH
JOHAN P. OLSEN

THE FREE PRESS

THE FREE PRESS
A Division of Simon & Schuster Inc.
1230 Avenue of the Americas
New York, NY 10020

Manufactured in the United States of America

10 9 8 7 6 5

Library of Congress Cataloging-in-Publication Data

March, James G.
    Rediscovering institutions : the organizational basis of politics /
James G. March, Johan P. Olsen.
      p.   cm.
    ISBN 0-02-920115-2
    1. Political science   2. Organization.   3. State, the.   4. Public
institutions.   I. Olsen, Johan P.   II. Title.
    JC249.M37   1989
    320—dc20   89-11639
                                         CIP

Contents

v

Acknowledgments

The research on which this book has been based was supported in part by the Spencer Foundation, the Norwegian Research Council for Science and the Humanities, the Norwegian Research Council for Applied Social Science, the Swedish Project on Power and Democracy, the Mellon Foundation, Norwegian Research Center in Organization and Management, the Stanford Graduate School of Business, the Stanford Hoover Institution, the Stanford Center for Organizations Research, and the Scandinavian Consortium for Organizational Research.

We are grateful to several publishers and professional journals for permission to base some sections of the present book on previously published articles. Chapters 5, 7, and 8 are revised versions of papers that appeared earlier (March and Olsen, 1983; 1986b; March, 1988c). The first part of Chapter 1 builds on another earlier paper (March and Olsen, 1984). We have drawn to a lesser degree from a number of other publications and have profited from comments made on a preliminary draft by Erik Eriksen, Helge Larsen, and Per Selle.

Barbara Beuche supervised the preparation of the manuscript and should receive primary credit for it.

Our wives, Jayne Dohr March and Helene Olsen, have contributed more than we know or they would admit. By persistent reminders of important things, they have confounded our collaboration with the pleasures of life.

James G. March
Johan P. Olsen

1

Institutional Perspectives on Politics

In most contemporary theories of politics, traditional political institutions, such as the legislature, the legal system, and the state, as well as traditional economic institutions, such as the firm, have receded in importance from the position they held in earlier theories of political scientists such as J. W. Burgess or W. W. Willoughby, economists such as Thorstein Veblen or John R. Commons, and sociologists such as Max Weber. From a behavioral point of view, formally organized political institutions have come to be portrayed simply as arenas within which political behavior, driven by more fundamental factors, occurs. From a normative point of view, ideas that embedded morality in institutions, such as law or bureaucracy, and that emphasized citizenship and community as foundations for political identity, have given way to ideas of moral individualism and an emphasis on bargaining among conflicting interests.

In recent years, however, institutional perspectives have reappeared in political science. They reflect an empirically based prejudice, an assertion that what we observe in the world is inconsistent with the ways in which contemporary theories ask us to think, that the organization of political life makes a difference. This resurgence of concern with institutions is a cumulative consequence of the modern transformation of social institutions and persistent commentary from their observers. Social, political, and economic institutions have become larger, considerably more complex and resourceful, and prima facie more important to collective life. Many of the major actors in modern economic and political systems are formal organizations, and the institutions of law and bureaucracy occupy a dominant role in contemporary life.

Attention to political institutions has increased in the literature on politics, in particular in studies of legislatures (Shepsle and Weingast, 1983; 1987a; 1987b), local government (Kjellberg, 1975), public law (Smith, 1988), political economy (Kiser and Ostrom, 1982), political culture (Wildavsky, 1987), budgets (Padgett, 1981), public policy making (Ashford, 1978; Scharpf, 1977b), rational choice (Ferejohn, 1987), and political elites (Robins, 1976). It is manifest in studies of the origin of the state (Wright, 1977), the development of national administrative capacity (Skowronek, 1982), the nation-state's relation to a world polity (Thomas et al., 1987), and the development of the welfare state (Ashford, 1986), as well as in analyses of the breakdown of democratic regimes (Potter, 1979), and in discussions of corporatism (Schmitter and Lehmbruch, 1979; Berger, 1981; Olsen, 1981). It is reflected in the Marxist rediscovery of the state as a problem in political economy (Jessop, 1977) and of the importance of organizational factors for understanding that role (Therborn, 1980). It is present in studies of formal organizations (Scott, 1987a; Zucker, 1987), including those of the place of such organizations in the implementation of public policy (Hanf and Scharpf, 1978). It is visible in attempts to link the study of the state to natural science (Masters, 1983) and to the humanities (Geertz, 1980), as well as in historical-comparative studies of the state (Hayward and Berki, 1979; Evans, Rueschemeyer, and Skocpol, 1985; Krasner 1984; 1988).

Renewed interest in institutions is not peculiar to political science. It is characteristic of recent trends in public law (Smith, 1988) and in economics, which has discovered law, contracts, hierarchies, professional codes, and social norms (Williamson, 1975; 1985; Furubotn and Richter, 1984; Akerlof, 1980). It is also seen in sociology (Meyer and Rowan, 1977; DiMaggio and Powell, 1983; Meyer and Scott, 1983; Thomas et al., 1987), although noninstitutionalist visions never succeeded in that field to the extent that they did in political science and economics. Cycles in ideas have brought us back to considerations that typified earlier forms of theory. The new and the old are not identical, however. It would probably be more accurate to describe recent thinking as blending elements of an old institutionalism into the noninstitutionalist styles of recent theories of politics.

STYLES OF CONTEMPORARY THEORIES OF POLITICS

Although the concept of institution never disappeared from theoretical political science, it has been largely supplanted in recent years by a conception of political life that is noninstitutional. The vision that has characterized theories of politics since about 1950 is (1) contextual, inclined to see politics as an integral part of society, less inclined to differentiate the polity from the rest of society; (2) reductionist, inclined to see political phenomena as the aggregate consequences of individual behavior, less inclined to ascribe the outcomes of politics to organizational structures and rules of appropriate behavior; (3) utilitarian, inclined to see action as stemming from calculated self-interest, less inclined to see action as a response to obligations and duties; (4) instrumentalist, inclined to define decision making and the allocation of resources as the central concerns of political life, less attentive to the ways in which political life is organized around the development of meaning through symbols, rituals, and ceremonies; and (5) functionalist, inclined to see history as an efficient mechanism for reaching uniquely appropriate equilibria, and less concerned with the possibilities for maladaptation and nonuniqueness in historical development.

Politics as Subordinate to Exogenous Forces: Contextualism

Historically, political scientists and political philosophers have tended to treat political institutions, particularly the state, as independent factors, important to the ordering and understanding of collective life (Heller, 1933). Modern political scientists, with few exceptions, do not. The state has lost its position of centrality in the discipline; interest in comprehensive forms of political organization has declined; political events are defined more as epiphenomena than as actions necessary to an understanding of society; politics mirrors its context (Easton, 1968).

The most conspicuously cited contextual factor cited is the social class structure (Dahrendorf, 1959). The social stratification of a modern society with its associated distribution of wealth and income has obvious major effects on political events. Class differences translate into political differences with great reliability across time and across cultures; differences in the organization and ideology of social class seem to lead to predictable differences in political organization and institutions (Tilly, 1978). Other analyses at the same level of aggregation make the structure and process of politics a function of physical environment, geography, and climate; of ethnicity, language, and culture; of economic conditions and development; or of demography, technology, ideology, or religion. Plausible arguments which make political life a derivative of one or more of these broad contextual forces have been developed, and it is not hard to find empirical data to support the arguments. Although there are a number of relatively precise contextual theories, the major theoretical significance of these ideas from the present point of view is less the specific forms of the theories than their general inclination to see the causal links between society and polity as running from the former to the latter, rather than the other way around. It is assumed that class, geography, climate, ethnicity, language, culture, economic conditions, demography, technology, ideology, and religion all affect politics but are not significantly affected by politics.

The Macro Consequences of Micro Behavior: Reductionism

Historically, political theory has treated political institutions as determining, ordering, or modifying individual motives, and as acting autonomously in terms of institutional interests. In contrast, substantial elements of modern theoretical work in political science assume that political phenomena are best understood as the aggregate consequences of behavior comprehensible at the individual or group level.

Such theories depend on two presumptions. The first presumption is that a polity consists of a number (often a large number) of elementary actors or events. Human behavior at the level of these elementary actors or events may be seen as conscious, calculated, and flexible, or as unconscious, habitual, and rigid. In either case, the preferences and powers of the actors are exogenous to the polity, depending on their positions in the social and economic system. The timing of events is exogenous, depending on external flows of problems and solutions. The second presumption is that collective behavior is best understood as stemming from the (possibly intricate) interweaving of behavior understandable at a lower level of aggregation. Discovering, or deducing, the collective consequences may be difficult, even impossible; but the central faith is that outcomes at the collective level depend only on the intricacies of the interactions among the individual actors or events, that concepts suggesting autonomous behavior at the aggregate level are certainly superfluous and probably deleterious.

Within such a perspective, for example, the behavior of an organization is the consequence of the interlocking choices by individuals and subunits, each acting in terms of expectations and preferences manifested at those levels (Niskanen, 1971). The behavior of a market is the consequence of the interlocking choices by individuals and firms, each acting in terms of a set of expectations and preferences manifested at those levels (Stigler, 1952). It is not necessary that the micro processes involve choice, of course. Aggregate behavior in a group can be defined as the consequence of the interlocking of trial-and-error learning occurring at the individual

4

level (Lave and March, 1975). Or the aggregate behavior of an industry can be defined as the consequence of the interlocking of standard operating procedures and accounting rules followed at the level of the individual firm, and of death and growth rates of those firms (Nelson and Winter, 1982). Or aggregate behavior in a decision process can be seen as the merging of independent flows of problems, solutions, decision makers, and choice opportunities (Cohen, March, and Olsen, 1972).

As is clear from the last example, there is nothing intrinsic to a perspective that emphasizes the macro consequences of micro actions which requires that the elementary units be individuals. All that is required is that the behavior of a more comprehensive system be decomposable to elementary behaviors explicable at a less comprehensive level. In practice, however, in most of the social sciences, the actions of individual human beings are considered to determine the flow of events in a larger social system. Outcomes at the system level are thought to be determined by the interactions of individuals acting consistently in terms of the axioms of individual behavior, whatever they may be. Thus, we make assumptions about individual consumers to understand markets, about voters to understand politics, and about bureaucrats to understand bureaucracies.

Action as the Making of Calculated Decisions: Utilitarianism

Historically, political science has emphasized the ways in which political behavior was embedded in an institutional structure of rules, norms, expectations, and traditions that severely limited the free play of individual will and calculation (Wolin, 1960). In contrast, modern political science has, for the most part, described political events as the consequence of calculated decisions. Not just in political science, but throughout modern theoretical work in the social sciences, the preeminent vision of human behavior is a vision of choice. Life is characterized as deliberate decision making.

The details of the choice metaphor vary from one treatment to another, but the characteristic form is one that assumes choices stem from two guesses about the future. The first is a guess about the uncertain future consequences of possible current action. Decision theorists recognize that human limitations may restrict the precision of the estimates, that the estimates may be biased, and that the information on which the estimates are based may be costly; but information about probable consequences is assumed to be important to a choice (Savage, 1954; Lindley, 1973). From this assumption comes an emphasis on the power of information and expertise (Crozier, 1964) and the importance of reliable and unbiased information sources (Nisbet and Ross, 1980). Although numerous psychological experiments have indicated that the guesses of human subjects are biased (Kahneman, Slovic, and Tversky, 1982; Schoemaker, 1982), it has not been easy to formulate alternatives to the simple notion that the guesses of experienced humans are, on average, accurate. As a result, most theories of choice present decisions as being, on average, sensible. In their political versions, choice theories assume that, on average, voters vote intelligently with respect to their interests; legislators organize sensible coalitions, given their interests; and nation-states voluntarily enter alliances that, on average, improve their positions.

The second guess on which intentional, anticipatory choice is based is a guess about a decision maker's uncertain future preferences for possible future outcomes. In any theory of deliberate choice, action depends on the decision maker's values. Since the consequences of interest are to be realized in the future, it is necessary to anticipate not only what will happen but how the decision maker will feel about those outcomes when they are experienced (March, 1978). The complexities of the second guess are largely ignored by theories of choice. In their standard forms, the theories assume that preferences are stable, thus that current preferences are good predictors of future preferences; that preferences are unambiguous and consistent, thus that a choice will be clearly indicated, given the first guess; and that preferences are exogenous, thus that whatever process generates preferences it precedes choice and is independent of the choice process. In one of the best-developed forms of choice theories, these assumptions about preferences are taken as axioms, and preferences are discovered not by asking decision makers to report them but by defining a "revealed preference" function that satisfies the axioms and is consistent with choices made by a decision maker (Luce and Raiffa, 1957). Although the empirical existence of consistent revealed preferences has been the subject of considerable debate (Becker and Stigler, 1977; Kahneman, Slovic, and Tversky, 1982), the theoretical idea forms the basis of extensive analytical development and empirical exploration.

The Primacy of Outcomes: Instrumentalism

Historically, theories of political institutions portrayed political decision making primarily as a process for developing a sense of purpose, direction, identity, and belonging. Politics was a vehicle for educating citizens and improving cultural values. Although there are exceptions, the modern perspective in political science has generally given primacy to outcomes and either ignored symbolic actions or seen symbols as part of manipulative efforts to control outcomes, rather than the other way around.

Modern polities are as replete with symbols, ritual, ceremony, and myth as the societies more familiar to anthropological tradition. Politicians announce public support for positions they fail to defend in private (Edelman, 1964). Legislators vote for legislation while remaining indifferent to its implementation (Pressman and Wildavsky, 1973). Administrators solicit public participation in decision making in order to secure public support for policies to which they are already committed. Chief executives advocate reorganization of the public bureaucracy, announce plans for making reorganizations, and regularly abandon the plans (see Chapter 5). Information is gathered, policy alternatives are defined, and cost-benefit analyses are pursued, but they seem more intended to reassure observers of the appropriateness of actions being taken than to influence the actions (Feldman and March, 1981).

In modern discussions of politics, these symbolic actions are characteristically portrayed as strategic moves by self-conscious political actors. Rituals and ceremonies are defined as window dressing for the real political processes, or as instruments by which the clever and the powerful exploit the naive and the weak. The hiring of experts lends legitimacy to policies (Meyer and Rowan, 1977); associating unpopular moves with popular symbols is reassuring (Edelman, 1964). Control over symbols is a basis of power, like control over other resources (Pfeffer, 1981a); and the use of symbols is part of a struggle over political outcomes (Cohen, 1974).

The Efficiency of History: Functionalism

Historically, political theory has been ambivalent about the efficiency of history. Like other social scientists, students of political development have been inclined to accept an idea of progress, the more or less inexorable historical movement toward some more "advanced" level. At the same time, political histories have often emphasized the unique significance of a particular sequence of events or choices, the impact of a particular campaign strategy or speech, or the particular tactics of international negotiation. In modern usage, the terminology of progress has been largely replaced by a terminology of survival, but for the most part, in contemporary theoretical political science, institutions and behavior are thought to evolve through some form of efficient historical process.

7

An efficient historical process, in these terms, is one that moves rapidly to a unique solution, conditional on current environmental conditions, and is thus independent of the historical path. The equilibrium may involve a stochastically stable distribution or a fixed point, but we require a solution that is achieved relatively rapidly and is independent of the details of historical events leading to it. The assumption of historical efficiency is a standard, although usually not explicit, assumption of much of modern social science. Economic theories of markets and ecological theories of competition, for example, are concerned with the characteristics of an equilibrium, if one exists. They are used to predict differences (e.g., in markets, organizational structures, populations, technologies) that will be observed, at equilibrium, in different environments. It is no accident that the most common principle of theories in the social sciences is the optimization principle, and that one of the greatest concerns in such theories is showing that a process has a unique optimum that is guaranteed to be achieved.

Similarly, some postwar theories of political parties see party orientation and organization as equilibrium solutions to problems of survival in a competitive political environment (Downs, 1957; Ordeshook, 1986). The assumption of historical efficiency makes such theories largely indifferent to the behavioral reality of the micro processes that are assumed. For example, competition can be assumed to eliminate action that is inconsistent with the logic of survival. Examples include theories of market equilibria, such as those found in recent ideas of efficient capital markets (Sharpe, 1970); theories of organizational structure, such as those found in recent ideas of industrial organization (Williamson, 1975); and theories of political parties, such as those found in ideas of political economy (Olson, 1965).

DISCOVERING ORDER IN AN INSTITUTION-FREE WORLD

The remainder of this book considers how styles of theories of politics that focus on institutions differ from the styles described above. Before proceeding to that topic, however, we examine briefly two examples of theories that portray politics as contextual and reductionist: theories that focus on the competitive interaction of rational actors and theories that focus on the temporal sorting of problems, solutions, decision makers, and choices. Although the two examples differ in other respects, they are both initially reductionist and contextual in style. That is, they imagine that the key attributes of a macro system are understandable as the consequence of the confluence of a large number of simple micro events within an exogenously determined social context. These theories are powerful contributors to our understanding of politics and should be seen as necessary correlates of the perspective that is offered in this book.

Politics as Rational Competition

Classical theories of competitive conflict in economic affairs assume that markets (particularly labor, capital, and product markets) mediate among conflicting demands through prices. Within any particular economic institution, entrepreneurs are imagined to impose their goals on other participants in exchange for mutually satisfactory wages paid to workers, rent paid to capital, and product quality paid to consumers. The behavior of a market is assumed to be understandable as a consequence of these individual actors making choices that, in aggregate, fit together into market phenomena.

The process can be treated as yielding a series of contracts by which participants confirm and regulate exchange. Decision making occurs in two stages. At the first stage, each individual negotiates the best possible terms for agreeing to pursue another's preferences, or for securing such an agreement from another. In the second stage, individuals execute the contracts. In more sophisticated versions, of course, the contracts are designed so that the terms negotiated at the first stage are self-enforcing at the second. The best developed version of contract theories of rational competitive conflict is found in n-person game theory (Ordeshook, 1986). These models assume that the outcomes depend on the rules of the game, including norms about trust, and those rules are sometimes portrayed as resulting from some kind of metagame; but interest in the constraints is typically subordinated to an interest in the equilibrium consequences of rational negotiation and action among the players, including the consequences of sequential games, and to the design of contracts to manage agreements (Shepsle and Weingast, 1987a; 1987b).

In political treatments of competitive conflict that are not heavily influenced by game theory and economics, the emphasis is less on designing a system of contracts between principals and agents, or partners, than it is on understanding a political process that allows decisions to be made without necessarily resolving conflict among the parties (Dahl, 1982). The core ideas are that individuals enter a political process with preferences and resources, and that each individual uses personal resources to pursue personal gain measured in terms of personal preferences. The

9

metaphors are those common to the literature of politics. There is a metaphor of combat. Disputes are settled by "force," that is, by reference to some measurable property by which individuals can be scaled. Collective decisions are weighted averages of individual desires, where the weights reflect the power distribution among individuals (Dahl, 1957; Nagel, 1975). There is a metaphor of exchange. Disputes are settled by offering or withholding resources and establishing a mutually acceptable structure of prices (Coleman, 1986). Markets facilitate cross-sector trading (e.g., bribery, blackmail) and encourage pursuit of resources with high exchange value (e.g., the taking of hostages). There is a metaphor of alliance. Disputes are settled by forming teams through exchange agreements and side payments and then engaging in combat regulated by rules (Harsanyi, 1977). Outcomes are (mostly) clear once the coalition structure is given, but this structure is problematic.

In a competitive system, information is an instrument of strategic actors (Akerlof, 1970; Demski, 1980). Information may be true or false; it is always serving a purpose. Actors may provide accurate information about their preferences; normally they will not, except as a possible tactic. They may provide accurate information about the consequences of possible alternative decisions; normally they will not, except as a possible tactic. As a result, information is itself a game. Except insofar as the structure of the game dictates honesty as a necessary tactic, all information is self-serving. Meaning is imputed to messages on the basis of theories of intention that are themselves subject to strategic manipulation. The result is a complicated concatenation of maneuver involving anticipated, as well as actual, action (Friedrich, 1937; Dahl, 1957; Krehbiel, 1987; Shepsle and Weingast, 1987b).

Alliances are formed and broken. They represent the heart of many political visions of choice, yet the real world of alliances is unlikely to be as simple as the world of the metaphor. Political alliances involve trades across time in the form of promises and implicit promises. Rarely can the terms of trade be specified with precision. Future occasions requiring coordinated action are unknown, as are the future sentiments with which individuals will confront them. It is often not a world of precise contracts, but one of informal loose understandings and expectations (Friedrich, 1937; Schelling, 1960).

Both economic and political perspectives on competitive conflict emphasize the problems of using self-interested individuals as agents for other self-interested individuals. It is a set of problems familiar to studies of legislators, lawyers, and bureaucrats (Eisenstadt, 1958; Dahl and Lindblom, 1953; Jacobsen, 1964). If we assume that agents act in their own self-interest, then ensuring that the self-interest of agents coincides with the self-interest of principals becomes a central concern. This has led to extensive discussions of incentive and contractual schemes designed to assure such a coincidence, and to the development of theories of agency (Ross, 1973; Fama, 1980; Moe, 1984; Levinthal, 1988). It is clear, however, that principals are not always successful in assuring the reliability of agents. Agents can be bribed or co-opted. As a result, politics often emphasizes trust and loyalty, in parallel with a widespread belief that they are hard to find (Friedrich, 1940; Finer, 1941; Hirschman, 1970). The temptations to revise contracts unilaterally are frequently substantial, and promises of uncertain future support are easily made worthless in the absence of some network of reciprocal favors.

Such complications lead to problems in controlling the implementation of decisions (Pressman and Wildavsky, 1973; Bardach, 1977). Decisions unfold through a series of interrelated actions. If all conflicts of interest were settled by the employment contract, the unfolding would present only problems of information and coordination, but such problems are confounded by the complications of unresolved conflict (Baier, March, and Sætren, 1986). For example, one complication in control is that any system of controls involves a system of accounts, and any system of accounts is a roadmap to cheating on them. As a result, control systems can be seen as an infinite game between controllers and the controlled in which advantage lies with relatively full-time players having direct personal interest in the outcomes.

Politics as Temporal Sorting

Ideas of temporal sorting are attempts to comprehend the relatively confusing picture of collective decision making drawn from empirical observations. Many things seem to be happening at once; technologies are changing and poorly understood; alliances, preferences, and perceptions are changing; solutions, opportunities, ideas, people, and outcomes are mixed together in ways that make interpretation uncertain and leave connections unclear (Kingdon, 1984). It has been observed that individuals fight for the right to participate in decision making and then do not exercise that right with any vigor (Olsen, 1976a). Decision makers ignore information they have, ask for more information, and then ignore the new information when it is available (Feldman and March, 1981; March and Sevón, 1984). Organizations buffer processes of thought and decision from processes of action (March, 1980; Brunsson, 1982; 1989). Managers spend substantial amounts of time in activities that appear to have few

11

consequences beyond acknowledging the importance of others, as well as themselves (Cohen and March, 1986). Minor issues create governmental crises and unexpected patterns of political activation, then fade away again (Olsen, 1983: Chapter 3). Participants contend acrimoniously over the adoption of a policy, but once that policy is adopted the same contenders appear to be largely indifferent to its implementation, or the lack of it (Christensen, 1976; Baier, March, and Sætren, 1982; Sætren, 1983).

The apparent disorderliness of many things in decision making has led some people ·to argue that there is very little order to collective choice and that it is best described as bedlam. Since the origin of the confusion may lie in the inadequacy of the theoretical ideas by which we try to order the observed events, rather than in the phenomena themselves (Glassman, 1973: 85; Weick, 1976: 9), a more conservative position is to assume that the ways in which order is imposed on disorder differ somewhat from those anticipated by conventional theories. In most theories of action, we assume things are ordered by their consequential connections. Deviations from consequential order are viewed as aberrations. They are disturbances of a system otherwise held together by the way wanting something leads to doing something connected to the want, and doing something leads to consequences related to the intention.

The central idea of temporal sorting models such as the garbage can is the substitution of a temporal order for a consequential order. In garbage can models (Cohen, March, and Olsen, 1972), for example, we find problems, solutions, decision makers, and choice opportunities coming together as a result of being simultaneously available. The linkages among them are assumed to be understandable as the consequence of the autonomous time-dependent flows of problem, solutions, and decision makers into choice arenas. In a culture with a strong sense of monthly or yearly cycles, or of birth cohorts, we should not be overly surprised by the idea of a decision process affected by timing. In many human situations the most easily identified property of objects or events is the time subscripts associated with them. Thus, students of time allocation in decision making have observed the ways in which attention to problems seems to be determined as much by the time of their arrival as by assessments of their importance (Cohen and March, 1986; Olsen, 1976c).

In pure form, garbage can models assume that problems, solutions, decision makers, and choice opportunities are independent, exogenous streams flowing through a system (Cohen, March, and Olsen, 1972; March and Olsen, 1976; 1986a). A problem is the concern of people inside and outside the system. It might arise over issues of lifestyle; family; frustrations of work; careers; internal group relations; distribution

12

of status, jobs, and money; ideology; or current crises of mankind as interpreted by the mass media or the next-door neighbor. All of these require attention. A solution is somebody's product or idea. A computer is not just a solution to a problem in payroll management, discovered when needed. It is an answer actively looking for a question. Despite the dictum that you cannot find the answer until you have formulated the question well, you often do not know what the public policy question is until you know the answer.

Participants come and go. Since every entrance is an exit somewhere else, the distribution of "entrances" depends on the attributes of the choice being left as much as it does on the attributes of the new choice. Substantial variation in participation stems from other demands on the participants' time (rather than from features of the decision under study). Choice opportunities are occasions when an institution is expected to produce behavior that can be called a decision. Opportunities arise regularly and occasions for choice are declared routinely. Contracts must be signed; people hired, promoted, or fired; money spent; and responsibilities allocated.

Although not completely independent of each other, each of the streams can be viewed as independent and exogenous to the system. Problems, solutions, decision makers, and choice opportunities are linked in a manner determined by their arrival and departure times and any structural constraints on the access of problems, solutions, and decision makers to choice opportunities. In the absence of structural constraints within a garbage can process, solutions are linked to problems, and decision makers to choices, primarily by their simultaneity. As a result, decision making becomes an occasion for exercising problems and solutions more than connecting them, for displaying decision making more than profiting from it, and for exhibiting virtue more than using it.

Most of the attention in the literature has been concentrated on examining the consequences of different rates and patterns of flows in each of the streams and different procedures for relating them (March and Olsen, 1986a). Two varieties of segmentation are reflected in the model. The first is the mapping of choices onto decision makers, the decision structure. The second is the mapping of problems onto choices, the access structure. In the purest garbage can situation we assume that any problem and any decision maker can be attached to any choice. An analysis of garbage can models reveals four major properties of the processes. First, resolution of problems is not the most common style of making decisions. Choices are normally made only when there are no problems attached to them. Second, the process is sensitive to variations in load. When load increases, problems are less likely to be solved, decision makers are likely to shift from one problem to another more frequently, choices are likely to take longer to make and are less likely to resolve problems. Third, there is a tendency for decision makers and problems to track each other through choices. Fourth, the process is frequently sharply interactive. Although some phenomena associated with the garbage can are regular and flow through nearly all of the cases, for example, the effect of overall load, other phenomena are much more dependent on the particular combination of structures involved.

Events within a garbage can decision process are understandable and, in some ways, predictable or even subject to manipulation, but neither the processes nor the outcomes appear to be closely related to the explicit intentions of actors. In situations in which load is heavy and the structure is relatively unsegmented, intention is lost in context-dependent flows of problems, solutions, people, and choice opportunities. Indeed, outcomes are frequently sufficiently dependent on elements of exogenously determined timing as to make the differences between what happens and what does not happen deceptively significant.

Finding Contextual Order in Reductionist Theories

Rational competition models and temporal sorting models are simultaneously models of decision makers and the environments in which they act. The two types of models are built on quite different views of the nature of decision making; but they both see the process in terms of a complex set of interactions among elementary events or actors. In rational competition models, for example, there is a large number of actors, each anticipating, over an indefinitely long future, the actions and reactions of the others. In temporal sorting models the process depends on a complicated mosaic of attention that makes the particular pattern of linkages among problems, solutions, and choice seem quite chaotic from a means-end point of view.

Similarly, empirical observations of polities often stress the complexity of modern polities (Ashford, 1986; Scharpf, 1977a; Offe, 1984; Suleiman, 1987; Held 1987). They identify politics as a rather complicated intertwining of institutions, individuals, and events. There are many institutions, some nested within others, with multiple, overlapping connections (Long, 1958). National political systems fit into international political systems and are composed of numerous subsystems, some of which extend beyond national boundaries (Thomas et al., 1987). The allocation of attention, as found in mobilization and agenda effects, for example, is critical to the flow of events (Kingdon, 1984).

14

Studies of decision processes in formal organizations reveal comparable complexity (Allison, 1971; March, 1988a). Alternatives are not automatically provided to a decision maker; they have to be found. Search for alternatives occurs in a context in which problems are not only looking for solutions, but solutions are looking for problems. Information about the consequences of alternatives is generated and communicated through institutional networks, so expectations depend on the structure or linkages within the system, as well as the ways in which biases and counterbiases cumulate (Simon, 1957a; 1957b). Guesses about future preferences are developed within institutions dedicated to defining and modifying values and the meanings of actions (Cyert and March, 1963; March and Olsen, 1976). The responsiveness of the system to environmental pressure may, at least in the short run, depend on the amount of slack in the system, and on the ways in which accounting numbers are produced and manipulated strategically. The system may not come close to trying to resolve conflict but simply attend sequentially to the demands placed on it (Cyert and March, 1963). Learning may be superstitious, and fallacious rules of inference may persist for long periods (Nisbet and Ross, 1980).

Theories of collective behavior most commonly simplify the potential morass of collective complexity by one of two classic routes. The first is statistical aggregation. In its usual guise, aggregation assumes that the factors affecting outcomes can be divided into two groups, one systematic and the other random. Thus, for example, we might assume that errors in expectations have a normal distribution with mean zero. Or we might assume that in a population of voters there are many factors affecting electoral choice. Some of those factors (e.g., income) have impacts on the vote that are strong and consistent across individuals. Other factors (e.g., specific policy issues) have impacts that are weaker or less consistent or less well understood. If we assume the latter factors can be treated as noise, that is, that they are independent, randomly distributed variables, the systematic factors will be clear in the aggregate results. In this way, conventional assumptions of aggregation impose a statistical order on the results.

The second classical simplification is the assumption of historical efficiency. Although the argument is usually associated with theories of natural selection and best specified in modern theories of population biology, the basic idea of historical efficiency is implicit in many modern theories. Regardless of the complexity or apparent anomalies of human behavior, historical processes are assumed to eliminate behaviors that are not solutions to an appropriate joint optimization problem. Thus, a prediction based on solving the optimization problem will correctly predict behavior, regardless of whether the actors involved formulate or solve

15

that problem explicitly (Friedman, 1953). In many cases, of course, solving the optimization problem is itself highly problematic.

In these ways, much of contemporary theory emphasizes the way order is imposed on political institutions by an external environment. In the case of rational actor models, order is produced through the invisible hand of competition. In the case of garbage can models, order is produced through temporal simultaneity. In both cases, the processes realize environmentally determined outcomes. From this perspective, for example, power within a political system is determined by possession of resources in the environment, interests are determined by position in the external world, and coherence within an institution is assured by the exigencies of existence. Order is effectively exogenous to the institution and does not depend on properties of the institution or processes within it.

THE ROLE OF INSTITUTIONS IN POLITICS

For most observers, including most people working within the two traditions identified above, politics does not seem to be either a pure case of environmentally constrained rational competition or a pure case of environmentally constrained temporal sorting. What happens is influenced by both, but it is also conspicuously influenced by the institutional structure within which politics occurs. This consciousness of the importance of institutions is manifest in concern with "nondecisions" (Bachrach and Baratz, 1962) and agenda effects (Kingdon, 1984), and some recent work in both the rational actor (Ferejohn, 1987) and the garbage can (March and Olsen, 1986a) traditions has emphasized the need to introduce institutions explicitly into such theories.

In the remainder of the present book we wish to explore some ways in which the institutions of politics, particularly administrative institutions, provide order and influence change in politics. This institutional perspective can be seen as an adjunct to theories such as those of rational competition or temporal sorting, and we are happy to endorse such a view. But our efforts proceed also from a more general concern with interpreting political institutions as fundamental features of politics and with understanding the ways in which they contribute to stability and change in political life.

Students of institutions emphasize the part played by political structures in creating and sustaining islands of imperfect and temporary organization in potentially inchoate political worlds. The premise of organization is that not everything can be attended to at once, though, in principle,

16

such attention is required for a comprehensive solution. Thus, a central anomaly of institutions is that they increase capability by reducing comprehensiveness. Some potential participants, issues, viewpoints, or values are ignored or suppressed (Schattschneider, 1960). Politics is uncoupled from administration, and various parts of administration are uncoupled from each other. Coordination among several components of a problem is uncoupled from the solving of the several parts. Some things are taken as given in deciding other things. Paradigms and ideologies focus attention on some things, distract attention from others. Institutions define individual, group, and societal identities, what it means to belong to a specific collective. Such identities represent barriers to trade—they signify something nonexchangeable and thus simplify the problems of trade.

As a result of these various forms of simplifications, political institutions are simultaneously an affront to our sense of comprehensive rationality and a primary instrument for approximating it. The uncouplings are justified not by a judgment that the aspects are independent but by the assumption that the errors introduced by treating them independently are less than the errors introduced by trying (and failing) to treat them as interdependent. The simplifications have political consequences. Internal institutional processes affect things like the distribution of power. As a result, they invite theoretical development of models of the ways in which interests and preferences develop within the context of institutional action, the ways reputations and expectations develop as a result of the outcomes of politics, and the ways in which the process of controlling purposive organizations produces unanticipated consequences and is tied to a symbolic system that evolves within an institution.

Without denying the importance of both the social context of politics and the motives of individual actors, therefore, institutional analysis posits a more independent role for political institutions. The state is not only affected by society but also affects it (Katzenstein, 1978; 1985; Krasner, 1978; 1988; Nordlinger, 1981; Skocpol, 1979; Stephan, 1978; Ashford, 1986; Thomas et al., 1987). Political democracy depends not only on economic and social conditions but also on the design of political institutions. Bureaucratic agencies, legislative committees, and appellate courts are arenas for contending social forces, but they are also collections of standard operating procedures and structures that define and defend values, norms, interests, identities, and beliefs.

The argument that institutions can be treated as political actors is a claim of institutional coherence and autonomy. A claim of coherence is necessary if we wish to treat institutions as decision makers. From such a point of view, the issue is whether we choose to picture the

17

state (or some other political institution) as making choices on the basis of some collective interest or intention (e.g., preferences, goals, purposes), alternatives, and expectations (Levi, 1981). There is no necessary answer to the question unless we impose one. Whether it makes pragmatic theoretical sense to impute interests, expectations, and the other paraphernalia of coherent intelligence to an institution is neither more nor less problematic, a priori, than whether it makes sense to impute them to an individual (Kahneman, 1982; March and Shapira, 1982). The pragmatic answer appears to be that the coherence of institutions varies but is sometimes substantial enough to justify viewing a collectivity as acting coherently. Traditional political theory involved considerable attention to ways coherence might be induced through constitutions, laws, and other stable rules, or by a community of moral obligation, often inspired and buttressed by religious dogma (Berki, 1979; Waterstone, 1966).

The claim of institutional autonomy is necessary to establish that political institutions are more than simple mirrors of social forces. Empirical observations seem to indicate that processes internal to political institutions, although possibly triggered by external events, affect the flow of history. Programs adopted as a simple political compromise by a legislature become endowed with separate meaning and force by having an agency established to deal with them (Skocpol and Finegold, 1982). The establishment of public policies, or competition among bureaucrats or legislators, activates and organizes otherwise quiescent identities and social cleavages (Olsen and Sætren, 1980; Tilly, 1978). Policy experts within the political system develop and shape the understanding of policy issues and alternatives (Heclo, 1974).

Thus, political institutions define the framework within which politics takes place (March and Olsen, 1984; Olsen, 1985). In the rest of this book we ask how those institutions function, how they affect political life, how they change, and how they might be improved. The book is too short and our competences too limited for the agenda. Our treatment is limited. It emphasizes ways in which contemporary thinking about political institutions may lead us astray. It is organized by a concern for understanding the place of political institutions in political stability and change. It draws particularly from research on formal organizations, thus is most directly concerned with institutions such as parliaments, ministries, courts, and administrative agencies. And it focuses primarily on political institutions within a context of democratic ideology.

In Chapter 2 we explore the way in which political action is governed by rules, rather than by utilitarian calculation. In Chapter 3 we describe how the noninstrumental construction of meaning can be seen as central

18

to politics. In Chapter 4 we examine a nonfunctionalist picture of institutional history. In the subsequent chapters we draw on such considerations to study institutional change in Western democracies, first (in chapters 5 and 6) by describing the process and then (in chapters 7 and 8) by suggesting some considerations in the design of democratic political institutions.

2

Rules and the Institutionalization of Action

In the classic open structures of free political competition and temporal sorting, action is potentially chaotic. It is not clear what will happen, or who will do what to whom when. The principles of rational consequential calculation or strict temporality are precise, but their interactive implications are obscure enough in complicated ecologies to make outcomes uncertain. In this chapter we examine the ways in which the institutionalization of action through rules reduces that ambiguity and affects politics.

THE UBIQUITY OF ROUTINES

The proposition that organizations follow rules, that much of the behavior in an organization is specified by standard operating procedures, is a common one in the bureaucratic and organizational literature (March and Simon, 1958; Weber, 1978). It can be extended to the institutions of politics. Much of the behavior we observe in political institutions reflects the routine way in which people do what they are supposed to do. Simple stimuli trigger complex, standardized patterns of action without extensive analysis, problem solving, or use of discretionary power. Institutions have a repertoire of procedures, and they use rules to select among them. The rules may be imposed and enforced by direct coercion and political or organizational authority, or they may be part of a code of appropriate behavior that is learned and internalized through socialization or education.

To say that behavior is governed by rules is not to say that it is either trivial or unreasoned. Rule-bound behavior is, or can be, carefully considered. Rules can reflect subtle lessons of cumulative experience, and the process by which appropriate rules are determined and applied is a process involving high levels of human intelligence, discourse, and deliberation. Intelligent, thoughtful political behavior, like other behavior, can be described in terms of duties, obligations, roles, and rules.

By "rules" we mean the routines, procedures, conventions, roles, strategies, organizational forms, and technologies around which political activity is constructed. We also mean the beliefs, paradigms, codes, cultures, and knowledge that surround, support, elaborate, and contradict those roles and routines. It is a commonplace observation in empirical social science that behavior is constrained or dictated by such cultural dicta and social norms. Action is often based more on identifying the normatively appropriate behavior than on calculating the return expected from alternative choices. Routines are independent of the individual actors who execute them and are capable of surviving considerable turnover in individuals.

These routines may be procedural rules specifying a process that is to be followed under certain circumstances. They may be decision rules specifying how inputs are to be converted into outputs. They may be evaluation rules specifying criteria for assessing results. Rules may regulate the allocation of authority and responsibility, record keeping, and information gathering and handling. They may specify who has access to what institutions or arenas under which conditions, including the rights of political oppositions. They may regulate the appropriate times for saying or doing things by providing deadlines or by imposing time periods when certain things cannot be said or done. They may regulate the changing of rules. Rules are codified to some extent, but the codification is often incomplete. Inconsistencies are common. As a result, compliance with any specific rule is not automatic.

Institutional routines are followed even when it is not obviously in the narrow self-interest of the person responsible to do so. Even in extreme situations like war, or in concentration camps, individuals seem to act on the basis of rules of appropriateness rather than rational consequential calculation (Geertz, 1980; Lundquist, 1988). The conformity to rules can be viewed as contractual, an implicit agreement to act appropriately in return for being treated appropriately, and to some extent there certainly is such a "contract." But socialization into a set of rules and acceptance of their appropriateness is ordinarily not a case of willfully entering into an explicit contract. Rules, including those of various professions, are learned as catechisms of expectations. They are constructed and elaborated through an exploration of the nature of things, of self-conceptions, and of institutional and personal images.

Some efforts have been made to rationalize normative rules, such as altruism (Kurz, 1978) and reciprocity (Axelrod, 1980), or to specify the conditions for their evolution (Axelrod and Hamilton, 1981; Trivers, 1971). Although such efforts have yielded important insights, they tend to limit attention to the comparative statics of individual norms. A broader theoretical examination of normative order would consider the relations among norms, the significance of their ambiguity and inconsistency, and the transformation of normative structures. A theoretical understanding of such conventional norms as those surrounding trust and legitimacy seems likely to be particularly germane to political analysis.

To describe behavior as driven by rules is to see action as a matching of a situation to the demands of a position. Rules define relationships among roles in terms of what an incumbent of one role owes to incumbents of other roles (Burns and Flam, 1987). The terminology is one of duties and obligations rather than anticipatory, consequential decision making. Political actors associate specific actions with specific situations by rules of appropriateness. What is appropriate for a particular person in a particular situation is defined by political and social institutions and transmitted through socialization. Search involves an inquiry into the characteristics of a particular situation, and choice involves matching a situation with behavior that fits it.

The contrast between the logic of appropriateness associated with obligatory action and the logic of consequentiality associated with anticipatory choice has been described as a basic distinction in the history of theories of justice and rationality (MacIntyre, 1988). It can be characterized by comparing the conventional litanies for action:

Anticipatory action:
1. What are my alternatives?
2. What are my values?
3. What are the consequences of my alternatives for my values?
4. Choose the alternative that has the best consequences.

Obligatory action:
1. What kind of a situation is this?
2. Who am I?
3. How appropriate are different actions for me in this situation?
4. Do what is most appropriate.

Despite the modern emphasis on the first litany as a justification for action, the second seems more often to describe action. The accountant asks: What does an accountant do in a situation such as this? The bureau chief asks: What does a bureau chief do in a situation such as this? Institutions are constructed around clusters of appropriate activities, around procedures for assuring their maintenance in the face of threats from turnover and from self-interest, and around procedures for modifying them.

The ubiquity of routines often makes political institutions appear to be bureaucratic, rigid, insensitive, or stupid. The simplification provided by rules is clearly imperfect, and the imperfection is often manifest, especially after the fact. But some of the major capabilities of modern institutions come from their effectiveness in substituting rule-bound behavior for individually autonomous behavior. Routines make it possible to coordinate many simultaneous activities in a way that makes them mutually consistent. Routines help avoid conflicts; they provide codes of meaning that facilitate interpretation of ambiguous worlds; they constrain bargaining within comprehensible terms and enforce agreements; they help mitigate the unpredictability created by open structures and garbage can processes by regulating the access of participants, problems, and solutions to choice opportunities. Routines embody collective and individual identities, interests, values, and worldviews, thus constraining the allocation of attention, standards of evaluation, priorities, perceptions, and resources (Hall, 1968; Van Maanen, 1973).

At the same time, the fact that most behavior is driven by routines does not, by itself, make most behavior routine. The number and variety of alternative rules assure that one of the primary factors affecting behavior is the process by which some of those rules, rather than others, are evoked in a particular situation. Institutions, traditions, and norms are not monolithic (Eisenstadt, 1964; Burns and Flam, 1987). The history that generates and changes rules is not a single cohesive history but consists in a variety of experiences in a variety of places under a variety of situations (Dahrendorf, 1968). Moreover, rules and their applicability to particular situations are often ambiguous. Individuals have multiple identities. Divisions of labor sometimes break down. Situations can be defined in different ways that call forth different rules. Rules are constructed by a process that sometimes encourages ambiguity.

Consequently, describing behavior as rule following is only the first step in understanding how rules affect behavior. The process includes the whole panoply of actions and constructions by which a logic of appropriateness is implemented in the face of conflict and ambiguity.

24

The criterion is appropriateness, but determining what is appropriate in a specific situation is a nontrivial exercise. One possibility is that rules are followed but choice among rules and among alternative interpretations of rules is determined by a consequential logic. That is, we could imagine political actors treating alternative rules and interpretations as alternatives in a rational choice problem. Some elements of such a calculus certainly occur, but it is not the dominant procedure. For example, potential conflict among rules is resolved partly by incomplete attention. Only a fraction of the relevant routines are evoked in a particular place at a particular time. Rules that are more familiar are more likely to be evoked, and so recently used or recently revised rules come to attention.

Where more than one potentially relevant rule is evoked, the problem is to apply criteria of similarity in order to use the most appropriate rule. In some cases, higher-order rules may be used to make the choice. The process seems quaint to a realpolitik tradition accustomed to cynicism with respect to judgments about "appropriateness." It is not a process that is well understood in the political context, but it is important to even the most political of situations. For example, during the Cuban missile crisis, when much of the language was a language of calculation and consequence, reports of decision making emphasize considerations of appropriateness and the matching of proper behavior to a particular situation (Allison, 1971).

Fitting a rule to a situation is an exercise more analogous to legal reasoning than to economic reasoning—even conceding modern obfuscations of the distinction (Posner, 1973; 1981). Levi (1949: 8–9) describes the process of legal reasoning:

> The first stage is the creation of the legal concept which is built up as cases are compared. The period is one in which the court fumbles for a phrase. Several phrases may be tried out; the misuse or misunderstanding of words itself may have an effect. The concept sounds like another, and the jump to the second is made. The second stage is the period when the concept is more or less fixed, although reasoning by example continues to classify items inside and out of the concept. The third stage is the breakdown of the concept, as reasoning by example has moved so far ahead as to make it clear that the suggestive influence of the word is no longer desired.

In establishing appropriateness, rules and situations are related by criteria of similarity or difference and through reasoning by analogy and metaphor. The process is mediated heavily by language, by the ways in which participants come to be able to talk about one situation as similar to or different from another; and the assignment of situations to rules is made at the same time as the rules change. Although the process is certainly affected by considerations of the consequences of action, it is organized by different principles of action, a logic of appropriateness and a comparison of cases in terms of similarities and differences. The process maintains consistency in action primarily through the creation of typologies of similarity, rather than through a derivation of action from stable interests or wants.

ACCESS, EXPERTISE, LEADERSHIP, AND TRUST

The Division of Labor

Since everything is, in principle, connected to everything else in politics, any action taken anywhere is of some interest to everyone. This suggests a political system, possibly imaginable, in which the effects of everything on everyone are simultaneously considered, and all conflicts resolved. Political institutions are not organized that way, at least not in the first instance. Many of the rules within political institutions are essentially devices for partitioning politics into relatively independent domains. The classical partitioning device is citizenship based on geography, a way of dividing a large world into a large number of small states.

Internal divisions of labor normally result in polities built around the principles of division of labor and specialization, and so a partitioning of citizens and officials into relatively self-contained collections of roles and rules. By suppressing links across partitions, the division of labor creates significant barriers between domains of legitimate action—areas of local rationality (Cyert and March, 1963) and responsibility. Coordination across boundaries is more difficult than within them. Different sets of rules tend to evolve independently in different domains. The division of labor identifies specialists not only with special access to a set of problems and solutions but also with responsibility for developing relatively stable rules for operating within that domain.

The division of labor and specialization are normally presented as principles of efficient organization. Efficiencies are seen as coming from increased competence at a small set of tasks and from gains in coordination produced by grouping together those tasks that are most closely related. In politics, of course, there is special interest in the gains attributable to grouping citizens having a particular set of demands with those agencies most involved in meeting them.

26

The boundaries also create buffers against conflict, and this is often their most significant political effect. One important example is the division of responsibility among legislatures, courts, and administrative agencies, each with a different set of rules for dealing with what is, in some sense, the same issue. Laws are made in one institutional sphere, where decision makers do not see many of the practical implications of what they are doing. When laws are implemented in courts of law or in an administrative agency, most potential participants and issues are excluded. There are rules limiting what matters can be considered by a court or an agency, buffering the court and the agency from certain types of conflict.

The resulting sporadic and sequential attention to potential issues of coordination and consistency in politics makes political systems feasible— if not always coherent. It exploits limitations in attention and energy on the part of participants. Regardless of the way in which institutions are structured, attention is a scarce good in politics; and control over the allocation of attention is important to a political actor. By inhibiting the discovery of and entry into some potential conflicts, a structure of rules organized into relatively discrete responsibilities channels political energies into certain kinds of conflicts and away from others.

At the same time, the buffers impose requirements for relatively high levels of trust across boundaries. Any boundary within a polity is a form of mutual delegation. The problems of delegation are well known. An agent may not, indeed in general will not, share precisely the same values as the person doing the delegation. Monitoring the behavior of the agent is difficult. Consciousness of these problems has led to various efforts to consider mutual delegation as involving a contract of reciprocity. That is, we imagine that mutual control is achieved through expectations of retaliation. Such implicit contracts are common in politics, but they deal crudely with many practical political situations.

They also probably misstate the nature of trust. The core idea of trust is that it is not based on an expectation of its justification. When trust is justified by expectations of positive reciprocal consequences, it is simply another version of economic exchange, as is clear from treatments of trust as reputation in repeated games (Kreps and Wilson, 1982). Trust explicitly conditional on reciprocity is often extended in politics. But the trust associated with delegation in political institutions is, like the division of labor itself, not an explicit contract but a rule of appropriate behavior. It is sustained by socialization into the structure of rules, and rarely considered as a deliberate willful action. Thus, trust can be undermined by persistent untrustworthiness, but it probably is more likely to be undermined by coming to see the granting of trust as part of a voluntary contractual arrangement, rather than as one of the normal obligations of political life.

The structure of rules within political institutions also affects the role of nonpolitical resources in politics. For example, we can compare a political system which uses complex, conditional rules and organization, on the one hand, with a polity that uses simple rules and sharp distinctions, on the other. Indications are that the more complex and conditional are a set of rules, the fuzzier the distinctions between responsibilities of agencies, and the greater the effort to map the complexity of the world onto the institutional structure, the greater the political advantage of persons possessing economic or intellectual resources (Schaffer, 1980; Bleiklie, 1983). In this way, modern developments of complicated institutional rules with many conditions, whether found in welfare state systems or in market systems, counter important principles of democracy. Simple rules with few exceptions reduce the bargaining advantages of wealth and education—though they pose other obvious problems.

Regulating Garbage Can Processes

Garbage can choice situations have been characterized in terms of two structures (Cohen, March, and Olsen, 1972): The first is the access structure, a relation between problems (or solutions) and choice opportunities. The access structure may require, allow, or not allow a particular problem or solution, if activated, to be attached to a particular choice. The second is the decision structure, a relation between decision makers and choice opportunities. This structure may require, allow, or not allow a particular decision maker to participate in the making of a particular choice. The unsegmented structures that are most commonly discussed are those in which any decision maker, any problem, and any solution has access to any choice situation.

Segmented access and decision structures can be imagined in any kind of arbitrary configuration, but two in particular have received formal consideration. The first, a specialized structure, is one that is decomposable into substructures that are unsegmented. Thus, a specialized decision structure is one in which it is possible to divide choice opportunities and decision makers into subgroups and match the two sets of subgroups so that every decision maker in a particular subgroup of decision makers has access to every choice opportunity in the matched set of choice opportunities, but to no other. The second, a hierarchical structure, is one in which access rights expand as a function of hierarchical rank.

For example, in a hierarchical access structure, problems and choices are ordered; and each problem has access to choices of the same or lower rank.

Garbage can processes within differing structures produce different problem-solving performances (i.e., effectiveness, efficiency) and result in different organizational climates (i.e., problem latency). Hierarchical structures tend to produce processes in which important (i.e., high-ranking) choices are particularly unlikely to resolve problems (Cohen, March, and Olsen, 1972). Attention to such structural features of garbage can processes has characterized several more recent discussions. Anderson and Fischer (1986) introduced solutions explicitly, associated problems and solutions with decision makers, and changed the rules for allocating decision makers to choices in order to reflect an individual focus on solving problems important to that individual. They obtained the same general results as were reported by Cohen, March, and Olsen (1972) but observed that the alternative assumptions had the effect of spreading decision makers among choice opportunities more evenly, thus reducing the consequences of bunching. Other theoretical analyses of garbage can processes in hierarchies have identified conditions for their relative efficiency (Carley, 1986).

Similarly, students of decision making have noted how garbage can processes are affected by structural features of the institutions within which they occur. March and Romelaer (1976) pointed out that the drift of decisions within a garbage can situation is not random but occurs in a context of beliefs and norms that produce a systematic bias. Powell (1978) and Levitt (1988) found that routines and norms were important to publishing decisions. Tyack (1976) showed how institutional norms produced considerable reliability in educational organizations. Rommetveit (1976) showed that moving a decision from one arena with certain structural features to another with different characteristics apparently changed the outcome. Weiner (1976) explored the consequences of having flows of problems and participants interconnected and showed that deadlines made a difference in a garbage can process. The effect of belief structures and normative duties was observed by Enderud (1976), Olsen (1976a), and Levitt (1988). Various studies have examined the structural constraints imposed by demographic orders (March and March, 1977; 1978; Pfeffer, 1981b), symbolic orders (Meyer and Rowan, 1977; Pondy, 1978; March, 1981a; Pfeffer, 1981a; March and Olsen, 1983), historical orders (Etheredge, 1976; Olsen, 1976b; Levinthal and March, 1981), normative orders (Christensen, 1976; Kreiner, 1976; Olsen, 1976c; Rommetveit, 1976; Stava, 1976), formal organizational structure (Egeberg,

29

1984; 1987; Olsen, 1983; Blichner and Olsen, 1986) and accounting systems (Cooper, Hayes, and Wolf, 1981).

Expertise and the Division of Labor

Within a political system, special expertise both justifies a division of labor and imposes boundaries on it; and the political complications associated with specialized expertise have concerned political philosophers since the Greeks. In modern times, the problems of expertise have been associated particularly with specialists such as scientists or technical experts (Gibbons and Wittrock, 1984; Weiss and Wollman, 1986), but the general problems extend to any form of specialized knowledge and any kind of division of labor. Expertise is a collection of rules. Although they may be rationalized to some degree, rules are learned by experts as catechisms: Physicists learn what physicists do; lawyers learn what lawyers do. The rules are enforced by the standards of professions and the expectations of patrons. As a result, within political institutions, physicists do what physicists do (and are expected to do); and lawyers do what lawyers do.

For most experts, the political process is an alien domain (Snow, 1961; Giplin and Wright, 1964; Kistiakowsky, 1976). Expertise presumes a process by which alternative theories are evaluated systematically against available data within a framework shared by "reasonable" (i.e., well-trained) people in order to rank ideas in terms of their plausibility. Politics presumes a process by which alternative policies are compared on the basis of the political resources of the people supporting them in order to rank programs in terms of their acceptability. On the surface, one process attempts to reduce subjectivity through standardized procedures designed to assure verifiable knowledge; the other attempts to organize subjectivity through a set of bargains designed to assure social stability. One process seeks data; the other seeks allies. The prototypic expert engages in research; the prototypic politician engages in logrolling. The classic outcome of confrontation of contending ideas among experts is the confirmation of one and the rejection of the others; the classic outcome of confrontation of political ideas is the building of a coalition that makes compromises among some in order to exclude others.

Despite these differences, a sharp division of labor between specialists and policy makers is impossible to sustain, either conceptually or behaviorally. Expert knowledge clearly rests on values that regulate the way knowledge is organized and validated (Primack and von Hippel, 1976). The structures of theories are partly arbitrary and do not necessarily

30

lead to the right questions, nor to the right answers. Like other people, experts seem to find facts and theoretical implications consistent with their policy preferences and forget facts and theoretical implications inconvenient for their purposes. Expert judgments are not magically shielded from personal commitments and professional biases (Lakoff, 1966).

For their part, policy makers often seem to use advice from specialists as an excuse for doing what is unpopular with some groups (Benveniste, 1972). They often seem to be inattentive to the cautions and fine details of expertise, and seem to have an inordinate confidence in the quality of advice given by specialists close to them (e.g., living in their own districts) compared to advice given by others. When experts disagree, policy makers often seem to view the disagreement as justification for accepting whatever advice is convenient. Agreement among specialists, on the other hand, is likely to be treated as a sign of conspiracy.

Confronted with these symptoms of breakdown in the division of labor, there is a tendency for political reformers to seek a comprehensive solution. In particular, experts have sometimes been urged not only to learn more about politics but also to develop a greater political consciousness, greater sophistication, and less innocence. It is said that innocence in politics, like innocence elsewhere, has its costs. There are personal costs, the embarrassment of naivete amplified by the patronizing amusement of friends. There are social costs, for example, when competent expert advice is ignored because it is given at a bad time, or in an incomprehensible way, or so that it offends a key political actor or belief. In these arguments, politically naive expert advice is pictured as bad advice.

The arguments are plausible, but they are not without some difficulties. It may be important for experts to distinguish ignorance about political processes from innocence in behavior. We may ask that experts avoid ignorance, that they understand politics, and appreciate the importance of political processes to sound public policies. At the same time, we may ask experts to be innocent about politics, to seek—as far as possible—to act without political intent. The greatest threat to innocence is the awareness that not everyone else is innocent. Knowledge, pride, and annoyance conspire to encourage cleverness, but cleverness is a trap also. When experts try to be politically clever, they honor sophistication at the expense of wisdom.

It is possible for a knowledgeable advisor to give advice with consciousness of the nuances of its political meaning. To do so, however, is to enter a game of political maneuver in which the other players are unusually suspicious and exceptionally adroit. Policy makers, for whom the threats of manipulation through information are clear, are more likely to see political maneuver when it does not exist than to fail to see it when it does. As a result, they may often have unwarranted suspicions; but they rarely mistake cleverness for naivete. And they are unlikely to be fooled for long. The chance that a politically ambitious expert will be trusted in politics is slight.

Moreover, from the point of view of society and expertise, success is no better than failure. Specialists unfortunate enough to be successful in political maneuver come to think of their role not as someone giving advice but as someone who has influence over policy. The changed frame of reference tends to compromise the quality of expert information in the political process and to undermine trust not only in the individual expert but in the institution of expertise. Such problems are conspicuous, for example, in assessing technological risk in public projects, such as space exploration or nuclear power plants.

The trust extended to an expert advisor by policy makers is affected by estimates of the competence, reliability, and irrelevance of the specialist (Moore, 1970). By competence we mean what any professional would mean about technical competence in the field. Determining competence is not always easy, but there are clues, informants, and past experiences. Policy makers trust people who are respected in the field. By reliability we mean the degree of congruence between the values and personal style of the expert and the values and personal style of the policy maker. Policy makers trust advisors whose values are close enough to theirs that the motivation to mislead them is modest and whose personal styles are familiar enough to allow advisors and policy makers to understand one another. By irrelevance we mean the extent to which the advisor is politically unambitious, and avoids basing advice on guessing what the policy maker will do with the advice, what is wanted, or what others are thinking. Policy makers trust advisors who leave the politics to them, who yearn neither for influence nor for martyrdom.

The implications are not complicated. Policy makers seek competence among experts, but competence alone is unlikely to be enough. Expertise needs to be reliable, not in the sense of being indistinguishable from advocacy, but in the sense of having a distribution of values and styles among competent experts that encourages a pairing of competent specialists with policy makers who trust them (Benveniste, 1972). In a relatively homogeneous, relatively stable society, this is not a serious problem. In a heterogeneous society, however, it is possible that politically important groups (most conspicuously lower-status groups and nonestablishment social movements) will have difficulty obtaining expert advice from competent advisors they trust.

Leadership and the Division of Labor

The division of labor in a political system grants considerable authority to leaders. Through their influence upon the government, the military, the media, and the course of events, political leaders can act with considerable autonomy even in a democratic system. Popular approval is not infinitely malleable, but leaders have considerable latitude in taking actions that will subsequently be deemed legitimate. Such a system assumes trust of and among political leaders. There needs to be confidence that tasks will be performed, agreements honored, and interests protected. Normally, such trust is an expected feature of a democratic political system. For instance, Olsen (1983: Chapter 3) observed through a detailed time study of the forty-five ministers, under secretaries of state, and political secretaries during a week in 1974 that, even when facing a possible political defeat and a cabinet crisis, the Norwegian social democratic government operated on the basis of established routines, division of labor, and trust. Most of the political leaders spent the week attending to prescheduled duties attached to their roles, feeling confident that the prime minister and a few others would take care of their, and their ministries', interests even in time of crisis.

An example of the ways in which trust and institutional autonomy are delicately intertwined is found in recent experience in Norway and Sweden with respect to comprehensive administrative reform (see Chapter 6). In both countries, traditions and political institutions associated with corporate democracy presume the development of a substantial consensus as a prerequisite for action. This consensus is built on the basis of two key features of politics in the two countries. The first is broad agreement on a host of social issues. The second is a predisposition to settle practical problems in a pragmatic way consistent with that broad consensus.

What is problematic in any such system is the relation between governmental actions and the wide range of ideological issues over which there is political conflict. Since the Second World War, democracy in both Norway and Sweden has been based on a fairly widespread social consensus, but the consensus does not exclude sharp ideological differences. In such a system trust in political institutions reflects confidence not only that the broad social consensus will be sustained but also that areas of ideological disagreements will not be preempted by concrete pragmatic actions. That trust is important, because it is known—on all sides— that piecemeal, pragmatic decisions (1) will usually secure post hoc popular approval, and (2) can effectively resolve political conflict without debate. In recent years, the erosion of trust has been reflected in concern by some major political interest groups that "pragmatic" institutional reform will lead to ideologically unacceptable solutions that are effectively undebated and irreversible. It is also reflected in the willingness of office holders to consider actions that, in effect, violate the rules.

Experience in the United States with a number of cases in which senior officials appear to have acted without regard for general norms of appropriate behavior have similarly raised issues of trust in the delegation of authority to political leaders. The response of the political system has been largely to try to improve the flow of information about violations of trust and to provide incentives for political leaders to be trustworthy, threats of sanctions in particular. In the end, however, any such strategy faces an impossible dilemma: A contract that will adequately control a major political leader will at the same time so circumscribe behavior in the role as to make effective leadership difficult. The alternative is to build a culture of trust in which trust is extended and honored because that is what is appropriate behavior by appropriate political figures. As recent history has indicated, such a culture is severely strained by exploitative political leaders, and may indeed be impossible to sustain in many heterogeneous societies with deep, persistent social cleavages and traditions of minimal regulation of political conflict.

INSTITUTIONAL ROUTINES
AND THE CHALLENGES OF NOVELTY

Routine procedures seem designed for routine situations, and it is conventional to predict that the ideas of standard operating procedures, logics of appropriateness, and norms of innocence will be particularly appropriate in dealing with repetitive, uncomplicated situations. The prediction undoubtedly has merit, but it exaggerates the case. A repertoire of routines is also the basis for an institutional approach to novel situations. For in the end, novelty is not a property of a situation so much as it is of our reaction to it; and the most standard organizational response to novelty is to find a set of routines that can be used. Rules and routines are shaped by a changing experience, and the process by which routines come to encode the novelties they encounter into new routines is vital to understanding the role of routines in political life.

The process may be illustrated by the encounters between the political institutions of Norway and a profusion of novel issues raised by the discovery of oil in the North Sea (Olsen, 1988c; 1989). Prior to 1969, Norway imported oil. Its relation to the oil industry was almost entirely as an importer. For the most part, petroleum was subordinated as a

34

source of energy to the abundant hydroelectric supplies of the country. After the Ekofisk discovery in 1969, it was clear that Norway could become an oil exporting country. Petroleum policy was a new field with an apparent lack of routines, and increasing political relevance. There were strong demands for rational action, protection of majority rule, and attention to national interests. It was unclear how to define the situation, what opportunities and problems the country faced, and what interests should be taken into consideration. It was unclear how decisions on oil issues should be made, what institutions would handle different decisions, and who were legitimate participants in various processes.

The ambiguity about procedures was paired with considerable environmental determinism. The history of oil exporting countries showed that large petroleum reserves and revenues have not assured the well-being of oil-endowed countries. Oil discoveries and their exploitation have created new power and dependency relations, social distortions, cost pressures, inflation, migration, and deindustrialization, despite the express intentions of authorities to avoid such developments (Tugwell, 1975; Coronel, 1983; Jenkins, 1986; Karl, 1986). Small countries with open economies are often assumed to have very little latitude in establishing economic policy (Katzenstein, 1985). They seem particularly ill-equipped to control their destinies in the face of the economics of petroleum. History seems to suggest that when a country becomes ''petrolized,'' oil and the money that accompany it change expectations, political institutions, political processes, and power relationships, regardless of decisions by political authorities (Karl, 1986).

The Norwegian case suggests that even in these extreme circumstances the political institutions of a small country were able to act somewhat autonomously. The parliament (Storting) declared that the state was to be involved in the industry at all levels, including production. The state would help coordinate private Norwegian interests in the industry and develop an integrated Norwegian oil production system. The state's autonomy is illustrated by several decisions with significant consequences for the structure of the industry. A state oil company (Statoil) was established and given a dominant position on the Norwegian continental shelf. In this respect, the Norwegian parliament echoed the general world trend of direct national involvement in oil production companies (Klapp, 1987). In addition, the state expanded to 51 percent its ownership in Norsk Hydro, a private company that was already involved in the oil industry. The state refused to give any of the newly created ''peoples' joint-stock companies'' any role in the industry. The state was active in coordinating private Norwegian interests and establishing the privately owned company Saga; and the state diversified the dependence on foreign oil companies by inviting companies from several countries and by not allowing any of them to achieve a dominant position.

Neither these decisions nor Norwegian oil policies in general were the result of careful rational calculations exploiting a nonrenewable resource by maximizing the net present value of investments (Aarrestad, 1984; Rees, 1985). The Norwegian government formulated many goals but never established a clear or stable preference function as a basis for economic planning. The policy makers seldom considered several choice alternatives or examined their various consequences in any great detail. Rather, the government followed a few simple, experience-based rules and standard operating procedures. Oil issues were interpreted and decided in the light of established routines. The various state agencies used existing rules and routines rather than develop special rules. Important decisions thus appeared obvious, natural, and reasonable.

The response of the Maritime Directorate, responsible for safety on floating oil rigs, is typical. The Directorate did not have much experience with oil rigs. But if a rig were viewed as a somewhat peculiar ship, the experts in the Directorate felt confident. They knew as much about safety on ships as anyone else in the world, and their standard routines and rules reflected that knowledge (Sangolt, 1984). They treated oil rigs as ships. Similarly, the Ministry of Industry followed standard operating procedures which have dominated industrial policy making in the postwar period. While the ownership of oil was a new situation, dependence on foreign capital and expertise was not. For instance, from the start of the oil age in Norway, the ministry used images and policies drawn from the country's struggles with international companies over the ownership and use of Norwegian waterfalls in the first part of the twentieth century.

Intervention in the industrial structure followed routines based on institutionalized norms and beliefs which can be traced to economic problems of the 1920s and 1930s. These included a strong faith in the value of developing an industrial society and the belief that the state had an important role to play in industrial development, that free markets would not produce desirable levels of employment, stability, and economic growth, and that the state was able to perform tasks the private sector could not. A key idea was to create national champions, a small number of big firms that could compete internationally. To do this the government was willing to use state capital, to activate and coordinate private Norwegian capital, and, if necessary, to attract foreign capital (Grønlie, 1977; 1989). Decisions in the petroleum sector were, for the most part, "business as usual'' more than innovations developed to fit the specific necessities of the oil sector.

Rule following, however, did not eliminate conflict. Different actors learn different rules and concepts of appropriateness as members of different national cultures, subcommunities, professions, and formal organizations. Frequently such rules are in disagreement or contradict each other. Major political conflicts are focused on which set of rules should prevail when and where. Actually, as observed by Burns and Flam (1987:ix), some of the more significant struggles in human history and contemporary society revolve around the formation and reformation of major rule systems, the core economic and political institutions of society. Norwegian oil policy making illustrates a collision between the rule sets and concepts of appropriateness of Norwegian social democratic political and industrial traditions, on the one hand, and both the free market traditions honored by the conservative opposition and ''good oil field practice'' as seen by the oil companies, on the other.

From the start, the oil companies organized themselves in terms of their standard procedures, especially those they used in the Gulf of Mexico. This resulted in the introduction of forms of organization and management that clearly deviated from postwar traditions in the Norwegian labor market (Andersen, 1988). At first, Norwegian authorities assumed that Norwegian traditions and rules would be followed in the North Sea. Conflicts between Norwegian standard operating procedures and ''good oil field practice'' made such an assumption subject to doubt. The Norwegian government made several efforts to ''normalize'' the situation. In issues such as the workers' right to organize, safety, and work conditions, the state supported the workers' demands for changes. With some success, the state also requested that oil companies follow Norwegian custom and join the Federation of Employers. The latter effort was closely linked to state efforts to control wages in the oil industry and to prevent ''wage contamination'' from oil to other sectors. The major trend over time, stemming both from the impact of state policies and from the fact that Norwegian companies and workers have achieved a more central role on the continental shelf over time, has been toward more emphasis on Norwegian customs, rules, and traditions.

RULES AND POLITICS

The centrality of rules and rule following has some implications for politics. We will explore a few of them in the following chapters, but it may be useful here to identify the key elements of our argument:

37

First, we see the logic of appropriateness as a fundamental logic of political action. Actions are fitted to situations by their appropriateness within a conception of identity. Second, we see action—including action in politically important and novel situations—as institutionalized through structures of rules and routines. Third, we see rules as reflecting historical experience in a way that ordinarily makes the rules, but not the experience, accessible to individuals who have not themselves lived through the experience. Thus, the specific experiential justifications for specific rules are likely to be irretrievable. Fourth, although rules bring order, we see sets of rules as potentially rich in conflict, contradiction, and ambiguity, and thus as producing deviation as well as conformity, variability as well as standardization. Fifth, we see the network of rules and rule-bound relations as sustained by trust, a confidence that appropriate behavior can be expected most of the time. Trust, like the rules it supports, is based on a conception of appropriateness more than a calculation of reciprocity.

Each of these observations is unexceptional, but collectively they present a picture of political life that differs from the picture in many contemporary theories of politics. The individual personality and will of political actors is less important; historical traditions as they are recorded and interpreted within a complex of rules are more important. A calculus of political costs and benefits is less important; a calculus of identity and appropriateness is more important. Learning as recorded in history-dependent routines and norms is more important; expectations of the future are less important. These differences have, as we shall see, implications both for understanding politics and for designing democratic political institutions.

3

Interpretation and
the Institutionalization
of Meaning

In Chapter 2 we considered how rules, routines, and standard operating procedures bring order to politics, how for example they reduce the potential for chaos in free political competition and in temporal sorting. In this chapter we examine the ways in which institutions constrain and shape politics through the construction and elaboration of meaning. Most theories of political action assume that action depends on an interpretation of life. In theories of calculated rationality, actors impute meaning to their expectations about the future and to their preferences. In theories of learning, actors impute meaning to their experiences. In theories of imitation, actors interpret the actions of others. Expectations, preferences, experience, and interpretations of the actions of others are all constructed within political institutions.

We consider three different features of the elaboration of meaning within political institutions. The first is the way in which individuals within political institutions come to attribute meaning and value to their pasts and their futures. The second is the way in which the process of comprehension of the world becomes, under some conditions, an enactment of that world. The third is the way in which interpretation is not only an instrument of other processes, such as decision making, but a central concern in its own right.

MAKING SENSE OF THE WORLD

Individuals try to make sense of their histories. They discover or impose order, attribute meanings, provide explanations, and experience pleasure or pain. Several biases in the construction of meaning are well known. Participants in events tend to overestimate low probabilities and underestimate high ones (Lee, 1971), and attach higher probabilities to desirable outcomes than to others (Slovic, 1966). They are likely to see history in a way that confirms their prior beliefs or reflects favorably on themselves (Deutsch and Gerard, 1955; Weary, 1979). They tend to attribute favorable outcomes to the intelligence of their actions and unfavorable outcomes to the actions of others, to exaggerate their own contributions to joint products (Ross and Sicoly, 1979), to come to prefer those things that they can achieve. But these biases are only part of the story. Because they are dedicated to the possibility of willful action, participants shape interpretations of history to emphasize the role of intention (Langer, 1975; Ross, 1977). Participants exaggerate the reliability not only of historical data but of history itself (Fischhoff, 1975). They overestimate the likelihood of events that actually occur and underestimate the likelihood of events that do not occur but might easily have occurred, and exaggerate in hindsight their own foresight (Fischhoff and Byeth, 1975).

Meaning is constructed in the context of becoming committed to action (Hedberg, Nystrom, and Starbuck, 1976; Swieringa and Waterhaus, 1982; Weick, 1986). Individuals organize arguments and information to create and sustain a belief in the wisdom of the action chosen, thus in the enthusiasm required to implement it. Where a decision process fails to do this, implementation is compromised (Brunsson, 1982; 1985; Baier, March, and Sætren, 1986). Where it does this too well, decisions are ill-considered and their consequences poorly evaluated (Janis and Mann, 1977; George, 1980). The extensive postdecision elaboration of the reasons for action already chosen, including the development of information to support it (Feldman and March, 1981), and the avoidance of postdecision evaluation (Meyer and Rowan, 1977; Harrison and March, 1984), can be seen as part of this process of commitment.

All of these factors shape the way beliefs develop within political institutions, but our present concern is with the ways in which the clusters of beliefs and norms that characterize political institutions are formed and change. In particular, it should be noted that the values and preferences of political actors are not exogenous to political institutions but develop within those institutions. The endogeneity of preferences is a major problem for theories of politics that picture action as stemming from prior preferences. If preferences are endogenous, the meaning of rational action becomes unclear, and the issues involved in the design of democratic political institutions are transformed. We return to these issues in later chapters.

For the present, we focus on the ways in which the development of preferences and beliefs under conditions of ambiguity accentuates the significance of institutions by strengthening preexisting structures of related values and cognitions. Understandings of events and their value are connected to previous understandings, to the understandings of other people, and to social linkages of friendship and trust (Daft and Weick, 1984). Political institutions organize these interactions in ways that shape interpretations and preferences. We can illustrate the kinds of considerations that are important by elaborating one version of ideas about structure—that associated with the idea that individuals and institutions seek to achieve some kind of cognitive consistency. The spirit of the effort is strongly in the tradition of Heider (1958), Kelley (1967), and Abelson (1968). It attempts to embed some basic notions of attitudinal consistency in an institutional structure (March and Olsen, 1975).

For expository purposes, a distinction can be made between beliefs about what a person "sees" and beliefs about what a person "likes." The beliefs about what a person sees include the ways in which actions and outcomes are defined, theories about the world are given credence, and interpretations of those theories are elaborated. The beliefs about what a person likes include affective sentiments, values, and tastes. By making this distinction, it is possible to link these ideas to common distinctions between expectations and preferences; but it should be clear that the process that is postulated for coming to believe that something exists or is true is not fundamentally different from the process for coming to believe that something is desirable.

To begin with, consider six assumptions about the elaboration of meaning in relatively unambiguous systems. First, individuals in politics see what is to be seen. There is an ordinary process of perceiving reality. The process is normatively well defined. Through it, individuals establish reliably what has happened in the phenomenal world. It is possible to relate observed events to their future consequences, and to their underlying causes. A correct link can be established between past choices and subsequent states of the world (i.e., it is possible to disentangle the effects of own choices and the effects of external factors). There exist some criteria for determining what choice situations are similar. Although much of what we want to discuss relates to other factors, we wish to acknowledge the possibility, and frequent dominance, of what is usually called objective reality.

41

Second, individuals in politics like what is to be liked. There are objective interests in the sense that, given an individual's position in society, it is possible to assert that some things are in his or her interest and others are not, even if that interest is not reflected in a present awareness. Although such a conception of interest is uncommon in modern social science, we consider it a defensible assumption of a theory that intends to predict actual behavior over time. Indeed, it is the basis of much effective prediction in social behavior.

Third, individuals in politics see what they expect to see. We assume that an individual approaches any situation with expectations. Those expectations may come from experience; they may come from a structure of beliefs about the world. In either case, the expectations help to control their own realization. Fourth, individuals in politics like what they expect to like. Individuals come to any particular choice situation with a set of values, attitudes, and opinions. These values are substantially fixed. Changes that occur within a relatively brief time period face problems of consistency with the preexisting attitude structure. In some cases, the restrictions imposed by this presumption will dominate the behavior.

Fifth, individuals in politics see what they are expected to see and, sixth, like what they are expected to like. The role of social norms in facilitating the interpretation of events and attitudes is a familiar theme in the analyses of social behavior. Among the best-known examples of social provision of precision are the studies of strongly ideological, religious, and political messianic movements (e.g., Festinger et al., 1956). The phenomenon extends well beyond such cases, however.

In many cases, seeing and liking are controlled by these elemental exogenous forces of objective reality, attitude structures, social reality, and social norms. In the rest of this section, however, we wish to examine the situations in which the elementary presumptions of "objective" seeing and liking do not completely determine the interpretation of events, where there is some degree of contextual ambiguity. Situations of ambiguity are common. The patterns of exposure to events and the channels for diffusing observations and interpretations often obscure the events. Despite ambiguity and uncertainty, individuals interpret and try to make sense out of their lives. They try to find meaning in happenings and provide or invent explanations. These explanations and their development over time are our primary focus.

In situations where interpretations and explanations are called forth some time after the events, the institutional "memory" (e.g., records, histories) and the retrieval system by which it is consulted will affect the degrees to which different participants can use past events, promises, goals, assumptions, behavior, etc. in different ways. Pluralism, decentralization, mobility, and volatility in attention all tend to produce perceptual and affective ambiguity in interpreting events. For present purposes a political system is considered to consist of individuals characterized by:

1. Varying patterns of interaction with each other. The frequency and duration of contacts between any two people may vary. In part this may reflect choice; in part it may be a consequence of social and political structure.

2. Varying degrees of trust in each other. The confidence in another person's ability, power, and motives varies.

3. Varying degrees of integration into the political system. Individuals are integrated to the extent to which they accept responsibility for the political system and feel that the actions of that system are fundamentally their actions or the actions of those they trust. The converse relation with the political system is alienation. We will view individuals as alienated from the political system to the extent to which they do not accept responsibility for it and feel that its actions are neither their actions nor the actions of others whom they trust.

4. Varying orientations to events in the phenomenal world. These orientations have four key dimensions: (a) The extent to which the event is seen. (b) The extent to which the event is liked. (c) The extent to which the event is relevant to different interpersonal relations. (d) The extent to which an event is seen as controlled by different individuals.

Suppose individuals in politics develop their interpretations of events in a way broadly consistent with standard hypotheses of cognitive and affective consistency (Einhorn and Hogarth, 1981; Kiesler and Sproull, 1982; Pitz and Sachs, 1984). That is, suppose there are clear interdependencies between cognitive organization (i.e., perceiving someone as causing something, owning something, being close, etc.) and the organization of preferences (i.e., liking or disliking something or someone). The interdependencies with which we will be concerned reflect various tendencies toward consistency. We believe that such tendencies are fundamental to understanding the formation of beliefs in politics. At the same time, however, it should be obvious that we do not anticipate that the attitude structures observed in politics will exhibit a high degree of consistency on some absolute scale. Ambiguity in the environment, short attention spans, and considerable human tolerance for inconsistency (Bem, 1970) conspire to maintain a high level of incongruence even in a process in which there are substantial efforts toward structure.

To focus on a simple set of ideas about movement toward cognitive and affective consistency, consider four propositions about seeing and liking: First, individuals will—to the extent to which they are integrated into the political system—see what they like. To the extent to which they are alienated from the political system they will see what they dislike. The elementary screening devices used by individuals in looking at the world tend to obscure those elements of reality that are not consonant with prior attitudes. As far as possible, individuals see what they want to see. The result of such wishful thinking is highly dependent upon integration into the political system. If individuals are alienated from the system, they will see evidence confirming their alienation.

Second, individuals will—to the degree they are integrated into the political system—like what they see. To the extent to which they are alienated from the political system they will dislike what they see. Not only do individuals modify perceptions to accommodate preferences, they also modify their preferences to accommodate their perceptions. Individuals tend to discover pleasures in outcomes arising from worlds into which they are integrated relatively independent of what those outcomes are; and displeasures from worlds from which they are alienated.

Third, individuals will—to the extent to which they trust others with whom they have contact—like what the others like. To the extent to which they distrust others with whom they have contact, they will dislike what the others like. Most individuals in politics most of the time will not be eyewitnesses to most relevant events. Both what they "see" and what they "like" will be dependent upon available sources of information, which of the available sources they are exposed to, and which of those they are exposed to they trust. Learning under such conditions becomes dependent both upon processes like discussions and persuasion, and upon relationships like trust and antagonism. Sentiments diffuse through the contact network characterized by variations in trust. They spread positively across trust relationships, negatively across distrust relationships. The frequency of interaction will be especially important when different trusted people hold different preferences. Individuals under such conditions will tend to like what those with whom they most frequently interact like.

Fourth, individuals will—to the degree they trust others with whom they have contact—see what the others see. To the extent to which they distrust others with whom they have contact, they will not see what the others see. Perceptions also diffuse through the contact network, mediated by the trust structure. Individuals (most of the time) have difficulties in seeing different things from what trusted associates see.

This elementary set of propositions results in a simple system for coming to believe what one believes. The basic system can be completed by adding a set of propositions that reflect the dynamics of balancing within the organizations of life for each participant: (1) Individuals will come to trust others whom they see as producing relevant events that they like and preventing relevant events that they dislike. (2) Individuals will come to believe that people they trust cause events they like and that people they distrust cause events they dislike. (3) Individuals will come to believe that events are relevant if they agree about them with people they trust and disagree about them with people they distrust. (4) Individuals will be active to the extent to which their seeing, liking, and trusting are unambiguous. (5) Individuals will—to the extent to which the political system and their activity levels permit—seek contact with people they trust and avoid contact with people they distrust. (6) Individuals will feel integrated into a political system to the extent to which they like the relevant events that they see.

Taken together, these propositions suggest a view of reality forming that emphasizes the impact of interpersonal connections within a political system and the affective connection between the system and the participant on the development of belief, as well as the interaction between seeing and liking. In keeping with ideas of cognitive consistency, the propositions emphasize the organization of belief as vital to the substance of belief, and accept a particular form of cognitive balance as an organizing device.

In general, the predictions that can be made depend on the fine detail of the ways an institution organizes contact and experience. However, a few broad predictions can be made. Where meaning develops within such a system, there is a tendency to partition a population of individuals into groups or institutions that share interpretations and preferences within groups but not across groups. This tendency is accentuated in situations in which cleavages that develop between groups are protected through contact or resource buffers. It is limited or breaks down where some of the internal mechanisms are overridden by other forces that induce changes in contact, trust, preferences, or perceptions that violate the consistency rules. For example, slack in an institution provides contact and experience buffers that allow subgroups to develop consistent sets of beliefs and to differentiate themselves from others. Subcultures develop and become sources of possible radical shifts. The removal of slack eliminates such buffers and results in conflict and a new constellation of beliefs. Whether that new constellation reflects new cleavages and how those cleavages cut across an institution depend not only on the institutional structure but also on the previous history of beliefs.

THE ENACTMENT OF SOCIAL REALITY

In simple ideas of adaptive institutions, it is usually assumed that institutions adapt to environments that are passive. The assumption is convenient. It permits us to see the processes of adaptation as mechanisms for matching appropriate institutions with exogenously created environments. In fact, institutions create their own environments in part, and the resulting complications are significant (Weick, 1979; Barley, 1987). For example, much of the richness of ecological theories of politics stems from the way in which the actions of each participant are part of the environments of the others. The environment of each political actor is, therefore, partly self-determined as each reacts to the other. The situation is familiar to studies of prey-predator relations and markets (Mayr, 1963; Kamien and Schwartz, 1975). When environments are created, the actions taken in adapting to an environment are partly responses to previous actions by the same actor, reflected through the environment. A common result is that small signals are amplified into large ones, and the general implication is that routine adaptive processes have consequences that cannot be understood without linking them to an environment that is simultaneously, and endogenously, changing.

Suppose, for example, that the success realized by each competitor in a political situation is a joint consequence of the allocation of resources to various constituencies by the several competitors, as well as their changing competences in dealing with the constituencies. In such situations, the various competitors come to learn different strategies for allocating effort; and the strategy of each depends on a variety of attributes of the others. If the situation is one of trial-and-error learning, there will be a tendency for the competitors to specialize with respect to constituencies, but which constituency becomes the specialty of which competitor depends on the mix of adaptation rates (Herriott, Levinthal, and March, 1985).

The situation in which an environment is reacting to actors at the same time as those actors are adapting to the environment is a standard one for social science. Parents adapt to children at the same time as children adapt to parents. Customers and suppliers adapt to each other. Political leaders and political followers adapt to each other. The outcomes are different from those observed when we have an adaptive learner in a stable environment. Equilibria depend on whether the process is one of mating or hunting and on the relative rates of adaptation of the institution on the one hand and its environment on the other (Lave and March, 1975).

There is a tendency for large, powerful actors to be able to specify their environments, thus forcing other actors to adapt to them. Dominant groups create environments to which others must respond, without themselves attending to the others. This is a fairly standard characterization of the position of dominant ethnic or gender groups, of persons in authority in totalitarian regimes, or of leading firms in a concentrated industry. The ability to ignore others can lead to long-term failure. Powerful institutions and individuals in them find it less important to monitor and learn from their experience and thus become less competent at doing so (Engwall, 1976). Such an apparent disability may not hurt, but there is some chance that a powerful institution will become dependent on its capability to enact its own environment and consequently be unable to cope with a world in which it does not have arbitrary control.

Finally, institutions create their own environments by the way they interpret and act in a confusing world. It is not simply that the world is incompletely or inaccurately perceived, but also that actions taken as a result of beliefs about an environment can, in fact, construct the environment. The classic examples are found in self-fulfilling prophecies and the construction of limits through avoidance of them (Meyer and Rowan, 1977; Weick, 1979). In politics, a standard example is the way in which a reputation for power is transformed into the reality of power.

POLITICS AS AN INTERPRETATION OF LIFE

A conception of politics as decision making and resource allocation is at least as old as Plato and Aristotle. It is reflected in the language and concerns of political thought, from the earliest political philosophers through Bentham to Merriam and Lasswell. Who gets what when and how? For the most part, contemporary theory in political science considers politics and political behavior in such instrumental terms. Although there are exceptions, the modern perspective in political science has generally given primacy to substantive outcomes and either ignored symbolic actions or seen symbols as part of manipulative efforts to control outcomes. The intent of actions is found in their outcomes, and the organizing principle of a political system is the allocation of scarce resources in the face of conflict of interest. Thus, action is choice, choice is made in terms of expectations about its consequences, meanings are organized to affect choices, and symbols are curtains that obscure the real politics, or artifacts of an effort to make decisions.

Parts of institutional analysis are challenges to this assumption of the primacy of outcomes. These challenges echo another ancient theme of political thought, the idea that politics creates, confirms, or modifies interpretations of life. Through politics, individuals develop their identities, their communities, and the public good. Historically, theories of political institutions portrayed political decision making primarily as a process for developing a sense of purpose, direction, and belonging. Politics was a vehicle for educating citizens and improving cultural values. In this view, participation in civic life is the highest form of activity for a civilized person. The ideas find post-Hellenistic voices in J. S. Mill, Pateman (1970), and Lafferty (1981). Politics is regarded as education, as a place for discovering, elaborating, and expressing meanings, establishing shared (or opposing) conceptions of experience, values, and the nature of existence. It is symbolic, not in the recent sense of symbols as devices of the powerful for confusing the weak (Edelman, 1964; Eriksen, 1987), but more in the sense of symbols as instruments of interpretive order.

The primary source of the institutionalist challenge is empirical. Observers of processes of decision making regularly discern features that are hard to relate to an outcome-oriented conception of collective choice. Information is gathered, policy alternatives are defined, and cost-benefit analyses are pursued, but they seem more intended to reassure observers of the appropriateness of actions being taken than to influence the actions. Potential participants seem to care as much for the right to participate as for the fact of participation; participants recall features of the process more easily and vividly than they do its outcomes; heated argument leads to decision without concern about its implementation; information relevant to a decision is requested but not considered; authority is demanded but not exercised (Feldman and March, 1981; March and Olsen, 1976).

The gathering and processing of information seems to be driven less by uncertainty about the consequences of specific action alternatives than by lack of clarity about how to talk about the world (Feldman and March, 1981; March and Sevón, 1984). Interpretive coherence for the ambiguities of political life is provided by the symbols, rituals, ceremonies, stories, and drama that permeate politics in a subtle and diffuse way (March, 1981a; March and Olsen, 1976; 1983; Meyer and Rowan,

1977; Pfeffer, 1981a; Pondy, 1978). Meaning develops within a context of action. Many of the activities and experiences of politics are defined by their relation to myths and symbols that antedate them and that are widely shared.

At the same time, symbolic behavior is also a strategic element in political competition. Individuals and groups are frequently hypocritical, reciting sacred myths without believing them and while violating their implications. Politicians announce public support for positions they fail to defend in private (Edelman, 1964; Brunsson, 1989). Legislators vote for legislation while remaining indifferent to its implementation (Pressman and Wildavsky, 1973). Administrators solicit public participation in decision making in order to secure public support for policies to which they are already committed. Chief executives advocate reorganization of the public bureaucracy, announce plans for making reorganizations, and regularly abandon the plans (see chapters 5 and 6).

These observations are often reported as anomalies, paradoxes, or symptoms of some other kind of perversity in the systems that are observed. The appearance of perversity, however, is a product of our theoretical presumption that the main point of a political process is action. For many purposes, that presumption may be misleading. These anomalous observations appear to reflect, at least in part, the extent to which politics is only partly—and often almost incidentally—concerned with producing outcomes. Decision processes are sacred rituals and decision making is linked to important symbolic concerns of politics and society (Olsen, 1970; Edlefson, 1978; Bartunek and Keys, 1979; Roos and Hall, 1980). These ritual, symbolic, and affirmative components of decisions are important aspects of the way institutions develop the common culture and vision that become primary mechanisms for effective action, control, and innovation.

At a simple instrumental level, political institutions and the individuals in them need to communicate to their observers that the decisions they make are legitimate (Meyer and Rowan, 1977). Legitimacy is established by showing that the decisions accomplish appropriate objectives or by showing that they are made in appropriate ways (Eriksen, 1987). So, political actors establish that they are good decision makers by making decisions in a way that symbolizes the qualities that are valued. They consult relevant people, consider alternatives, gather information, and act decisively but prudently. Plans, information gathering, analysis, consultation, and other observable features of normatively approved decision making are explicable less in terms of their contribution to decision outcomes than as symbols and signals of decision making propriety (Feldman and March, 1981). Since legitimacy often depends as much on the appropriateness of intentions as it does on outcomes, political processes are more effective in reinforcing values and celebrating different values sequentially than they are in articulating those values through action (Brunsson, 1989).

Thus, choice in political institutions is orchestrated to assure its audience of three essential things: First, that the choice has been made intelligently, that it reflects planning, thinking, analysis, and the systematic use of information. Second, that the choice is sensitive to the concerns of relevant people, that the right interests have been heard in the process. Decisions themselves and the intentions they exhibit are important, independent of their implementation. Indeed, they have been described as the primary product of organizations (Brunsson, 1989). Third, that the political system is controlled by its leadership, and appropriately so. For example, part of the drama of decision making reinforces the idea that policy makers and their policies affect outcomes in the political system. Such a belief is, in fact, difficult to confirm using the kinds of data routinely generated in a confusing world. But the belief is important to a political system. It allocates responsibility, thus simultaneously reaffirming human control over history and absolving most individuals of responsibility for it.

The symbolism of the decision process also sustains broader social visions. The idea of intelligent choice is a central idea of modern ideology, and political institutions are dedicated to that vision of life. Consequently, activities within political institutions, and particularly decision activities, are part of a set of rituals by which a society assures itself that human existence is built around choice. Such rituals confirm that human institutions are manifestations of the intelligent control of human destiny through intentional action. These sacred values are interpreted and reinforced through the processes of politics. Individuals establish their reputations for virtue; an interpretation of history is developed, shared, and enforced; dissent is nurtured and contained; new ideas are grafted to old ones or disassociated from them; alliances are developed, tested, and displayed; the young are socialized (Olsen, 1970; March and Sevón, 1984).

In older worlds in which the major causal force producing historical experience was the will of the gods, social rituals were organized around ceremonies by which that will was discovered and influenced. Most contemporary developed societies, being somewhat more secular in their conceptions of causality, believe that experience is produced by a combination of natural laws and intentional human action. In these societies, social and political rituals are organized around the consultation of expertise and the making of decisions (Olsen, 1970). The procedures of decision that we observed are reflections and reminders of this modern, secular conception of the social order. The rituals of choice infuse participants with an appreciation of the good sense of life's arrangements. They tie routine events to beliefs about the nature of things (Pfeffer, 1981a; Brunsson, 1989).

Political processes are as much concerned with managing interpretations and creating visions as they are with clarifying decisions, but the distinction is easily overdrawn. As a structure of meaning evolves from the process of politics, specific actions are fitted into it (Burgelman, 1988). Standard procedures and records are part of the social language by which organizations comprehend what they are doing, why they are doing it, and how they might do it better. New institutional instruments stimulate interest in new dimensions of description and redefine decision alternatives (Burchell, Colin, and Hopwood, 1985). Information that is generated for decision-irrelevant reasons becomes a topic of conversation, and ultimately contributes to redefining the way we think about decision strategies and options (Feldman, 1989). As a result, a political process may remove uncertainty from a prestructured array of decision alternatives connected to a predetermined array of preferences, but it is probably better seen as a set of procedures that move the whole apparatus of information, desires, and options in a productive direction, simultaneously developing ideas of what is "productive" and instruments for achieving it.

We are led to a perspective that challenges the first premise of many theories of politics, the premise that life is organized around choice. Rather, we might observe that life is not only, or primarily, choice but also interpretation. Outcomes can be less significant—both behaviorally and ethically—than process. The process gives meaning to life, and meaning is a major part of life. The reason that people involved in politics devote so much time to symbols, myth, and rituals is that they (appropriately) care about them. These trappings of action are signals and symbols of the appropriateness of events, not in the sense that what happened needs to be viewed as desirable or pleasant, but in the sense that what happened can be viewed as having occurred in the way things happen (Feldman and March, 1981). The usual term is "legitimate"; but legitimacy may denote something narrower than is intended, for what rituals seek to establish is not only the moral virtue of events but also their necessity (Holmberg, 1989).

Thus, to recognize the symbolic significance of politics is not to denigrate it. Symbols and social ritual may be a way of concealing political reality. In modern discussions of politics, symbolic actions are often portrayed as strategic moves by self-conscious political actors. Rituals and ceremonies are defined as window dressing for real political processes, or as instruments by which the clever and powerful exploit the naive and weak. The hiring of experts lends legitimacy to policies (Meyer and Rowan, 1977); associating unpopular moves with popular symbols is reassuring (Edelman, 1964). Control over symbols is a basis of power, like control over other resources (Pfeffer, 1981a); and the use of symbols is part of a struggle over political outcomes (Cohen, 1974).

Unquestionably, symbols sometimes mask realities (Edelman, 1964; Eriksen, 1987). However, the converse can also be true. Students of politics probably have a systematic tendency to exaggerate the significance of explicit substantive results from the process and to underestimate the significance of the symbolic contributions that politics makes. They tend to underestimate the diffuse, interactive way in which meaning, intentions, and action are woven together. For such students, symbols obfuscate outcomes. Yet it is hard to imagine a society with modern Western ideology that would not require a well-elaborated and reinforced myth of intentional choice through politics, both to sustain a semblance of social orderliness and meaning and to facilitate change. We may quarrel with the ideology and seek a different interpretive frame; but, by most reasonable measures, the symbolic consequences of political decision making are at least as important as the substantive consequences.

In many respects, substantive results can be seen as the embellishments of a life of interpretation. By providing a structure of routines, roles, forms, and rules, political institutions organize a potentially disorderly political process. By shaping meaning, political institutions create an interpretive order within which political behavior can be understood and provided continuity. It is from this perspective of institutional stability and coherence that we turn to an examination of institutional change. As we shall see in the remainder of the book, the character of political institutions as systems of rules and structures of meaning frames our discussion of institutional change and the role of political institutions in democracy.

4

Transforming
Political Institutions

In previous chapters we have emphasized the ways in which the institutionalization of action through routines and the institutionalization of values and beliefs through the development of meaning affect political life. These features of institutions constrain the free flow of rational action and competition in a rational actor model, and they constrain the free flow of people, problems, and solutions in a garbage can decision model. From this point of view, political institutions are sources of order and stability in an interactive world that might otherwise appear quite chaotic.

In this chapter and the following ones we shift from this view of institutions as sources of order and stability and consider an institutional perspective on institutional change. Since such a perspective is built on an argument that the institutional bases of routines and meaning tend to limit the efficiency of history and to make politics history dependent, we begin by examining that proposition. Then we consider the difficulties and possibilities for producing intentional transformations of institutions. In general, we argue that efforts to reform political institutions are often unsuccessful in accomplishing precisely what was intended, but that institutional processes make change possible and make talking about the justification and mechanisms of change useful.

INSTITUTIONAL STABILITY
AND THE INEFFICIENCY OF HISTORY

Political institutions provide important elements of order in politics. The relative stability of institutions is important to understanding how history confounds theories of comparative statics. It will be recalled from Chapter 1 that most contemporary theories of politics emphasize the efficiency of historical processes, the ways in which history moves quickly and inexorably to a unique outcome dictated by environmental conditions. Such theories presume that regardless of the process or the time path of history, its outcomes are implicit in the environment.

These evolutionary equilibrium arguments were originally made in economics and other social sciences as justification for assuming that surviving institutions and institutional rules reflected implicit solutions to an optimization problem. The argument was simple: Competition for scarce resources resulted in differential survival of institutions and rules that were optimal. The presumption was not one of conscious calculation but of evolution. It was argued that surviving rules, whatever their apparent source, intention, or character, would be optimal. The notion that rules gain intelligence from cumulative experience that cannot be fully comprehended, or even assessed, by individual actors is a familiar one to political discourse. It has been a part of conservative doctrine for hundreds of years, forming a basis for defending both traditional rules of behavior and the existing political order (Brennan and Buchanan, 1985).

Although the argument has a certain charm to it, the fact that institutions encode experience into standard operating procedures, professional rules, practical rules of thumb, and identities does not imply that the rules necessarily reflect intelligence (Brehmer, 1980; March, 1981b). Neither does it imply that institutions will necessarily fail if they do not adapt precisely and immediately. Most close students of adaptive processes in institutions are less than confident that the processes reliably and quickly lead to unique equilibria, or that selection will reliably guarantee that rules will be optimal at any arbitrary point in time (Maynard Smith, 1978; Carroll, 1984).

Not all rules are necessarily good ones, least of all indefinitely. It has been pointed out, for example, that species that have disappeared were once survivors, and unless selection processes are instantaneous, some currently "surviving" rules are in the process of disappearing. Good sense is not guaranteed. At the least, it seems to require occasional deviation from the rules, some general consistency between adaptation rates and environmental rates of change, and a reasonable likelihood

54

that networks of imitation are organized in a manner that allows intelligent action to be diffused somewhat more rapidly and more extensively than silliness. Extensive adjustment periods may be required (and tolerated) during which diverse, conflicting, and inefficient solutions survive (North, 1981: 9). Institutions develop a character that discourages arbitrary structural changes (Selznick, 1957), and sometimes they change their environments rather than adapt to them (Nystrom and Starbuck, 1981).

More generally, there are several obvious problems in assuming historical efficiency. An equilibrium may not exist, or it may not be unique, or it may not be achievable. Even if there is an equilibrium that is, in principle, achievable, historical processes can easily be slow enough relative to the rate of change in the environment that the equilibrium of the process is unlikely to be achieved before the environment, and thus the equilibrium, changes. Unless an environment is perfectly stable, or an institution instantaneously adaptive, of course, there will always be some delay in an adaptive process, thus some degree of mismatch between an environment and the institutions existing in it. But where an environment changes quickly relative to the rate at which an institution adapts, an adaptive process can easily and persistently fail to reach an equilibrium. For example, when it is predicted that political parties will come to identical positions in an environment of single-peaked voter preferences, it is assumed that party adjustment will be as rapid as changes in voter preferences.

The environment of political institutions is not stable and adaptation to it is not instantaneous. For example, European party systems of the 1960s reflected, with few significant exceptions, the cleavages of the 1920s. The cleavages were older than the electorates (Lipset and Rokkan, 1967). Institutions preserve themselves, partly by being resistant to many forms of change, partly by developing their own criteria of appropriateness and success, resource distributions, and constitutional rules. Routines are sustained by being embedded in a structure of routines, by socialization, and by the way they organize attention. The order that comes from the development of meaning tends similarly to be stable. Meaning is conserved by the processes described in Chapter 3. It is sustained by social pressure and education.

Theories of political behavior that assume historical efficiency avoid focusing on transient phenomena that might be less predictable from environmental conditions and more subject to effects from the details of the processes involved. Institutional theories of politics, on the other hand, tend to replace the assumption that history is efficient with explicit consideration of how historical processes are affected by specific characteristics of political institutions. The theories assume, and are particularly relevant to, historical processes that do not have equilibria, take extended periods of time, lead to nonunique equilibria, or result in unique but suboptimal outcomes.

Processes without equilibria or with multiple equilibria are, of course, easily specified and frequently observed. What makes them unattractive theoretically is not their rarity, but their intractability and the indeterminacy of their outcomes. Thus, the advantage to treating behavior as rule driven, in addition to its apparent consistency with numerous observations, is not that it is possible thereby to "save" a belief in historical efficiency. Rather, it is that it leads more naturally than does treating behavior as optimization to an examination of the specific ways in which history is encoded into institutions, and thus to making theories of behavior more attentive to the conditions for inefficiency, and more likely to generate interesting predictions about multiple equilibria or long time paths. In fact, the assumption of historical efficiency becomes mostly a matter of faith if the joint optimization problem cannot be specified or solved by the observer, or if it is impossible to identify the precise mechanisms by which historical experience is transformed into current action. Unless the process is specified, it is difficult to examine either the likelihood that a particular equilibrium will be achieved or how long it will take.

Theoretical attention to the inefficiencies of history involves a greater concern for the ways in which institutions learn from their experience (Levitt and March, 1988) and the possibilities that learning will produce adjustments that are slower or faster than are appropriate, or are misguided. It involves trying to specify the conditions under which the sequential branches of history turn back upon each other and the conditions under which they diverge. It involves characterizing the role of standard operating procedures, professions, and expertise in storing and recalling history. It involves attention to the ways in which the preferences (interests), resources, and rules of the game of politics are not exogenous to politics but heavily influenced by institutional processes.

INTENTIONAL REFORM OF POLITICAL INSTITUTIONS

Institutions change, but the idea that they can be transformed intentionally to any arbitrary form is much more problematic. The political difficulties in changing political institutions are well documented. For example, major deliberate structural reform of legislatures is rare, and virtually unknown in many Western democracies. Arguably, the effects of expansion and professionalization of legislative staffs might qualify as exceptions, but it is hard to argue that the effects, as distinct from the changes, resulted from a conscious intention on the part of political authorities to produce them.

Change in Complex Institutions

There are some classic difficulties associated with making sensible, intentional changes in complex institutions. Changes in the environment of any complex system produce a series of actions and reactions that need to be calibrated before the ultimate consequences can be understood. Complexity obscures the causal structure of the system being changed. If causal links are ignored because they are new, because their effects in the past have been benign, or because the world is inherently too complex, then changes that seem locally adaptive may produce unanticipated or confusing consequences. Concurrent intentional changes of prima facie intelligence may combine to produce joint outcomes that are not intended by anyone and are directly counter to the interests motivating the individual actions (Schelling, 1978). Such outcomes are particularly likely in situations in which belief in a false or incomplete model of causality can be reinforced by confounded experience.

These problems are particularly acute in any structure of nested intentions and interests. It is possible to see an institution as the intermeshing of three systems: the individual, the institution, and the collection of institutions that can be called the environment. Many of the complications in the study of change are related to the way those three systems intermesh. The problems are well known in the literature on formal organizations where there are a large number of studies that discuss managing change in terms of the relations between organizations and the individuals who inhabit them (Coch and French, 1948; Burns and Stalker, 1961; Argyris, 1965), between organizations and their environment (Starbuck, 1976; Aldrich, 1979), and among organizations (Evan, 1966; Benson, 1975). Much of classical organization theory addresses the problems of making the demands of organizations and individuals consistent (Barnard, 1938; Simon, 1957a; March and Simon, 1958); the same theme is frequent in modern treatments of information (Hirschleifer and Riley, 1979; Levinthal, 1988) and incentives (Downs, 1967).

Although the problems are old, they continue to be interesting for the analysis of institutional change. In particular, it seems very likely that both the individuals involved in institutions and systems of institutions have different requirements for change than do the institutions themselves. There is no particular a priori reason for assuming that individual desires for change and stability will be mutually consistent or will match requirements for institutional survival. Moreover, the survival of an institution is a more compelling requirement for the institution than it is for a system of institutions. Complications such as these are common in any combination of autonomous systems. They form a focus for some standard issues in contemporary population genetics (Maynard Smith, 1978; Wright, 1978), as well as extensions of those ideas into the social and behavioral sciences (Wilson, 1975; Hannan and Freeman, 1977; Vaughan and Herrnstein, 1987; Levitt and March, 1988).

For such reasons and as we shall elaborate more fully in the following chapters, the contemporary record with respect to intentional change does not encourage boundless confidence in the possibilities for deliberate, controlled change. Nevertheless, a completely conservative perspective can be misleading in three ways. First, there is considerable mundane adaptiveness in institutions that can be influenced. Although the course of change cannot be arbitrarily dictated, it is possible to influence the gradual transformation by stimulating or inhibiting predictable adaptive processes. Second, although the rules and routines of institutional life are relatively stable, they are incomplete. It is possible to influence the resolution of ambiguity surrounding the rules. Third, it is possible to produce comprehensive shocks in institutions that transform them relatively abruptly. As in the case of the more mundane changes, the transformation cannot be controlled with any great precision; but change can be produced intentionally.

Intentional Transformation Through Exploiting Stable Processes

Most institutional action results neither from extraordinary processes or forces, nor from heroic interventions, but from relatively stable, routine processes that relate institutions to their environments. The stable rules and meanings described in chapters 3 and 4 produce a great variety of behavior flexibly responsive to environmental changes. If the environment changes rapidly, so will the responses of stable institutions. As a result, with respect to many aspects of their behavior, political institutions change quickly in response to environmental signals.

Research on institutions as routine adaptive systems emphasizes six basic perspectives for interpreting action and changes in them (March, 1981a): Action can be seen as the application of standard operating procedures or other rules that evolve through a process of *variation and selection.* Duties, obligation, and roles match a set of rules to a situation by criteria of appropriateness. The duties, obligations, roles, rules, and criteria evolve through experimentation, competition, and survival. Those followed by institutions that survive, grow, and multiply come to dominate the pool of procedures. The model is essentially a model of evolution (Nelson and Winter, 1982).

Action can be seen as *problem solving.* The underlying process involves choosing among alternatives by using some decision rule that compares alternatives in terms of their expected consequences for antecedent goals. The model is one of intendedly rational choice under conditions of risk and is familiar in statistical decision theory, as well as in microeconomic and behavioral theories of choice (Lindblom, 1959; Cyert and March, 1963).

Action can be seen as stemming from *experiential learning.* The underlying process is one in which an institution is conditioned through trial and error to maintain rules that have been successful in the past and to abandon rules that have been unsuccessful. The model is one of trial and error learning (Day and Groves, 1975).

Action can be seen as resulting from *conflict* among individuals or groups representing diverse interests. The underlying process is one of confrontation, bargaining, and coalition, in which outcomes depend on the initial preferences of actors weighted by their power. Changes result from shifts in the mobilization of participants or in the resources they control. The model is one of bargaining and negotiation (March, 1962; Gamson, 1968; Pfeffer, 1981c).

Action can be seen as spreading by *contagion* from one institution to another. The underlying process is one in which variations in contact and in the attractiveness of the behaviors or beliefs being imitated affect the rate and pattern of spread. The model is one of contagion and borrows from studies of epidemiology (Rogers, 1962; Walker, 1969; Rogers and Shoemaker, 1971).

Action can be seen as resulting from the intentions and competencies of actors and changing through *turnover.* Turnover in institutions introduces new members with different attitudes, abilities, and goals. The underlying process is one in which conditions in the institution (e.g., growth, decline, changing requirements for skills) or deliberate strategies (e.g., co-optation, raiding of competitors) affect action by changing the mix of participants. The model is one of regeneration (White, 1970; McNeil and Thompson, 1971).

These six mechanisms are neither esoteric, complicated, nor mutually exclusive. They are also responsive to signals that can, to some extent,

59

be controlled. For example, consider signals related to success and failure. Changes through problem solving or learning are particularly sensitive to information that indicates a gap between aspirations and performance. Institutions devote more attention to activities that are failing to meet targets than to activities that are meeting them (Cyert and March, 1963). The riskiness of action taken is systematically related to evaluations of success or failure (Lopes, 1987; March and Shapira, 1987; March, 1988b). The magnitude of slack buffers, and thus the level of conflict in an institution is likewise related to the extent to which performance exceeds aspirations (Cyert and March, 1963; Singh, 1986).

Unfortunately (from the point of view of simplicity), failure does not always produce change, and success often does. There is evidence that failure-induced stress in social systems can produce persistence in behavior rather than change (Staw, 1976; 1981). And when change is produced from failure, there is indication that the resulting changes tend to be modifications in effort or refinements in procedures more often than major innovative changes (Staw and Szwajkowski, 1975; Manns and March, 1978). Success-induced changes, on the other hand, come from a sense of competence and the freedom to experiment that slack provides (Daft and Becker, 1978; March and Shapira, 1987). Although many of those changes are likely to be dysfunctional from the point of view of the larger social system, reflecting pursuit of various subunit or individual objectives, they are also more likely to include major shifts in procedures or strategies.

Success and failure are normally seen as subject to intentional control primarily through effects on performance. So, efforts to control change through signals of success and failure involve trying to affect performance. The classic example is the boycott or strike. Defining success in terms of the relation between an aspiration level and a performance level, however, suggests that an important mechanisms for inducing change might be to influence the aspiration level (Berg, 1986; Olsen, 1989). For example, we might try to modify the subjective sense of success by changing the reference group of social comparisons. Aspiration-level changes have been shown to have important consequences for the long-run distribution of risk taking in a society (March, 1988b) and for relative stability in success/failure rates (Levinthal and March, 1981).

Although modifying performance or aspirations affects the subjective sense of success, and thereby affects institutional change, the precise nature of the change cannot be controlled. When failure induces search, the results of that search are only partly predictable or controllable. When success induces slack search or illusions of efficacy, the exact directions of change are not easily anticipated. Thus, the signals of success and failure are important to change, and those signals can be managed intentionally to some extent; but other procedures are required to sustain intentional control over the character as well as the magnitude of change.

Intentional Transformation Through Exploiting the Incompleteness of Stable Processes

Stable processes of action are conservative. That is, they tend to maintain stable relations, sustain existing rules, and reduce differences among organizations. The processes are also incomplete. This incompleteness is reflected in, and invites, three somewhat different forms of intentional control. The first is control over attention. Neither institutions nor the individuals in them are able to maintain completely consistent cognitive systems or to attend to everything that they might want to attend to. As a result, their focus of attention is important. The second form of control is control exercised through some anomalies of adaptive processes, the ways in which they generate unanticipated consequences. The third form of control is control over broad systems of meaning. Stable processes of action depend on the structure of meaning within which they occur.

The centrality of attention allocation to decision making in social institutions is a standard feature of behavioral theories of collective choice (March, 1988a). What happens depends on which rule is evoked, which action is imitated, which value is considered, which competitors are mobilized, which opportunities are seen, which problems and solutions are connected, or which worldview is considered. Consequently, a major means of intentional control over institutions is the management of attention. For example, mobilization is important to systems of alliance. In order to be active in forming and maintaining a coalition and monitoring agreements within a coalition, it is useful to be present; but attention is a scarce resource, and some potential power in one domain is sacrificed in the name of another. Allies have claims on their time also, and those claims may make their support unreliable at critical moments. To some extent the problems of attention can be managed by making threats of mobilization, or developing fears on the part of others about potential mobilization, or using agents as representatives. However, each of those introduces more uncertainties into the process. Difficulties of attention, in fact, form the basis for one of the classic anomalies of political behavior—the sequential attention to goals. If all participants were activated fully all of the time, it would not be possible to attend to one problem at one time and another later. Since attention fluctuates, it is possible to sustain a coalition among members who have what appear to be strictly inconsistent objectives (Brunsson, 1989).

The incompleteness of stable processes of change is also reflected in anomalies of adaptive processes, the ways in which ordinary learning, problem solving, contagion, conflict, selection, and regeneration all produce unanticipated consequences. Consider, for example, solution-driven problem solving. Although there seems to be ample evidence that when performance fails to meet aspirations, institutions search for new solutions (Cyert and March, 1963), changes often seem to be driven less by problems than by solutions. Daft and Becker (1978) have argued the case for educational organizations and Kay (1979) for industrial organizations; but the idea is an established one, typical of diffusion theories of change.

The linkage between individual solutions and individual problems is often difficult to make unambiguously. Almost any solution can be linked to almost any problem, provided they arise at approximately the same time (Cohen, March, and Olsen, 1972: March and Olsen, 1976; 1986a). When causality and technology are ambiguous, the motivation to have particular solutions adopted is likely to be as powerful as the motivation to have particular problems solved, and changes can be more easily induced by a focus on solutions than by a focus on problems. Solutions and opportunities stimulate awareness of previously unsalient or unnoticed problems or preferences.

A second anomaly of adaptive processes is the tendency for innovations to be transformed during the process of adoption (Browning, 1968; Brewer, 1973; Hyman, 1973). This is sometimes treated as a measurement problem. In that guise, the problem is to decide whether a change observed in one institution is equivalent to a change in another, to determine when a change has been implemented sufficiently to be considered a change, or to disentangle the labeling of a change from the change itself. To treat such problems as measurement problems, however, is probably misleading. Seeing innovations as spreading unchanged helps link studies of innovation to models drawn from epidemiology; but where a fundamental feature of a change is the way it is transformed as it moves from invention to adoption to implementation to contagion, such a linkage is not helpful.

Change develops meaning through the process by which it occurs. Some parts of that process tend to standardize the multiple meanings of a change, but standardization can be very slow, in some cases so slow as to be almost undetectable. When a government (Nelson and Yates, 1978) or a business firm (Cyert, Dill, and March, 1958) adopts a new policy, or a university a new program (March and Romelaer, 1976), specifying what the change means can be difficult, not because of poor information or inadequate analysis, but because of the fundamental ways in which changes are transformed by the processes of change. The developing character of change makes it difficult to use standard ideas of decision, problem solving, diffusion, and the like, because it is difficult to describe a decision, problem solution, or innovation with precision, to say when it was adopted, and to treat the process as having an ending.

These problems for the student of diffusion are also problems for the activist interested in changing institutions. By shaping a change to make it more consistent with existing procedures and practices, institutions maintain stability in the face of pressure to change. At the same time, however, the same indeterminacy of a change that allows an institution to redefine stability as change, invites redefinition of one change into another. Desired solutions can be described as equivalent to solutions desired by others, and allies can be obtained through flexible definitions of what a particular change is (Bardach, 1977).

A third common anomaly of adaptive processes is the competency trap (March, 1981b; Levitt and March, 1988). Suppose an institution learns from its experience, simultaneously learning what strategies or technologies to use and improving its capabilities in using those with which it has experience. In such a situation, the process of learning from experience which technology to use is confounded by the process of increasing efficiency at using the various technologies. In the typical situation increasing efficiency at a particular technology increases its use, which in turn further increases the efficiency. The system tends to become very efficient at the technology being used, and that efficiency reinforces the likelihood of using it. The process is entirely sensible, provided it does not lead to a level of efficiency with a suboptimal technology that is high enough to make that technology preferable (in the short run) to a better technology, with which the system has less experience and is less efficient.

Competency traps are inhibitors of change and instruments of induced change. They inhibit change by building competency barriers to new strategies, procedures, or technologies. They are instruments of change when it is possible to provide arbitrary experience with a new technology, increasing efficiency at it, and thus inducing its selection over alternatives that would be better with equal experience.

The third form of intentional control over stable processes is the control exercised by influencing the structure of meaning. Problem solving, learning, conflict, contagion, and turnover all depend on an interpretive structure. What happened? Why did it happen? What are the possible ways of thinking about what happened? The control can be rather precise, as for example in the case above of influencing the definitions of success and failure. It can also be rather diffuse, as for example in the case of redefining what are legitimate ways of talking about "interests" or of writing history. These diffuse forms of influence include control over worldviews, that is, over visions of the nature of things. In politics, they include influences over definitions of legitimate authority and appropriate institutions. As should be clear, these methods of intentional control are powerful but doubly imprecise. Influence over the development of a worldview is difficult to establish, and the influence of a worldview over specific actions is indirect and often subtle. As a result, such techniques as "consciousness raising" or "ideology" are often unreliable instruments for affecting concrete political actions in precise ways, but they are major factors in shaping political institutions.

Intentional Transformation Through Processes of Radical Shock

Producing change through radical shock is, of course, a classic revolutionary procedure. Major structural changes in institutions are made in hopes that such changes will destabilize political arrangements and force a permanent realignment of the existing system.

The effectiveness of a strategy of radical shock depends on the inefficiency of history. Changes through radical shock depend on the way in which institutions affect interests and resources, thus on the history dependence of outcomes. If the outcomes of politics depended only on the interaction of exogenously specified interests and resources, institutional reform could, at most, have a quite transient effect. The equilibrium achieved would depend only on the interests and the resources. Where historical processes are inefficient, it is possible to imagine moving the political system from one (relatively) stable equilibrium to another one that is quite different. This is the sense in which political institutions are essential elements of political change. They are instruments for the branching of history. The Thatcher government's attempts to reform the British civil service may turn out to be an example of such a process (Metcalfe and Richards, 1987).

Intentional radical shocks can transform political institutions and politics, but the same factors of institutional autonomy and stability that make shock strategies possible also make them difficult to implement and to control. Formal changes in structure are resisted or corrupted, and efforts to make radical changes are often frustrated (see chapters 5 and 6).

The long-run nature of the transformation is not itself easily controlled. Thus, it is easier to produce change through shock than it is to control what new combination of institutions and practices will evolve from the shock. The outcomes stemming from substituting one set of institutions for another appear to be the consequence of two somewhat contradictory processes. On the one hand, the destruction of existing institutions tends to reduce institutional constraints on noninstitutional forces, thus reinforcing forces associated with the possession of noninstitutional resources and moving a temporal sorting system more toward an unsegmented structure. At the same time, the creation of new institutions and their spontaneous elaboration establish new institution-based resources and constraints. The conflict produced by inconsistencies between the two processes is the story of postrevolutionary change.

For example, great revolutions have destroyed state institutions, gone through periods of vacillation and experimentation, and then set other state institutions in their place. In most cases the new states emerging from the revolutionary situations have been stronger and of a quite different character from the ones destroyed. The new states have been more centralized, bureaucratic, and autonomously powerful at home and abroad. The original revolutionary crises have set in motion political and social processes. But the outcomes of those processes have been influenced less by the ideological worldviews or programs of the revolutionary vanguards than by the legacies of the old regimes and the situations in which revolutionary leaders have found themselves. The new states have often been consolidated during armed domestic conflicts, as well as threatening international military circumstances—situations usually not easily controlled (Borkenau, 1937; Skocpol, 1979:172, 285–287).

THE CONCEPT OF INTENTION IN THE STUDY OF CHANGE

We have argued that institutional change rarely satisfies the prior intentions of those who initiate it. Change cannot be controlled precisely. Such a perspective, however, is itself misleading, for it presumes that intention is clear, fixed, and unitary. Understanding the transformation of political institutions requires recognizing that there are frequently multiple, not necessarily consistent, intentions, that intentions are often ambiguous, that intentions are part of a system of values, goals, and attitudes that embeds intention in a structure of other beliefs and aspirations, and that this structure of values and intentions is shaped, interpreted, and created during the course of the change in the institution.

Institutions develop and redefine goals while making decisions and adapting to environmental pressures, and initial intent can be lost (Hauschildt, 1986). For example, an organization of evangelists becomes a gym with services attached (Zald, 1970); a social movement becomes a commercial establishment (Messinger, 1955; Sills, 1957); a radical rock radio station becomes an almost respectable part of a large corporation (Krieger, 1979); and a new governmental agency becomes an old one (Selznick, 1949; Sproull, Weiner, and Wolf, 1978). These transformations seem often to reflect occasions on which actions taken (for whatever reasons) become the source of a new definition of objectives.

The possibility that preferences and goals may change in response to behavior is a serious complication for rational theories of choice (March, 1978; 1987). Goals change in the course of introducing deliberate innovations, or in the course of normal institutional drift. As a result, actions affect the preferences in the name of which they are taken, and the discovery of new intentions is a common consequence of intentional behavior. The transformation of intention is particularly significant to studying institutional change, because institutional change typically takes time and intentional control over it depends on persistence in a diffuse process. Requirements for persistence and diffuseness seem to suggest that intention must be stable and pervasive, rather than changing, in order to affect the process of change in a consistent way. Alternatively, understanding the course of institutional change will entail a comprehension of the way in which intentions are transformed along the way.

These complications are somewhat moderated by the fact that intentions are part of a structure of values and beliefs. The study of values is plagued with an abundance of terminology, distinguishing among such concepts as those of attitudes, preferences, values, intentions, wants, needs, interests, utilities, and goals with an enthusiasm that belies the confusion. At least part of the terminological cacophony stems from a desire to recognize that there is structure in intentions or desires, that there are more general sets of beliefs that change more slowly than less general beliefs but which are linked to them (Ashford, 1986).

Disparities in rates of change of different parts of a structure of preferences or intentions provide elements of stability in institutional change and in the pressures for change. Political actors discover and construct their intentions through the process of acting on them, but those processes of discovery and construction occur within a context of broader beliefs that are changing at a slower pace. Thus, intentions are simultaneously persistent and shifting, simultaneously pervasive and idiosyncratic. Intentions change in the process of producing change, but they do not change in a capricious manner. They develop and the linkage between yesterday's intentions and those of tomorrow gives coherence to the process even in the face of substantial long-term drift.

The two following chapters focus on some of the complications of intentional institutional reform. Chapter 5 attends to nonroutine attempts at comprehensive administrative reorganization in the United States. In Chapter 6 we consider, on the basis of some observations from the Nordic countries, how the content, organization, and implementation of deliberate attempts to routinize comprehensive administrative reform are influenced by the institutional and historical context within which they take place.

5

Institutional Reform as an Ad Hoc Activity

D espite the persistence of many forms of organizational routines and structures, any discussion of bureaucratic stability must be prefaced by a recognition of substantial bureaucratic change over time (March, 1981b). Most modern governments have experienced a recent history of exceptional growth and change. Many new agencies have been added, agencies have been merged or transferred, their responsibilities have been changed, and the relations among agencies or between agencies and their clients have changed. These changes have been produced by law, by executive fiat, by legislative committee mandate, and by internal transformation (Seidman, 1980; Szanton, 1981).

Such more or less continual, but piecemeal, changes in administrative structures and procedures have been supplemented periodically by more grandiose, and more explicit, efforts to review and reorganize the administrative apparatus of government. These comprehensive reviews of administrative structure and practices have been undertaken by governments of all political persuasions and under a wide variety of political circumstances. They have often involved considerable investment of money, time, and political discussion. They are a characteristic feature of twentieth-century bureaucratic and political life.

Administrative reorganizations are interesting in their own right. The effectiveness of political systems depends to a substantial extent on the effectiveness of administrative institutions, and the design and control of bureaucratic structures is a central concern of any polity. At the same time, because of their generality, visibility, and frequency, administrative reorganizations provide useful insights into the nature of politics more broadly conceived. Politics operates within highly structured situations (e.g., budgeting) using repetitive, routinized procedures; and it operates within unstructured, relatively rare situations (e.g., revolutions) using ad hoc and unprogrammed procedures. Much of political life, however, is neither so regular as budgeting nor so unusual as revolution; the study of (major efforts at) administrative organization may illuminate those intermediate situations.

In Chapter 6 we will consider recent attempts to place administrative reform on the primary agenda of politics. In the present chapter, we examine the history of ad hoc efforts at comprehensive reorganization in the United States during the twentieth century.[1] Reorganization of the federal bureaucracy is not a routine activity. The contrast between the improvisation of reorganization and the routinization of budgeting procedures is marked. Since the Budget and Accounting Act of 1921, budgeting has come to be highly institutionalized, whereas over the same period, the institutionalization of administrative reorganization has been fitful. Major efforts at administrative reform in the United States are, in fact, natural experiments in governance. They occur frequently enough to provide repeated experience with similar issues under different conditions, but not frequently enough to be completely routinized. Over the years there has been a gradual shift of reorganization initiative away from Congress (Weber, 1919; Harding, 1921; Kraines, 1958; White, 1958; Karl, 1963; Arnold, 1976), and toward the president (Herring, 1934; Millett and Rogers, 1941; Harris, 1946; Heady, 1947; 1949b; 1949c; Hobbs, 1953; Pinkett, 1965; Mansfield, 1970; Emmerich, 1971), but congressional resistance to presidential initiatives is persistent (Hurt, 1932; Hobbs, 1953; Mansfield, 1970; Berg, 1975; Brown, 1977; Moe, 1978) and reorganizational procedures remain far from routine.

For the most part, discussions of comprehensive reorganizations have focused on understanding single cases in particular historical contexts. Our observations depend extensively on those previous studies, but our interests are different. We consider some general lessons to be learned about the institutional nature of politics and the organization of political life from an examination of major efforts to reorganize the public bureaucracy, when those efforts apparently account for an insignificant share of the total administrative changes that occur, are seldom followed by systematic efforts to assess their effects, seem to be a source of frustration and an object of ridicule, become regular and unlamented casualties of experience with trying to achieve significant reform, and yet are persistently resurrected by the political system. We suggest a few speculations about the process that might be used as a base for examination of similar phenomena in other countries. Those speculations focus on the ways in which the rhetorical and symbolic organization of political events is linked to the outcomes and interpretation of politics.

THE REORGANIZATION STORY IN THE UNITED STATES

During the last part of the nineteenth century, Congress held the initiative in reorganization. Presidents were relatively uninterested, or uncooperative, defenders of the administrative status quo (White, 1958: 86–87). The Cockrell Committee (1887–1889) and the Dockery-Cockrell Commission (1893–1895) both assumed administrative accountability to Congress. They ignored the idea of executive supervision of administration, as well as ideas of hierarchy and chain of command. Indeed, both initiatives manifested clear antipresidential moods (Weber, 1919; Kraines, 1958; 1970; Arnold, 1976).

Theodore Roosevelt tried to strengthen the role of the president in administration. The Keep Commission (1905–1909) was an explicit assertion of executive authority and a move in the direction of a managerial presidency. The Commission changed the connotation of the word administration from its long-held simple meaning of the personnel of executive departments to the art of managing the public business. In company with the traditional words of economy and efficiency, the Commission paid respect to coordination, communication, control, cost accounting, decision making, employee morale, interdepartmental relations, lump sum budgeting, methods and procedures, planning, organization, records management, relations with public interest groups, simplification, specialization, systems analysis, task forces, training, and work auditing (Kraines, 1970: 52). The Commission was a "landmark" (Emmerich, 1971), and a "milestone" (Karl, 1963). It helped to provide reasons for new mechanisms such as interbureau and interdepartmental committees and system inspection offices (Pinkett, 1965: 311). In reaction to all of this, Congress refused to authorize official publication of the Commission's report and moved to forbid the expenditures of federal funds in the future by any commission on administration unless the creation of the commission had been specifically authorized by Congress (Hobbs, 1953: 10–11; Kraines, 1970: 39). Similarly, when the Taft Commission on Economy and Efficiency suggested new budgeting procedures, Congress enacted a law prohibiting the wasting of government employees'

71

time in the preparation of any more executive budgets (Hobbs, 1953: 16; Harding, 1921).

From this original reluctance to allow presidents to assume responsibility for the administration and from seeing commissions on reorganization as presidential encroachments on congressional domains, there has been a long-term—but not entirely steady—expansion of the managerial role of the president, and an acceptance of its legitimacy. The authority to reorganize has been granted to presidents, but hesitantly and with considerable qualification. The authority has been used sparingly. It has been claimed that delegation to the president of the authority to reorganize is unconstitutional, or at least improper, and attempts to restrict the use of such plans have sometimes been successful (Hurt, 1932; Hobbs, 1953; Mansfield, 1970; Berg, 1975; Moe, 1978).

In 1917 the First World War induced Congress to grant authority to the president to reorganize in order to achieve a more effective conduct of the war (Emmerich, 1971: 42; Redford and Blissett, 1981: 9). Similarly, presidents have been given reorganization powers in other crisis situations (e.g., the Economy Acts of March 3 and March 20, 1933; the War Powers Act of December 1941). During the past sixty to seventy years, Congresses and presidents have gradually accepted the idea that the usual process of legislation needs to be supplemented by some special procedures for administrative change, not only to deal with crises but also to deal with the ordinary problems of management of a large bureaucracy (Herring, 1934; Millett and Rogers, 1941; Harris, 1946; Heady, 1947; 1949b; 1949c; Hobbs, 1953; Pinkett, 1965; Mansfield, 1970; Emmerich, 1971).

The idea of presidential initiative, subject to legislative veto, was suggested by Herbert Hoover, then secretary of commerce, in 1920 (Emmerich, 1971: 43–44). As president, Hoover saw most of his specific proposals for reorganization rejected, but the reorganization plan method was established through the Executive Act of 1932 (Moe, 1978: 41) and the Reorganization Acts of 1939 and 1949 (Mansfield, 1970; Fain, 1977). The reorganization plan method seems to provide a compromise procedure for safeguarding congressional interests while permitting presidential initiative and thus preventing deadlocks (President's Advisory Committee on Management, 1952; Mansfield, 1969; 1970), but there is little consensus on the details of appropriate procedures. Over the years presidential authority has sometimes been expanded, but the expansion has been temporary and circumstantial (Brown, 1977; Moe, 1978). On occasion, Congress has granted more reorganization authority to department heads than it has given to the president.

Recently, the idea that the president would be an active manager of the executive branch has been eroded (Moe, 1978: 72). The problems of administering new social programs raised questions about the cognitive and coordinative demands on the role (Redford and Blissett, 1981), and Watergate exposed some moral limitations (Roberts, 1973; Mosher et al., 1974; Nathan, 1975). These doubts contributed to a revival of fears of a presidency that was too strong, produced a number of congressional bills intended to give agencies greater autonomy, and probably augmented themes of federalism, decentralization, and participation (Hess, 1976: 150; Fain, 1977: 649–662; Moe, 1978: 100; Seidman, 1980: 12). These developments made Hess (1976) propose that the office should be made less managerial and more political. And it made Heineman and Hessler (1980) worry how to arrest the decline in the power of the presidency. Since then, the Reagan administration seems to have contributed to some increase in confidence in the presidency and in the workability of the political system (Nathan, 1986; Salamon and Lund, 1987; Jones, 1988).

An effort to reshape the organization and administrative apparatus used to carry out government's role was an integral component of the Reagan program. The administration perceived its reform program as one of the most comprehensive and ambitious efforts to improve management and reduce costs ever undertaken by any administration. Important issues were the proper scope of government, the appropriate machinery of government, the role of government employees in the policy process, and the respective roles of the public, private, and nonprofit sector workforce in the service delivery process (Levine, 1986; Benda and Levine, 1988). But the budget, rather than the ideas about supply-side management, was the principle vehicle the Reagan administration used (Carroll, Fritschler, and Smith, 1985; Salamon and Lund, 1987; Benda and Levine, 1988). During his first eighteen months in office Reagan generally neglected federal government management policy (Newland, 1984:165). At the same time an extraordinary effort was made to appoint subcabinet officials who shared the administration's basic ideology. The Reagan administration filled a larger proportion of the executive positions in government with noncareer political appointees than was the case in any prior administration (Goldberg, 1987).

UNDERSTANDING AD HOC
COMPREHENSIVE REORGANIZATION

Behind this history of frustration and renewed enthusiasm lies a political system. Understanding that system through looking at comprehensive reorganization involves a consideration of reorganization rhetoric, of the political terms of trade, of the garbage can character of ad hoc comprehensive reorganizations, of the record of short-term failures and long-term successes that runs through the history, and of the relation between reorganization and social values.

Reorganization Rhetoric

The history of administrative reorganization in the twentieth century is a history of rhetoric. Efforts at reorganization in the United States have produced a litany for conventional discourse. Two orthodox rhetorics infuse the speaking and writing of persons involved in reorganization as well as students of it. The first is that of orthodox administrative theory. This rhetoric speaks of the design of administrative structures and procedures to facilitate the efficiency and effectiveness of bureaucratic hierarchies. Mainly prescriptive in its orientation, administrative orthodoxy has been linked to religious and moral movements (Emmerich, 1971; Cohen, 1977; Moe, 1978) and is deeply ingrained in American culture (Waldo, 1961).

The rhetoric of administration proclaims that explicit, comprehensive planning of administrative structures is possible and necessary, that piecemeal change creates chaos. Since Theodore Roosevelt claimed in 1907 that the executive branch had grown up entirely without plan (Emmerich, 1971: 39), it has become a standard cliche to see the bureaucracy as having grown, "like Topsy," in a haphazard fashion without unity of purpose. As new tasks and constituencies have been identified, office has been piled upon office, with little attention to fitting new structures into old ones and resultant administrative confusion (Willoughby, 1923; President's Committee on Administrative Management [Brownlow Committee], 1937: 29; U. S. Commission on the Organization of the Executive Branch of the Government [Hoover Commission], 1949; Graves, 1949; Executive Office of the President [Nixon], [Nixon Papers], 1972: 9). Thus, it is argued that conventional processes of change in bureaucracies are too decentralized to be effective, that there is a need to consider the entire organization of the administrative branch of government at one time, and to eliminate "antiquated machinery" through comprehensive reorganization (Willoughby, 1923; Gulick, 1937; Meriam and Schmeckebier, 1939).

Administrative orthodoxy emphasizes economy and control. It speaks of offices that could be abolished, salaries that could be reduced, positions that could be eliminated, and expenses that could be curtailed (White,

1958: 85). It calls for strong managerial leadership, clear lines of authority and responsibility, manageable spans of control, meritocratic personnel procedures, and the utilization of modern techniques for management. It sees administration as the neutral instrument of public policies, and reorganization as a way of making that instrument more efficient and effective through the application of some simple, organizational principles. Failures of reorganization are interpreted as being the result of the way parochial or special interests overcome efforts to implement administrative policies in the public interest (Brownlow Committee, 1937: 3, 52; First Hoover Commission, 1949: viii; Nixon Papers, 1972: 20; Nathan, 1975: 115–16, 124; Weinberger, 1978: 47; Redford and Blissett, 1981: 200).

Administrative rhetoric is the official language of laws governing reorganizations, many public statements about it, and the obligatory terminology of reports. Although for many years most analyses of governmental expenditures have indicated that reorganizations cannot result in major savings (Holcombe, 1921; Hurt, 1932; Meriam and Schmeckebier, 1939; Price, 1975), the rituals of reorganization seem to require symbols of economy and efficiency to be used (Harris, 1946; Aikin and Koenig, 1949; Pemberton, 1979: 15). Franklin Roosevelt argued that "we have to get over the notion that the purpose of reorganization is economy" (Polenberg, 1966: 8), but in public he often paid tribute to the same notion.

Since 1949 the reorganization statute has specified explicitly that reorganizations should be presented and justified in terms of their contribution: "(1) to promote the better execution of the laws, the more effective management of the executive branch and of its agencies and functions, and the expeditious administration of the public business; (2) to reduce expenditures and promote economy to the fullest extent consistent with the efficient operation of the Government; (3) to increase the efficiency of the operations of the Government to the fullest extent practicable; (4) to group, coordinate, and consolidate agencies and functions of the Government, as nearly as may be, according to major purposes; (5) to reduce the number of agencies by consolidating those having similar functions under a single head, and to abolish such agencies or advisory functions thereof as may not be necessary for the efficient conduct of the Government; and (6) to eliminate overlapping and duplication of effort."

The language could have been taken from any of a number of early pioneers in administrative theory. Similar terminology fills discussions of organization wherever bureaucracies are found—in business firms, armies, hospitals, and schools. And it persists. When President Carter proposed that the Reorganization Act of 1949 be amended to eliminate the requirement for detailed savings estimates and to substitute information on improvements in service, Congress defended the faith and retained the requirement that the president estimate any reduction or increase in expenditures, itemized as far as practical (Seidman, 1980: 12).

The second rhetoric of reorganization is the rhetoric of realpolitik. It is equally conventional. It speaks of reorganization, like organization, in terms of a political struggle among contending interests. Fundamental political interests, within the bureaucracy and outside, seek access, representation, control, and policy benefits. Organizational forms reflect victorious interests and establish a mechanism for future dominance (Redford and Blissett, 1981: 224). Conflicts and inconsistencies found in statutes, authorizations, and contradictory legislative mandates cannot be coordinated through reorganization. Congress, bureaucrats, and organized interests in society are linked in ways substantially less hierarchical than is assumed in orthodox administrative theory. Within such a breviary, the idea of a neatly effective administrative structure is a dangerous illusion. Because the design of an administrative structure is an important political issue, to be effective the reorganization process must reflect the heterogeneous milieu and the values, beliefs, and interests present in ordinary legislative processes (Herring, 1934; Graham, 1938; Coy, 1946; Harris, 1946; Leiserson, 1947; Durham, 1949; Heady, 1949a; Millett, 1949; Redford, 1950; Fesler, 1957; Rourke, 1957; Scher, 1962; Mansfield, 1970; Noll, 1971; Ostrom, 1973; Arnold, 1974; Schick, 1975; Beam, 1978; Moe, 1978; Seidman, 1980; Salamon, 1981a; 1981b).

The rhetoric of realpolitik is an empirical and prescriptive counterpoint to an orthodox administrative perspective. To the emphasis on managerial control, it juxtaposes an emphasis on political control. It argues that a single individual has neither the cognitive capacity, nor the time and energy, nor the moral and representational abilities assumed by the managerial perspective. The dangers of a too powerful executive are real; good government cannot be reduced to good administration; and congressional and interest group parity or dominance in administrative affairs is a precondition for a good political system (Hyneman, 1939; 1950; Millett and Rogers, 1941; Woods, 1943; Coy, 1946; La Follette, 1947; Durham, 1949; Finer, 1949; Simon, Smithburg, and Thompson, 1950; Dimock, 1951; Fesler, 1957; Simon, 1957a; Roberts, 1973; Arnold and Roos, 1974; Mosher et al., 1974; Nathan, 1975; 1976; Hess, 1976). In the realpolitik story, the formal administrative hierarchy is a minor part of the structure of proper administrative control. Agencies are established as responses to group demands, or they subsequently develop a close following in society. If they do not, they do not last long (Herring, 1934; Millett, 1949). Thus, administrators have several competing loyalties, constituencies, and bosses.

This second orthodoxy pictures policies, organizational structures, and day-to-day organizational actions as formed through a political struggle in which the president is only one of the actors. Other main participants include congressional committees and subcommittees, administrative agencies and bureaus, and organized interests in societies—often cooperating in "iron triangles." Reorganization efforts that ignore such networks of power and interests will fail or be inconsequential. Indeed, it would appear that the real interests of political actors will find expression proportionate to their power, regardless of administrative arrangements (Coy, 1946; Dimock, 1951). For example, in a case study of federal employment security policy, Rourke (1957) observed that power over policy continued to rest with a coalition of state agencies and employer groups even after a reorganization that moved this activity into the Department of Labor.

Realpolitik rhetoric is conventional for commentaries on administrative organization; the litany of interests, politics, conflict, bargaining, and power is as stylized as the litany of coordination, chains of command, authority, and responsibility. The rhetoric is largely rejected as an official basis for reorganization (Moe, 1978), but it is sometimes argued that awareness of realpolitik makes it possible to accomplish some limited modifications of the administrative structure (Arnold, 1974; Nathan, 1975; 1976; Seidman, 1980). The political process does not respond to "true power" instantaneously, automatically, or precisely. As a result, policy environments may be changed; new groups may be given access; or program emphases may be modified incrementally (Seidman, 1980; Redford and Blissett, 1981; Salamon, 1981a; 1981b).

Realpolitik rhetoric, in fact, appears to be as sacred, and as well known, as the rhetoric of administration. Far from being concealed in the activities of governance, including the activities of bureaucratic agencies, realpolitik is confirmed by the language and performances of political actors and their observers. We would require an assumption of uncommon ignorance on the part of political participants to imagine that they do not know the gospel of political realism. Moreover, it would be an assumption easily refuted. The events of governance are routinely explained by reference to a political metaphor; bureaucrats routinely speak of their "constituencies"; and newspaper reports routinely use concepts of power, interest, and conflict as the fundamental basis for interpreting the events of government. If the political nature of bureaucratic life is a secret from the participants in the process, it is certainly a widely shared one. Most knowledgeable administrators and other political actors as well as students of administration and organization know both rhetorics and recite one or the other when appropriate. They jointly help define the basic frame of reference for public discussion and action, a set of understandings within which incremental changes can occur (Musicus, 1964; Mosher, 1967; 497; March and Olsen, 1976; Grafton, 1979; Mansfield, 1969; March, 1981a; 1984).

A compelling feature of the history of administrative reorganization is the way these two rhetorics have persisted throughout the twentieth century. It is not the case that an older (administrative) orthodoxy has gradually been replaced by a newer (realpolitik) orthodoxy (Garnett and Levine, 1980). Some of the earliest comments on reorganization were comments on power, interests, and the interplay among self-interested actors (Holcombe, 1921; Coker, 1922; Willoughby, 1923; Herring, 1934; Harris, 1937; Graham, 1938; Hyneman, 1939) and some of the most recent pronouncements on reorganization and organizational design have made it possible to describe the past few years as a high-water mark for administrative rhetoric (Zoffer, 1976: xi; Beam, 1978: 72; Weinberger, 1978). The canons of administrative thought and the canons of political realism are interdependent elements of contemporary faith, and both secure expression in reorganization.

The Terms of Political Trade

Neither presidents nor congresses succeed often in major reorganization projects. What is proposed is regularly defeated or abandoned. Presidents, in particular, go through a cycle of enthusiasm and disappointment. Most commonly (Franklin Roosevelt and Nixon are partial counterexamples), they start reorganization studies at the beginning of their terms; but by the time the studies are completed, they seem to have concluded that reorganization either will not solve their administrative problems or will not be worth the political costs (Mansfield, 1969: 338; Musicus, 1964; Brown, 1977: 165; Miles, 1977: 155; Pemberton, 1979: 52; Redford and Blissett, 1981; Szanton, 1981; 5). Many observers of the early days of a presidency, including some presidents, comment on the innocence, ignorance, and naivete of new presidents about reorganization (Hess, 1976: 33; Nathan, 1976; Moe, 1978; Pemberton, 1979; Heineman and Hessler, 1980: 9; Seidman, 1980; Califano, 1981: 14, 60–61). Presidents report that they miscalculated the difficulties of achieving substantial reform in the national government. Truman said he knew it would be difficult, but still he was surprised. "To talk about it and to do it are two different things" (Pemberton, 1979: 47, 175). Yet, reorganization efforts, ad hoc committees, and commissions are undertaken again and again.

Although there are occasional political confrontations over reorganization, as when more than 100 Democratic congressmen deserted a Democratic president (Franklin Roosevelt) to defeat the 1938 Executive Reorganization Bill despite an overwhelming Democratic majority in the House of Representatives (Polenberg, 1966), pitched battles have usually been avoided by conventional political bargaining among the parties involved; and most plans for major reorganizations fail to survive normal political trading. Presidents are reluctant to use the reorganization authority they have in the face of opposition (Hurt, 1932; Herring, 1934; Rogers, 1938; Zink, 1950; Polenberg, 1966; Mansfield, 1969; Seidman, 1980; Redford and Blissett, 1981). They are often unwilling to submit reorganization plans that are controversial or that they think will not pass (Seidman, 1980: 106; Redford and Blissett, 1981: 120).

The inclination of presidents to retreat from reorganization proposals when faced with opposition is illustrated by studies of Presidents Wilson (Hobbs, 1953; 18), Johnson (Redford and Blissett, 1981), Nixon (Nathan, 1975; Leibfried, 1979), Carter (Heineman and Hessler, 1980: 34), and Reagan (Benda and Levine, 1988: 128). Even President Truman, one of the most successful reorganizers, hesitated when confronted with conflicts within the executive branch and with Congress. When he finally acted, he submitted mild, relatively uncontroversial proposals (Pemberton, 1979: 28, 154–157). Hess (1976: 19) observed that presidents complain about the ill-fitting shape of government but generally see attempts at serious restructuring as no-win propositions. Neither the voters nor the annals of history seem likely to reward them for such efforts.

In general, the historical pattern of political bargaining over administrative organization indicates that the structure of the bureaucracy is less important politically to the president than it is to many legislators. Particularly in times of war or during periods of active social reform, presidents tend to give priority to substantive problems, especially those with an apparent deadline (Holcombe, 1921: 249; Woods, 1943; Hess, 1976; Miles, 1977; Redford and Blissett, 1981). For example, Franklin Roosevelt, who agreed with the Brownlow Committee (1937: 29) that most of the 100 agencies outside the executive departments ought to be included in those departments, nevertheless created numerous new agencies on an ad hoc basis to solve immediate problems (Zink, 1950; Polenberg, 1966).

Recent presidents have apparently considered reorganization an important part of their personal agendas, even a duty; but they have not considered it important enough to make significant political trades involving substantive legislative projects. For the most part, the political trading goes the other way. Presidents give up reorganization projects in order to secure legislative support for other things, and legislators give up opposition on other things in order to block administrative change. The somewhat paradoxical observation that presidents are more interested in legislation and Congress more interested in administration was made as early as 1910 by Senator Jonathan Dolliver in opposing the creation of the Taft Commission (Mansfield, 1970: 493), and the political bargains struck between presidents and Congresses subsequently seem generally susceptible to such an interpretation.

Reorganization threatens prime perquisites of legislative office—access to bureaucratic operations and the linkages between agencies and committees. The internal structure of an agency and its location in the departmental structure of the government are perceived by congressmen as affecting legislative influence and control and thus the capability of furthering political careers through constituency services (Scher, 1962; Pemberton, 1979: 18). As a result, presidential proposals for reorganization have the consequence of providing a convenient trading chip in bargaining with Congress. Although explicit presidential cleverness cannot be excluded, it seems unlikely that reorganization efforts are deliberate sacrificial lambs, the result of conscious attempts to provide trading resources. It seems more likely that the persistent presidential pattern of generating and then abandoning reorganization is likely to be more a personal than a political one; the political sacrifice of reorganization projects, although unplanned, becomes convenient as the political situation unfolds.

Reorganizations as Garbage Cans

Although some features of political trading are fairly stable over the history we have examined, political bargaining over reorganization is sensitive to contextual fluctuations and to short-run changes in political attention. Ad hoc comprehensive reorganization is an ecology of games (Long, 1958) in which attention is problematic. Access rules for participants and issues change over time in response to experience, conscious attempts to control reorganizations, and the cumulative twists of history, but the general absence of precise rules controlling access makes it likely that reorganizations will become garbage cans, highly contextual combinations of people, choice opportunities, problems, and solutions (Cohen, March, and Olsen, 1972; March and Olsen, 1976; 1986a; Olsen, 1976d:

314–315). Thus, the course of events surrounding a reorganization seems to depend less on properties of the reorganization proposals or efforts than on the happenstance of short-run political attention, over which reorganization committees typically have little control.

On the one hand, reorganization efforts have difficulty in sustaining the attention of major political actors. Although administrative reorganizations involve committees or commissions that are expected to proceed in parallel with activities in the rest of the government, the necessity of securing attention from political actors in order to be effective drives reorganization into competition for scarce resources of attention (Brown, 1979: 172). Presidents, congressional leaders, major interest groups, and higher civil servants are typically too busy to be more than very occasional participants. As a result, reorganization efforts often operate in an attention vacuum with respect to those political figures who are likely to be most supportive; and improbable promises of economies are made in an effort to secure attention (Aikin and Koenig, 1949; Fox, 1974; Brown, 1979: 200).

The history with respect to presidential attention is clear. Although it is hard to predict what specific crisis, scandal, or war will divert presidential and other supporters of reorganization from the reorganization arena, it is easy to predict that something will. The destiny of the Commission on Economy and Efficiency was heavily affected by the way in which the Taft administration was overcome by political tumult in 1912 (Mansfield, 1970: 478). The First World War diverted Wilson from his administrative principles (Herring, 1934). The Joint Committee on Reorganization, initiated by Congress and supported by Harding, was a casualty of the scandals around Harding's administration and of his death (Herring, 1934; Mansfield, 1970; Emmerich, 1971: 43). Hoover initiated a major reorganization when he was elected in 1928, but economic events of his years in office deflected the thrust. It was 1932 before he received reorganization authority, and after he lost the election in 1932, Congress rejected all plans that were submitted (Emmerich, 1971: 45).

In his first term, Franklin Roosevelt was continually diverted from his reorganization plans by immediate needs. Roosevelt's press conferences during 1933 document grand schemes giving way to the immediate stress of events. Emergencies claimed his time and forced him to abandon reorganization plans in favor of less orthodox administrative strategies (Polenberg, 1966: 9; Emmerich, 1971: 62). The first Hoover Commission was supposed to prepare for a Republican administration, but Truman's unexpected victory completely changed the premises of its work (Aikin and Koenig, 1949; Arnold, 1976; Pemberton, 1979). A well-organized public relations campaign created an unusual level of support for administrative change at the time of the second Hoover Commission; but by the time the Commission submitted its report, the mood had changed toward expansion of governmental involvement in economic and social affairs (Fesler, 1957; Emmerich, 1971). When the Price task force presented its recommendations on reorganization to Johnson, he talked about the Vietnam War (Redford and Blisset, 1981: 189, 209, 236). Subsequently, he promised to make reorganization an important part of his agenda, but when he decided not to run for another term, the fate of the Heineman task force was decided. The Watergate scandal swamped the Nixon administration, providing a familiar destiny for the proposals from the Ash Council (Nathan, 1975; Leibfried, 1979).

At the same time as presidents and other major political supporters for reorganization are hard-pressed to maintain attention on the issue, less central actors become active. Like discussions of institutional goals and long-run planning (Cohen and March, 1986), reorganizations attract numerous otherwise-unoccupied participants and unresolved issues. Any particular reorganization proposal or topic for discussion is an arena for debating a wide range of current concerns and ancient philosophies. Since there are few established rules of relevance and access, reorganizations tend to become collections of solutions looking for problems, ideologies looking for soapboxes, pet projects looking for supporters, and people looking for jobs, reputations, or entertainment. The linkages among these concerns seem to be testimony more to their simultaneity than to their content, and administrative reform becomes associated with issues, symbols, and projects that sometimes seem remote from the initial impetus behind the effort (Cohen, March, and Olsen, 1972; March and Olsen, 1986a).

For example, the defeat of Roosevelt's proposed reorganization in 1938 resulted in large part from an extraordinary mobilization of opposition to it, a mobilization that stemmed from a linkage between the reorganization plan and a variety of other issues, like the Supreme Court controversy, problems in other agencies and in the Democratic party, as well as an antilynching bill (Rogers, 1938; Mansfield, 1970: 479; Emmerich, 1971: 214). The result of this garbage can collection of issues was that a reorganization that was first received with indifference or moderately positive attitudes was transformed into a major confrontation and defeat of the president.

The garbage can character of reorganization discussions is accentuated by the ambiguities of problems and solutions. Different participants act on the basis of different definitions of the situation. For example, Truman and Hoover agreed on specific suggestions made by the first Hoover Commission, but they had different interpretations of the problems as well as the solutions (Mansfield, 1970; Arnold, 1976; Pemberton, 1979; Seidman, 1980). Recommendations that Franklin Roosevelt saw as strengthening democratic institutions were perceived by others as a move toward presidential dictatorship (Harris, 1937; Polenberg, 1966: 16; Emmerich, 1971: 56–57). Hoover, a strong believer in the possibility of efficiency gains through administrative changes, heard his director of the budget testify before a congressional committee that there was no such thing as a logical grouping of functions in an organization and no possibilities of major savings through reorganization (Hobbs, 1953: 6–7, 36). Carter made comprehensive reorganization a major issue in his campaign, but the man he chose to lead the reorganization effort noted: "History teaches that efforts to redesign the Executive Branch in a single scheme or plan are not digestible by our political system. More importantly, such efforts are themselves difficult to comprehend. They ignore the underlying complexities of our government" (Lance, 1977: xi). A senior advisor also told the president that it was people, rather than organizational structures, that counted (Heineman and Hessler, 1980: 48, 371).

Different perspectives and expectations may facilitate agreement, as they apparently did in the case of Hoover and Truman; but they make coherent action, implementation, and evaluation difficult. In the course of the development of a reorganization effort, change comes to mean many different things to different participants (Brown, 1979: 180). Participants may try to attach their pet projects to a reorganization to make it something they can support. In such a case, the ambiguity of reorganization is a political asset since it allows the possibility of strange bedfellows; however, it also allows a variety of negative interpretations. It appears that under most circumstances more attention is attracted from groups with objections to proposed changes than from groups in favor of them (Rogers, 1938). While incremental and less visible changes not linked to a major reorganization effort often succeed (Emmerich, 1971; Seidman, 1980; Redford and Blissett, 1981; Szanton, 1981: 120), comprehensive reorganization tends to consolidate an opposition (Coy, 1946; Harris, 1946; Hobbs, 1953: 49; Polenberg, 1966; Kaufman, 1977: 410; Lance, 1977: xi), provide an occasion for negative logrolling in Congress (Mansfield, 1970: 472), and an opportunity to deal a blow to presidential prestige (Rogers, 1938). Reorganizations also become vulnerable to the focused attention of significant actors. For instance, in their study of the Department of Transportation, Redford and Blisset (1981: 71–76) discussed how the presumed power of a president was nullified by the attention of a single strategically located person, in this case the president of the seafarers' union.

In such a context, it has been argued that inviting people into the process involves compromises on the changes to be proposed (Kaufman, 1971: 76), that extended participation delays the process, and that radical changes need to be made fairly quickly if they are to occur at all. Conversely, it has been proposed that reorganization efforts would be more successful if they involved a more explicitly participatory style (Lance, 1977: x). Although the latter argument is drawn from research on participation that has received a good deal of attention in recent years, the empirical support that can be drawn from this situation is limited (Mosher, 1967). For example, President Taft learned from Theodore Roosevelt's problems and tried cooperating with Congress rather than confronting it, but without notable success (Kraines, 1970: 43). The idea of placing key members of Congress on a commission in order to facilitate subsequent congressional acceptance of commission recommendations was tried by the first Hoover Commission. The major apparent effect was to increase the number of dissents; and one of the two senators thus co-opted opposed the recommendations when they came to Congress; the other was not reelected (Heady, 1949b; 1949c).

Short-run Failures and Long-run Successes

Although the process of institutional reform is important, irrespective of its outcomes, it is the outcomes by which reform is ordinarily justified. In those terms, efforts at reform entail two assumptions: first, that organizational form can affect administrative performance, and second, that organizational forms can be modified by deliberate choice. The latter assumption emphasizes the role of human will, reason, effort, and power in the transformation of political institutions. The former portrays public administration as part of modern technology. It leads to mechanical metaphors picturing administration as the "instrument," "tool," "apparatus," and "machinery" of governance.

Neither assumption seems well supported by experience with comprehensive reform in the United States. Despite the frequency and intensity of serious efforts, major reorganizations seem to have been largely unsuccessful. Most reorganization efforts produce some formal administrative change. Of 102 reorganization plans submitted to Congress between 1939 and 1970, only 22 were rejected (Moe, 1978: 90), and 72 percent of the proposals from the First Hoover Commission have been listed as implemented (MacNeil and Metz, 1956). The tabulation of successes, however, seems inflated by counting minor matters and details that were implemented by the president on his own. Changes resulting from efforts at comprehensive reorganization seem small compared to changes produced by continuous, incremental change (Herring, 1934; Hart, 1948; Hobbs, 1953; Polenberg, 1966; Mansfield, 1969; Kaufman, 1971; 1976; Arnold, 1974; Nathan, 1976; Sproull, Weiner, and Wolf, 1978; Dempsey, 1979; Pemberton, 1979; Redford and Blissett, 1981). Frequently, organizational change seems to occur first, and formal reorganization later, rather than the other way around. As observed by Short (1923), a common pattern is that offices are initially created by a department head, later acquire implicit statutory recognition in an appropriation act or hearing, and only much later are formally recognized in substantive legislation.

In terms of their effects on administrative costs, size of staff, productivity, or spending, most major reorganization efforts have been described by outsiders, and frequently by participants, as substantial failures. Few efficiencies are achieved; little gain in responsiveness is recorded; control seems as elusive after the efforts as before. In its report to President Reagan, the President's Private Sector Survey on Cost Control (the Grace Commission) promised savings of $424 billion over a three-year period, rising to $1.9 trillion yearly by the year 2000. The forty-eight–volume report, based on one and a half million pages of documentation, and the 2478 recommendations were controversial. Supporters and opponents of the Commission disagreed about the estimated cost savings, the basic assumptions underlying the report, and the feasibility of the recommendations, as well as their political substance (Grace, 1984; Kennedy and Lee, 1984; Goodsell, 1984; Kelman, 1985; Hansen, 1985; Downs and Larkey, 1986; Newland, 1984). The Grace Commission had as much difficulty translating its philosophical beliefs into concrete forms as did many of its predecessors (Salamon and Lund, 1987), and many of its key recommendations were not implemented (Benda and Levine, 1986; 1988).

In general, the reorganization story is a record of "problems identified, but not solved, of promises made but not kept . . . the source of frustration and disillusionment" (Lance, 1977: ix). Moreover, the effects of presidential reforms are sometimes modified by policies and actions at the state and local level (Nathan, 1986). The same conclusions have been reached about reorganizations at the state and local level in the United States (Buck, 1938; Meier, 1980; Morgan and Pelissero, 1980), and about reorganizations at the national level in other countries (Siegel and Kleber, 1965; Argyrades, 1965; Gorvine, 1966; Groves, 1967; Mayntz and

Scharpf, 1975; Leemans, 1976; Brown, 1979; Roness, 1979; Chapman and Greenaway, 1980).

Any specific major reorganization project is likely to fail, but persistent repetition of similar ideas and similar arguments over a relatively long period of time appears to make some difference. Bureaucratic reform seems to require long-run commitment, patience, and perseverance (Brownlow Committee, 1937: 18; Heady, 1949a; 1949b; 1949c; Brown, 1977: 164, 18). Persistence both increases the likelihood that a proposal will be current at an opportune time and creates a diffuse climate of availability and legitimacy for it. Recommendations that produce a storm at one time are later accepted with little opposition (Hurt, 1932; Harris, 1946; Musicus, 1964; Nathan, 1975; Moe, 1978). For example, one year after the acrimonious defeat of his 1938 reorganization plan, Franklin Roosevelt was able to get the Reorganization Act of 1939 passed without serious controversy (Mansfield, 1970: 480). Different times, different meanings. The same groups that had seen the recommendations of the Brownlow Committee and the 1938 plan as an aggrandizement of presidential power described the very similar suggestions in the 1945 reorganizations, and later by the first Hoover Commission, in positive terms. Now, a strong, unified executive was considered to be essential to democratic institutions. Instead of talking about presidential dictatorship, the themes harked back to Hamilton's quest for leadership, and the Hoover proposals became a "monumental effort to bring order out of chaos" (Harris, 1946; Emmerich, 1971: 87; Fesler, 1975: 101). Truman's proposals of 1949 and 1950 to establish a department consolidating health, education, and welfare were rejected, but the proposal was approved in 1953 when made by Eisenhower (Fesler, 1975: 102).

Persistence in the face of success is necessary also (Nathan, 1976: 44). Easy victories contain the seed of easy defeats (Garnett and Levine, 1980). The Presidential Management Initiatives launched by President Ford in July 1976 were terminated when Carter came into office and thereby became the most short-lived of recent major presidential management reforms (Haider, 1979). Success in establishing a new agency or department may be illusory. It is likely to be composed of several old agencies with well-defined programs and constituencies; it begins with a broad and imprecise mandate; there are conflicting views about the nature of the agency; and its structure has to be worked out (Sproull, Weiner, and Wolf, 1978; Redford and Blissett, 1981: 13, 30).

Reorganization can be viewed as a form of civic education (Herring, 1934; Short, 1947; Aikin and Koenig, 1949; Finer, 1949; Heady, 1949a; 1949b; 1949c; Hobbs, 1953; Musicus, 1964; Polenberg, 1966; Mansfield,

1969, 1970; Emmerich, 1971; Arnold, 1976; Fain, 1977: xxi, 357; Moe, 1978: 16; Redford and Blissett, 1981: 203, 208, 214). Finer (1949: 407) observed that while any reorganization effort is at the mercy of a hundred irrelevant political hazards and thus cannot be sure of practical results, one thing is in its power—it can educate the public and help to change the climate of opinion. The President's Advisory Committee on Management (1952) also suggested that such "secondary consequences" as a general change in the climate of opinion could well turn out in the long run to be more consequential than the immediate recommendations; and Herbert Hoover listed as one of the purposes of the Hoover Commission "to open the doors of understanding of the functions of government to our people at large. They are a lesson in civil government of significant educational value" (MacNeil and Metz, 1956: v).

Reorganization studies provide concepts and ideas; they keep theories and proposals alive. They create precedents. They develop a logic of argument that is carried over to subsequent reorganization efforts. They develop "solutions" waiting for "problems" and circumstances. They organize support and motivation for administrative change. Each of these occurs over relatively long time periods, and the relevant ideas evolve in a subtle way over a series of experiences. Successive reorganizations have enlarged the concept of reorganization itself well beyond its original connotation of changes in office procedures (White, 1958: 86), and have shifted the definition of the responsibility of the president in reorganization (Harding, 1921; Kraines, 1970; Emmerich, 1971; Moe, 1978; Redford and Blisset, 1981); they have participated in elaborating the role of the president as manager. The possibility of reorganization stimulates self-inspection on the part of agencies and offices, and sometimes fulfills the intentions of the reorganization without formal structural change (Pinkett, 1965: 310–312). Finally, an imitative burst of state reorganizations typically follows federal commissions (Buck, 1938; Council of State Governments, 1950; Kaufman, 1963; Brademas, 1978; Garnett, 1980; Garnett and Levine, 1980).

Because of these secondary returns to persistence, the achievement record of reorganization efforts seems more impressive in the long run than in the short run. Proposals for change that have been made in the context of reorganization committees frequently are implemented years later. To credit such implementation to the reorganization commission in which the proposal first appeared, or to the series of efforts through which it is repeated, would be an overstatement. The same political forces that place an issue on the agenda of a committee often keep it on the agendas of other groups. However, formal considerations of administrative reorganization are part of the broad education process by which possible changes gain credence and support. That long-run educational process cannot easily be justified in terms of short-run observable effects. As a result, it depends heavily on the ways in which each new administration comes to see reform as feasible and desirable, despite the long history of disappointments with administrative reorganization. And it depends on the somewhat irrational and arbitrary commitments of professional students of administrative reform and the handful of political leaders for whom this is an enduring concern.

Reorganization and Social Values

For the most part, reorganizations have been proposed and understood in instrumental terms, as possible solutions to perceived problems (Mosher, 1967; Olsen, 1976a). Nevertheless, there are few attempts by the initiators of reorganizations to discover what really happened as a consequence of their efforts. Salamon argued that "serious empirical work on the real effects of reorganization is not only deficient, it is nonexistent. . . . Given the millions of dollars and thousands of person-years of effort that have gone into the generation of proposals for organizational change in the federal government over the past half century, this situation would be scandalous were it not so common" (Salamon, 1981b: 60). Similar comments can be found in Mosher (1965), Kaufman (1977), Miles (1977), Brown (1979), and Garnett (1980). In those rare cases where information is available, it is not attended to reliably (Heady, 1949c; Polenberg, 1966); Seidman (1974: 489) observed that one of his greatest frustrations as a reorganizer was that "we never had the time or staff to analyze the results of reorganization." He reported that the White House typically lost interest in reorganization as soon as a decision was made.

One possible reason for the reluctance to evaluate such results, of course, is an awareness that it is hard to cite much success in improving either efficiency or control through major reorganization. Although struggles over organization charts can be emotional (Emmerich, 1971: 129–30; Sproull, Weiner, and Wolf, 1978: 160), most observers agree on the limited success of reorganization in achieving manifest instrumental goals. Since the two Hoover Commissions alone spent almost five million dollars (in direct costs) and generated about six million words of reports (Emmerich, 1971: 101), a formal cost-benefit analysis may not be appealing to someone who has faith in the importance of reorganization efforts.

Persistence in the face of apparent failure and indifference to careful evaluation of the consequences of action are, of course, often observed in human behavior—particularly in domains of strong beliefs and ambiguous experience. If a favorite social reform fails to achieve its promised success, we may conclude that the problem lies not in the reform, but in our failure to push it hard enough, far enough, or long enough (Staw, 1976; 1981). In such cases, it is not only that our interpretation of the outcomes of action is confounded by our ideologies, but also that our actions have symbolic meaning that is independent of their instrumental consequences. Action is an affirmation of belief and an assertion of virtue. Similarly, organization and reorganization are expressions of social values (Miles, 1977; Seidman, 1980). Organizations are cultural systems embedded in a wider culture; and reorganizations are symbolic and rhetorical events of some significance to that wide culture (Meyer and Rowan, 1977; Meyer and Scott, 1983; Thomas et al., 1987).

Although personal or group influences make it difficult to secure agreement on the specifics of any reorganization, the idea of reorganization rarely produces dissent. Everyone is for it, in principle (Seidman, 1980: 126). One of the major themes of White House mail after Truman became president was the need for reorganization and reform (Arnold, 1976: 57); in Truman's twenty-one–point address of September 1945, reorganization ranked tenth in public interest, a higher ranking than either the full employment bill, the regulation of prices and wages, the control of the atomic bomb, or the housing shortage (Pemberton, 1979: 30). Congress is more ready to approve the creation of new departments than the consolidation or elimination of them, but it is more ready to talk about simplification than growth (Miles, 1977). Congressional actors protect their own committees; bureaucratic actors protect their own agencies; presidents protect their own pet projects; but all of them advocate the principles of simplification, reduction in government, and reorganization (Holcombe, 1921; Hurt, 1932; Herring, 1934: 191; Harris, 1937; Polenberg, 1966; Emmerich, 1971: 129; Seidman, 1980). Observers report that reorganizers who want to succeed must exhibit substantive neutrality, claim a distinction between administration and policy (Mansfield, 1969: 335), and appear to eschew politics (Seidman, 1980: 10–11). Similarly, although his secretary of health, education, and welfare planned the largest reorganization in the history of HEW under conditions of extreme secrecy and began to execute it during the 1978–1979 congressional recess, President Carter spoke of an open and participatory reorganization process (Califano, 1981: 42–45).

Reorganization sometimes appears to be a code word symbolizing a general frustration with bureaucracy and governmental intrusion in private lives (Seidman, 1980: 125). When President Carter promised to "bring the horrible bureaucratic mess under control" and restore sound principles of organization and management (Moe, 1978: 49; Seidman, 1980: 125), he was reciting a traditional theme. The Brownlow Committee argued that "the safeguarding of the citizen from narrow-minded and dictatorial bureaucratic interference and control is one of the primary obligations of democratic government" and that "the forward march of American democracy at this point in history depends more on effective management than upon any other single factor" (Brownlow Committee, 1937: 33, 53). The argument was repeated by Truman (Pemberton, 1979: 3); and Nixon announced that restoring confidence in government "requires us to give more profound and more critical attention to the question of government organization than any single group of national leaders since the Constitutional Convention adjourned in Philadelphia in September 1787 (Nixon Papers, 1972: 4, reprinted in Nathan, 1975: 134–35). Reagan in his first inaugural address promised to check and reverse the growth of government which showed signs of having grown beyond the consent of the governed (Levine, 1986; Benda and Levine, 1988).

More generally, efforts at comprehensive administrative reorganization, like other governmental programs, are symbols of the possibility of meaningful action. Confessions of impotence are not acceptable; leaders are expected to act (Vickers, 1965; Mosher, 1967; Brown, 1979), and reorganizations provide an opportunity to symbolize action (Johnson, 1976; Dahl, 1980a). Presidents who promise reforms apparently do not suffer if they fail to implement them (Destler, 1981: 166). Announcing a major reorganization symbolizes the possibilty of effective leadership, and the belief in that possibility may be of greater significance than the execution of it (Fain, 1977: xxiii; Sproull, Weiner, and Wolf, 1978). The most important things appear to be statements of intent, an assurance of proper values, and a willingness to try (Edelman, 1964: 78–79).

It is tempting in looking at such disparities between action and words to see the actions as reflecting basic underlying forces, and the words as deceits (Harris, 1946; Aikin and Koenig, 1949; Pemberton, 1979: 15). Thus, Salamon (1981b: 76) argues that reorganization often becomes an alternative to action, a way to express concern about a program for which no resources are available. And Seidman (1980: 115, 316) discusses reorganization as a tactic for creating an illusion of progress where none exists. The history leaves no doubt that some consciousness of such tactics is present throughout the period we have been examining. Neither presidents nor other political actors are completely innocent. But such a view may be misleading.

90

Any effective deceit is testimony to a belief deeply enough held to warrant the costs of hypocrisy. If we observe that everyone says the same thing, we are observing something important about the political system and the beliefs on which it rests. Virtuous words sustain the meaning and importance of virtue, even among sinners. To view the symbols of politics as intentional efforts by sophisticated actors to deceive the innocent is likely to exaggerate the extent to which things as fundamental as the optimism that mankind can direct and control its environment for the better (Mosher, 1975: 4) can be manipulated arbitrarily as a tactic. Leaders need reassurance, too. More generally, organization and reorganization, like much action, are tied to the discovery, clarification, and elaboration of meaning as well as to immediate action or decision making (March and Sevón, 1984). It is part of the process by which a society develops an understanding of what constitutes a good society, without necessarily being able to achieve it, and how alternative institutions may be imagined to contribute to such a world (Wolin, 1960; March and Olsen, 1976; Hawkins, 1978).

The preponderant evidence is that symbols of administrative reform are important to politicians, not only as ways to fool the voters but also as reflections of their own beliefs. Incoming administrations, like their supporters, believe in the possibility of making a difference; and the recurrence of major reorganization efforts is tied to that belief. Since progress through intentional action is an enduring part of American secular religion and since sacred beliefs must be exhibited by sacred institutions, the necessary logic of public life is efficacy. In the case of leaders, a belief in the efficacy of action is less difficult to sustain than it might be among others. Political success makes it relatively easy for political leaders to resolve the ambiguities of experience by an interpretation that confirms their own competence and sagacity. Winning an election is likely to lead them to believe in their skill, intelligence, political understanding, and hard work (Hess, 1976: 18). They are surrounded by evidence of their own capabilities for control, evidence that is partly a consequence of the staging and rhetoric of their activities. They sustain those beliefs through the acting out of decisiveness and decision. Efforts at administration reform, like other political efforts, express—and thereby confirm—a fundamental confidence in the possibility of directing and controlling human existence, or, more specifically, the government.

Such a perspective may provide an interpretation of the cultural ritual of reorganization and of the rhetorical duality of that ritual. The rhetoric of administration and the rhetoric of realpolitik are mutually supporting and embedded in a culture in which each is important. The ritual of reorganization is a reminder of both sets of beliefs and testimony to their efficacy. On the one hand, a commitment to administrative purity is made tolerable by an appreciation of realpolitik, much as a commitment to personal purity is made tolerable by an appreciation of human weakness. At the same time, a commitment to a realpolitik rhetoric is made consistent with human hopes by a faith in the possibility of improvement through human intelligence. It should not be surprising to find that both rhetorics survive and thrive, and both find expression in the symbols of reorganization. The orthodoxy of administration is the voice of the prologue to comprehensive administrative reform; the orthodoxy of realpolitik is the voice of the epilogue; the myths of the first shade into the myths of the second over the course of a major effort at reorganization; and both sets of myths are needed for a normatively proper interpretation of the reorganization saga.

The simultaneous recitation of the stories of classical administration and the stories of political realism are a reflection of the duality of social beliefs, as are the uses of the sacred symbols of economy, efficiency, constituency pressure, and interest groups. Because immediate structural change may be of less consequence than the reinforcement of social beliefs and long-term educational effects, there is little interest in studies of the immediate results of reorganizations, and what people say and what they do is only loosely linked. Presidents make only modest use of the reorganization authority they have fought to achieve, at least in part because the symbolic value of the authority is more critical to them than its exercise. And presidents are more likely to be punished for not making promises of administrative reform than for not implementing them, because providing rhetorical support for the administrative and realpolitik orthodoxies is of greater significance for their roles as leaders of the public bureaucracy than is rearranging organizational structure (Cohen and March, 1986; Peters, 1978; Pondy, 1978; Weick, 1979; March, 1984; Pfeffer, 1981a).

IMPLICATIONS FOR GOVERNANCE

Reorganization is a domain of rhetoric, trading, problematic attention, and symbolic action. It is described both as fundamental to governmental power (Fain, 1977: xxiii; Hawkins, 1978) and as not worth the time and effort involved (Dimock, 1951). Its effects are uncertain; hopes for a firm theoretical basis for institutional design have been mostly unfulfilled (Fox, 1974; Seidman, 1974; 1980; Szanton, 1981); and prescriptions tend to be contradictory (Simon, 1957a; Kaufman, 1977). No matter what principles of organization are followed, it seems to be inevitable that administrative problems will persist (March and Simon, 1958; Miles, 1977). The balancing of leadership, expertise, and interest representation is delicate (Kaufman, 1956; Lægereid and Olsen, 1984). There is little agreement on criteria (Millett, 1949); goals are discovered as well as implemented (March and Olsen, 1976); and post hoc revision of intentions and desires is common. One result is that few presidents have been comfortable with a role as overseer of the bureaucracy (Moe, 1978: 60; Dahl, 1980a: xvi); and comprehensive reorganization seems more valuable as a proposal than as a project.

Although history shows long-run changes that may be partly attributable to the cumulative effect of major reorganization efforts, short-run achievements are meagre. Powerful figures receive both easy victories and seemingly inexplicable defeats. Attempts to interpret reorganization through simple models of political competition tend to miss the mark (Garnett and Levine, 1980). An open structure makes attention critical, but hard to arrange arbitrarily. As participants move onto and off the stage, short-run outcomes are hard to predict or control. Woven around this experience are two conventional rhetorics, widely known and routinely recited, by which individuals talk about the problems of reorganization and interpret their experience with it. The rhetorics exhibit and reaffirm fundamental social values, particularly those associated with personal efficacy, intention, interest, power, and rational choice.

These features of reorganization are not unique to that arena. They are cited frequently as general features of political life. As a result, it may be possible to extend some features of the interpretation we have made to a more general consideration of political institutions and processes, to the problems of governance. The history of reorganization leads us to some of the most honored traditions in political thought: the role of intentions, reflection, and choice in the development of political institutions (Hamilton, Jay, and Madison, [1787] 1964; Mill, [1861] 1962; the importance of legitimacy and the relation between political drama and social values; and the contrast between the vision of coherence found in relatively macro theories of broad political and social trends and the vision of confusion often found in their micro political cousins.

We focus on three basic observations about governance, drawn from the history of major reorganization efforts in the United States. The first observation is that the short-run course of action in most political domains is heavily influenced by the problematics of attention, by the ways in which choice opportunities, problems, solutions, and participants are associated in terms of their simultaneous availability. The idea that attention is a prime scarce resource in governing is not a new one. In most cases, however, concerns about attention or activation arise as an annoying, but ultimately minor, constraint or complication within some more "basic" vision. The basic idea is that political processes and outcomes are determined by power based on the possession of valued resources. Our observations suggest that perhaps we should shift the focus, that the core reality is the organization of attention, and that metaphors like the ecology of games or garbage can decision processes capture a key essential of political events (March and Olsen, 1976: Chapter 3; Kingdon, 1984).

The second observation is that the long-run development of political institutions is less a product of intentions, plans, and consistent decisions than incremental adaptation to changing problems with available solutions within gradually evolving structures of meaning. Sait (1938: vi) argued that "the great monuments of human activity—such as the state itself or the common law—have taken shape like the coral islands, planlessly, by a series of minor adjustments that result from the more or less mechanical reaction of man to his environment." The statistical properties of that long-run development may, in fact, be both predictable and, to some extent, controllable. Although it is difficult to guess when an opportunity to attach a favorite solution to some problem will arise, a solution that is persistently available is likely to find an occasion. The implication is not that governing is impossible. Rather, it is that governance becomes less a matter of engineering than of gardening (Szanton, 1981: 24); less a matter of hunting than of gathering.

The third observation is that governance is an interpretation of life and an affirmation of legitimate values and institutions. In a society that emphasizes rationality, self-interest, and efficacy, politics honors administrative and realpolitik rhetoric. It provides symbolic and ritual confirmation of the possibility of meaningful individual and collective action. The argument is not that symbols are important to politics, although they certainly are. Rather, the argument is the reverse—that politics is important to symbols, that a primary contribution of politics to life is in the development of meaning. It is not necessary to decide here whether decision making and the allocation of resources or symbols and the construction of meaning are more fundamental. They are heavily intertwined and discussions of primacy may obscure that fact. But it seems unlikely that a theory of governance can represent or improve the phenomena of governing without including the ways political institutions, rhetoric, and the rituals of decisions facilitate the maintenance and change of social values, and the interpretation of human existence.

6

Institutional Reform as
Public Policy

The political history of institutional reform is not a history of sustained political attention or concern. The occasional forays of politics into administrative reform have not led to the development of a general institutional capability for such reform. Although the political system has fairly often been attracted to some of the rhetoric of administrative reform, political interventions tend to produce sporadic crusades, primarily in situations of crisis, separated by long periods of relative quiet (Krasner, 1988). The solutions selected at critical junctures in history are frozen into structures within which changes are piecemeal, reflecting what Skowronek (1982) calls patchwork and Johnson (1976) describes as opportunistic pragmatism.

Chapter 5 has detailed one country's experience with ad hoc reform of administrative institutions. Comprehensive reforms based on special committees, commissions, or task forces often seem to fail from the point of view of the manifest intentions and aspirations of their sponsors, and they tend to fade quickly from memory (Berger, 1987: 211). Such reform attempts create loosely structured situations with few limitations on access, making the reform process highly sensitive to the details of the political environment. Frequently the result is a complex mixture of participants, problems, and solutions in garbage can processes. The political system seems unable to digest comprehensive reforms in one single operation, and the development of meaning becomes a more significant aspect of the reform process than the structural changes achieved.

As shown in Chapter 5, such experience is not unique to the United States, but extends to several other countries where such efforts have been made.

This chapter explores deliberate attempts to place policies for comprehensive institutional reform on the main political agenda and to organize to develop and implement those policies. These efforts involve both increased political consciousness of the relevance of political institutions to specific political programs and increased attention to the organizational requirements for persistent reform. We consider the possibilities for political attention to reform and how the content, organization, and implementation of attempts to make comprehensive administrative reform a major public policy issue are influenced by the institutional and historical context within which the attempts take place.

EFFORTS TO PUT REFORM ON THE POLITICAL AGENDA

Contemporary Pressures

Contemporary politics in many countries in Western Europe and North America, as well as in Australia, exhibits unease. The social democratic order associated with the post–World War II era is less secure than it once appeared. There is a tendency for a majority of citizens in each country to be relatively supportive of the social democratic policies of economic and social welfare around which much of the political debate in these countries from 1945 to 1970 was organized (Rose, 1984: 225; Ladd, 1987). However, public confidence in public institutions has eroded. Levels of trust are down (Crozier, Huntington, and Watanuki, 1975; Scharpf, 1977a; Allardt et al., 1981; Deutsch, 1981; Lipset and Schneider, 1987). It has become more difficult to justify results that seem particularistic or willful to those not favored by them (Rueschemeyer and Evans, 1985).

Demands for institutional reform are major components of current political argument and governmental policies. These demands are exemplified by critiques of administrative institutions but extend beyond them. Public bureaucracies have become too complex, centralized, sectorized, and rigid as well as too difficult to influence. They are not oriented toward the needs of citizens, service, effectiveness, economy, efficiency, and productivity. They do not respond to political initiatives. A fairly general disenchantment with the performance and structure of public institutions is reported even by people whose personal, direct experience with those institutions is positive (Katz et al., 1975). Demands for reappraisal and reform are supported by the mass media, political parties, organized interests, national governments, and international organizations such as the OECD.

Contemporary criticism is really threefold: First, political institutions are portrayed as rigid and incompetent. They are unable to adjust intelligently and rapidly to changes in the economy, demography, or mood of a country, and unable to cope with the most pressing problems of society. Second, political institutions are described as too interventionist and powerful. There is a criticism of the loss of individual and institutional integrity and freedom. Even though there has been a considerable transfer of task and responsibility from the national government to regional and local government in many countries, a frequent theme is the need for more decentralization, including the transfer of tasks and authority to local or regional governments, and the private sector. Proposals for privatization, deregulation, and debureaucratization reflect, at least in part, discontent with governmental encroachments on individual autonomy (Savas, 1982; LeGrand and Robinson, 1984).

At the same time, the third criticism is about the loss of national purpose and central direction. The political system is pictured as having surrendered to major organized interest groups, especially economic interests, while neglecting the national interests and the interests of less well-organized groups. This criticism has led to proposals aimed at strengthening the hand of institutions with broad national concerns, at increasing attention to the economy and society at large, or at making institutions accountable to society as a whole, rather than just a part of it (Lowi, 1969; Olson, 1982; OECD, 1983; Olsen, 1986a; 1988b).

These criticisms of the competence, scope, and institutional forms of the state are part of a long-term political development. Since 1945 the growth and diversification of the public agenda has been so extensive that it amounts to a public revolution (Tarschys, 1978; Rose, 1984; Kristensen, 1987b; Olsen, 1986a; 1988b). Likewise, changes in the organization of the public administration have been substantial. Three interrelated developments stand out: First, the number of nondepartmental bodies "at the margin of the state" has grown. Administrative functions have been entrusted to semi-autonomous governmental or quasi-private agencies (Hague, Mackenzie, and Barker, 1975; Hood, 1986; Hood and Schuppert, 1988). Second, there has been an extensive and complicated interpenetration of governmental agencies and organized interests. Public policy making and the administration of public programs have been turned over to a network of collegial bodies in which civil servants,

experts, and the representatives of organized interests are the major participants (Heisler and Kvavik, 1974; Schmitter and Lehmbruch, 1979; Olsen,
1981; Berger, 1981). Third, the actual working of the administrative
apparatus has become more complex and more obscure. Institutional
structures defy simple description (Bozeman, 1987). It is difficult to
say precisely who influences the administrative system, to whom it is
accountable, or how it works.

Just as a growing, interventionist welfare state challenged earlier liberal-
democratic ideas of governance and institutional forms (Ashford, 1986),
the idea that an interventionist, planning state is a suitable means for
promoting the welfare of citizens is being tested by market-oriented
ideas. The state is pictured as an overgrown, expanding, intrusive, and
unwieldy Leviathan (Salamon and Lund, 1987; Jones, 1988). For instance,
when President Reagan promised the nation a "new beginning" in his
first inaugural address, he argued that government was not a solution
to the problem, government *was* the problem (Levine, 1986; Benda
and Levine, 1988). Privatization, together with the introduction of competition and marketlike arrangements in the public sector, once rejected
in many countries as intolerable intrusions of alien principles, are now
taken seriously. "More managerial thinking and marketing mentality"
(OECD, 1987: 125) is assumed to help. The challenge is revolutionary
in spirit. Incremental change is viewed as inadequate. It is argued that
"major surgery" is needed (OECD, 1980: 13).

In such a spirit, recent governments of many Western countries, as
well as their political oppositions, have formulated comprehensive reform
programs for the public sector. The programs are collections of reform
ideas (many of which have existed for years) rather than coherent philosophies and unitary strategies of change. Most of the programs reveal a
strong belief in the relevance of institutional design. It is assumed that
the organization of agencies has a significant impact upon the policies
made, that it is important to have an institutional policy, and that government has a right and a duty to design administrative organization to
facilitate the achievement of political goals.

Programs of administrative reform seek to reduce the perceived discrep-
ancies between the demands made upon the public sector and its capabilities, but they differ from one another with regard to how they will
accomplish that task. Some want to reduce the demands by rolling back
the state—by eliminating or privatizing services, or minimizing costs
almost regardless of outputs (Gray and Jenkins, 1985). Others want to
increase the capabilities and performance of the public sector by reforming
its structures and processes. Reform programs also differ in the political

strategies they reflect. Some view reorganization as an issue of confrontational politics, organized along the major cleavage lines of society. Others view reorganization as part of a consensual change affected through gradual education and stable processes of adaptation within a shared normative structure.

The Politics of Comprehensive Reform

Experience with institutional reform suggests that successful comprehensive reform may depend on expanding the time horizons of reform efforts and buffering them from short-term fluctuations in attention. The political implication is to give institutional reform higher status and priority through attention from top levels in the political hierarchy and through linkage with key policy issues. The organizational implication is to establish institutional reform as a program or policy of its own. When institutional reform is made a policy area of its own in these ways, reform issues are seen as continuous rather than episodic. Permanent attention to reform issues is augmented by creating special offices and roles responsible for reforms. Rules regulate the access of participants, problems, and solutions. Larger reforms are divided into smaller, planned steps with which the political system can cope.

These imperatives for success in comprehensive institutional reform are, of course, not necessarily imperatives for the political system. Treating institutional design as a major political issue excludes similar treatment for some other issues. The political system cannot proliferate "major issues" indefinitely. Organization involves delegation, but creating new institutions in order to reform institutions leaves the details of those reforms to the possibly perverse niceties of bureaucratic behavior. The political requirements for the institutionalization of comprehensive administrative reform are not easily met.

To examine how one set of Western democracies has responded to pressures for comprehensive reform, we consider some aspects of recent political history in the Nordic countries of Denmark, Finland, Norway, and Sweden, particularly Norway (Olsen, 1988b).[1] The Nordic case may be of some general interest. For example, Heisler and Kvavik (1974) have described Norway as the archetype of the "European polity model." The Nordic welfare state model has been viewed as a success story, combining an active welfare state with a welfare society. The last decade has seen the emergence of a less optimistic mood, and more doubt about the present situation and future possibilities (Allardt et al., 1981). Political debate has focused on whether a large welfare state necessarily makes a better society. The political and economic situation seems to provide an opportunity for major modifications of public institutions, and governments in all the Nordic countries have become more interested in exploring the possibility of administrative reform.

The Norwegian conservative-center Willoch government, in a report to the parliament, described the Norwegian state as too expansive and expensive. It was seen as too rigid and sectorized—unable to change its own structures, work processes, and priorities. Its ability to reallocate goods was doubted. It was argued that the organization of the state made society less innovative and enterprising, as well as less flexible and less able to adapt to technological and economic necessities. Special interests were described as too powerful in public policy making. Professions were criticized for acting in self-interested ways, rather than as experts driven by codes of ethics and the needs of citizens. Elected leaders and individual citizens were seen as having problems asserting their rights.

While the main tendency in Norway since 1945 has been to integrate organized interests, and thus social conflicts, into the administrative apparatus, the key argument of the conservative-center program was that the state, in order to govern, needed a certain distance and independence from the various interests. The lines of responsibility between public authorities and organized interests were to be drawn more clearly, and the number of collegial bodies reduced. Efforts were made to reduce the access to the state of organized, major sector-oriented interests and to strengthen the access of weakly organized interests or commonweal organizations. Although workplace democracy was valued, it was not to replace or constrain the operation of political democracy. In short, some of the "corporatist" aspects of the postwar welfare state were questioned.

The solution suggested was not to collect all power in the hands of government. Such a move would have been counter to the Willoch government's ideology and principles of decentralization and power sharing. It was also judged to be unrealistic because hierarchical channels were seen as having limited capacity and as being cumbersome to use. Thus, the task was to relieve central government of decisions, and to increase the integrative capacity and the ability to establish general goals, frameworks, and principles for decisions to be made elsewhere. The sovereign consumer, the private corporation, and the competitive market were to be given more central places in public administration. A powerful bureaucracy was to become more productive and more directed toward public needs and preferences. Where marketlike conditions could not be established, an incentive structure was to be constructed to simulate markets.

The program was also concerned with the value base of society and political life. It emphasized that democratic governance needed both (1) a sense of community, joint interests, shared loyalties, identification, a sense of justice, due process, and predictability, and (2) institutional spheres beyond political intervention and majority rule that guarantee the rights of citizens and protect private initiative. These issues were viewed as being made particularly important by trends in Norwegian society as it moved from a relatively homogeneous Christian-humanitarian culture to a more heterogeneous one. These pluralistic trends were reflected in efforts to give the (state) Church of Norway more autonomy from political intervention and to establish more nonpolitical appellate institutions, independent courtlike agencies, similar to the present ombudsmen and the Insurance Court.

This program of the Norwegian conservative-center government embodied a desire to move away from the "corporatist" organizational basis of the welfare state that had evolved in Norway since 1945. Politics was to be insulated more from corporations and organized interests. Public corporations were to be treated in the same way as private firms and were expected to compete on equal terms. Business and service agencies were to be given more autonomy where competition could be established. The basic framework for social life was to be provided through the political system. The rights of citizens and other social values were to be protected from majoritarian principles. And the market was to be used to assure the provision of public services with the highest possible productivity and flexibility.

The reform program was implemented to some degree before the conservative-center government was replaced in 1986 by a social democratic government. Between 1981 and 1986 the number of governmental boards and committees was reduced by more than 200. Partly this reduction was cosmetic, a result of updating statistical records more than changing patterns of representation. But partly the reduction was real, and a break with the trend of growth since 1945. Some separation of political, administrative, expertise, and businesslike functions was accomplished, as well as some separation between functions exposed to competition and those not. While the ideals of the competitive market were emphasized in most of the steps that were taken, the importance of strengthening political control was also emphasized, for instance in the reorganization of the health service (Christensen, 1985), the administration of aid to developing countries (Kloster, 1984), the state oil company (Krogh, 1987), and the Bank of Norway. The granting of more autonomy based on institutional arguments was most obvious in the case of the Norwegian state church.

The story was different when it came to issues of privatization and deregulation. Privatization is an ambiguous policy term covering a variety of changes in the relationship between the public and the private sector (Kristensen, 1984; 1987a; 1987b; 1987c; Kay and Thompson, 1986), but it is a term with strong, and opposite, symbolic meaning in different political cultures. For instance, in the United States President Reagan could appeal to a political culture and a rhetoric that, for the most part, assumed the superiority of private sector solutions to public solutions (Downs and Larkey, 1986), and privatization was accorded an even higher priority in the president's second term than in the first one (Benda and Levine, 1988: 124). In the Nordic countries "privatization" provoked strong negative reactions even when the term was used to refer to ordinary processes of adjustment between the public and the private sector, usually widely accepted (Olsen, 1986b; Christensen, 1987; Kristensen, 1987a).

For instance, in Norway privatization was described as turning back the clock. Privatization proposals were viewed as a general attack on the welfare state—as a "cookbook for the destruction of the welfare state" and as the "starting signal of an extensive ideological battle that may shatter hard-won unity and solidarity, reinforce old injustices and infuse life into destructive adversarial relationships between groups and classes" (Olsen, 1986b). A consequence of this response was that the privatization issue faded, at least temporarily.

In Denmark, a similar debate took place and the government removed privatization from the agenda long before an attempt to implement a privatization policy was really tried. The word disappeared from the Danish political vocabulary (Kristensen, 1987a). "Deregulation" also became politicized in Denmark. Christensen (1987) describes deregulation as the story of an ambitious political initiative which gradually fell victim to bureaucratic reluctance and disinterest on the part of economic interest organizations. Among ministers there never was much enthusiasm for it or it gradually eroded. In Sweden and Finland, governments have seen privatization as even less attractive as an explicit policy, and the new Norwegian social democratic government in its 1987-program was very negative toward privatization as a solution to contemporary problems.

The lesson learned by the nonsocialist government in Denmark, like its counterpart in Norway, was to de-emphasize the political and ideological aspects of administrative reform. As deregulation turned out to be more onerous and less popular than expected, the Danish government presented to Parliament in November 1983 a much-publicized plan for modernizing the public sector (Finansministeriet, 1983). "Modernization'' was not expected to provoke anyone.[2] Christensen (1987) argues that the very looseness of this plan guaranteed that it would not meet the same kind of fierce opposition as deregulation. The Ministry of Finance commented that since redistribution turned out to be problematic, it was necessary to improve productivity (Finansministeriet, 1987: 8). Likewise, Mellbourn, commenting on the Swedish policy (1986: 103), argues that it was tempting to refer to management theories from private business because they were perceived as apolitical and noncontroversial.

The Danish government, while resisting any link to ''privatization,'' was eager to be in the forefront of ''modernizing'' the public sector. The new philosophy was the best possible service at lowest costs. ''It shall become easier to be a Dane'' (Finansministeriet, 1987). The Swedish social democratic government, in its statement on the modernization of the public sector, said that the welfare of citizens was the goal of all public activity. The program was for citizens and against bureaucracy (Regeringens skrivelse, 1984-1985: 202; Mellbourn, 1986: 20). Similar formulations could be found in the other programs. The goals were better service, better economy and efficiency, better workplaces for the employees, and more democracy through more influence for elected leaders and citizens. Notably lacking was any explicit discussion of the trade-offs among such goals or between them and the institutional principles they imply. The programs included some operational goals, but the ''philosophy'' of the administrative policy was coached in grand, symbolic terms open to many different interpretations.

INSTITUTIONAL FRICTIONS
IN COMPREHENSIVE REFORM

Reorganization efforts in the Nordic countries were couched substantially within an apolitical rhetoric. The task of reform was seen as organizing the public sector to serve shared, prior goals with economy and efficiency. The language of programs for reform retreated from themes, such as privatization and cutbacks, that were politically divisive. The reform programs, and particularly the specific policies implemented, seemed to be what Anderson (1983) called a bland alternative, a choice with a low probability of producing either highly negative or highly positive effects. They involved a fair amount of rhetoric about institutional reform, but that rhetoric seemed to have a greater immediate effect on subsequent rhetoric than it did on subsequent policies or practice.

This Nordic experience with comprehensive reform was in some respects reminiscent of the American experience discussed in Chapter 5, even if the rhetoric and the symbolic meaning of key terms were different. Ideological differences were aired, but the general tendency was either to avoid ideological battles or to debate ideology at a level of generality at which differences are indistinguishable from agreements. The apolitical approach, the tendency to avoid major institutional dilemmas, and the modest resources invested in institutionalizing reform all suggest that institutional reform in the Nordic countries had rather little direct effect upon either institutions or ideology, at least up to 1988.

On the other hand, during the first part of the 1980s there was widespread, and growing, political support for reforming the public bureaucracy in the Nordic countries. Political leaders emphasized a desire to pursue comprehensive reforms. They formulated programs and policies, established some new agencies, and routinized reporting on reform achievements. Some initiatives were also being taken to improve the knowledge basis of administrative reforms. For instance, in Norway the Research Council for Applied Social Research was established with a special responsibility for the public sector. Also, the mood of the political debate changed somewhat. It became more legitimate to question public monopolies, to oppose subsidies to inefficient industries, agriculture, and the fisheries, and to ask for changes in the rules of social welfare systems. The self-images of civil servants started to change (Czarniawska, 1985). Likewise, the symbols of the state began to change (Harbo, 1985; Høgetveit, 1985). For instance, in Sweden two-thirds of the central boards and agencies of the state changed or modified their graphic symbols between 1980 and 1985. They replaced the traditional three-crown symbol of the Swedish state with modern logotypes associated with private companies and mass advertising (Petersson and Freden, 1987). Finally, it also became more unusual for governments to make important decisions without the participation of organized interest groups. A possible implication is that the reform efforts set off, or became a part of, a long-term process of change in institutional norms, interpretations, and, eventually, standard operating procedures.

This history can be contrasted with the related experience in Great Britain, where the political tone was sharply confrontational and ideological. The task of changing "the machinery of government" absorbed a generous slice of the energies of several recent prime ministers and their most senior advisors—despite the argument that such activities lacked popular appeal, were unglamorous, and remained politically unrewarding (Pollit, 1984).

The organization of comprehensive reforms in Britain was institutionalized rather than ad hoc. Arnold (1988) compared reorganizations in the United States and Great Britain in the twentieth century and argued that the cabinet became the main arena for executive reorganization planning in Britain. While the use of committees and commissions was not unknown, administrative reform was viewed in Britain as inseparable from the task of the cabinet—a process which could not be referred to a body outside the cabinet and its instruments. Decisions about such matters could be made within the cabinet and without specific public justification. The process was political and guarded. In contrast, as we have seen in Chapter 5, the tradition in the United States was to attempt large-scale reorganization through ad hoc commissions, committees, and task forces. Outside experts were heavily represented, and the official language and justifications for reorganization were apolitical, that is couched in efficiency terms rather than in policy terms.

The differences were related to institutional and historical differences. In Britain administrative reform became a policy tool for the prime minister precisely because responsible administrative authority was located within the cabinet. In contrast, American administrative reform was enmeshed in the political struggle between the Congress and the presidency. Thus, administrative reform assumed a political role defined by the drama of authority and governance specific to a political regime (Arnold, 1988). To a larger extent than in the Nordic countries, both the British and the American experience during the 1980s was one in which reform was actively defined as political, but the structure and traditions of American politics drove the issue from the main political agenda. Thus, the seemingly apolitical character of reform in the United States, like that in the Nordic countries, stemmed in part from a political reluctance to deal explicitly with unresolved conflict in this domain. But the process in the Nordic countries, more than in the United States, was affected by a tradition of seeking consensus on major political issues.

Metcalfe and Richards (1987) relate the course of administrative reform in Britain to the fact that the prime minister herself exhibited a long-term commitment to institutional reform, and that feedback and evaluation processes were established at the highest political level to monitor departmental programs. By 1985 it became common to claim that the British civil service was at a crossroads (Wass, 1985; Harrison and Gratton, 1987; Fry, 1988), and the changes introduced in the British civil service after the Conservative victory in 1979 were described as a watershed in the evolution of British government (Metcalfe and Richards, 1987). While the reform plans were expected to fade away, the Thatcher government set a new direction and instigated changes in the culture of Whitehall which may be difficult to reverse.[3] Issues like the elimination or cutback of agencies and services, privatization and deregulation, as well as economy and efficiency, were placed at the top of the agenda. The style was one of political confrontation, between political parties, as well as in relation to civil servants, unions, and affected interest groups.

Without claiming that this simple analysis adequately characterizes the differences between the Nordic countries and others, we wish to examine the implications of the apparent differences for understanding institutional reform and politics more generally. To do so, we shall consider two institutional friction interpretations of the development of the politics of comprehensive reform that are consistent with the apparent differences between Nordic experience and experience in Great Britain and the United States. The first is the idea that a political system does not respond instantly to small deviations in power. The second is the idea that comprehensive reform requires strong organizational capabilities.

Institutional friction is assumed by virtually any institutional perspective. That is, it is assumed that institutional arrangements, once established, survive until the external demands for change are fairly substantial. Institutions are stabilized through absorption of protest and co-optation (Selznick, 1949), or by rejecting deviants (Lægreid and Olsen, 1978). They are also stabilized when they allow what Merton (1957: 318) called institutionalized evasions. For instance, citizens' initiatives and civil disobedience might work as an institutional evasion of the normative prescription of representative democracy, making representative democracy more robust against change. The more an institution is integrated into a larger political order so that changes in one institution require changes in several other institutions, the less likely is change (Krasner, 1988). Thus, the expectation is one of historical junctures which provide the opportunity for major change. Whether that opportunity is exploited depends partly on the level of support from key political groups and figures, in short on political leadership (OECD, 1980: 13). The solutions introduced at such unusual times are frozen into new structures which constrain future change.

From such a point of view, radical shocks to a public administration, like the one the Thatcher government gave the British civil service, are only likely to succeed if there are significant inefficiencies in the historical development of political institutions. That is, if the authority and power exercised by civil servants and the leaders of organized interest groups deviate considerably from what they would have been at equilibrium (a clearance of the "authority and power market"). A comparative study of the institutions, interests, resources, conflicts, and alliances organized around reform issues would probably show that those traditionally support-ing the integration of organized interests into public policy making (i.e., social democratic parties, trade unions, bureaucrats, and interest groups benefiting from governmental programs) were relatively stronger in the Nordic countries during the 1980s than they were in the United Kingdom and in the United States (Olsen, 1981).

Institutional friction is also linked to the relation between proposed changes and the normative order of an institution (March and Olsen, 1975). The idea of comprehensive reforms is not alien to the Nordic countries. On the contrary, all the Nordic countries, and in particular Sweden, have traditionally shown great confidence in their capacity for reform and in their ability to design effective and efficient bureaucracies (Hedborg and Meidner, 1984). Governments have also intervened success-fully and achieved specified goals (Roness, 1979; J. G. Christensen, 1980; Lundquist and Ståhlberg, 1982; Egeberg, 1984;1987; T. Christen-sen, 1985; Söderlind and Petersson, 1986). The specific administrative reforms suggested in the international debate of the 1980s, however, were inconsistent with political traditions of the Nordic countries, as was abrupt, radical change. The welfare state in the Nordic countries was the result of historical compromises among political parties and among economic interest groups. After the mid 1930s, a political style of fact-oriented cooperation, compromise, and trust developed. Talking each other into consensus through a ''sounding out''–process, peaceful coexistence, and revolution in slow motion were institutionalized as the appropriate way of approaching pressing social problems (Olsen, 1972; Olsen, Roness, and Sætren, 1982; Øvrelid, 1984).

In contrast, the British political system had a postwar history of confron-tations over the nationalization and denationalization of industry. Impos-ing privatization and the elimination of agencies and programs was consistent with this tradition. It helped to focus cleavages and alliances, and thus to facilitate political mobilization. Within the British tradition, conflict and criticism were exploited to facilitate change. Through atten-tion to major cleavages, the themes of reform were kept alive politically. Through such a sense of political relevance, reform issues and the mundane reports that came from reform agencies retained their political relevance.

Conflict and criticism also stimulate efforts to quell them. Consider the conflict over ''privatization'' and the threat it provided to public agencies. It is often argued that the likelihood of cutbacks in public agencies decrease if the agencies are able to restructure themselves. Less attention is paid to the possibility that reforms may be easier in the face of cutbacks or threats of cutbacks. For instance, ''privatization''

107

proposals create conflict and political attention. Such proposals are likely to be viewed as provocations and external threats by civil servants. Civil servants may leave or try to resist all changes, and the climate of cooperation may deteriorate. But, threats of privatization may also make civil servants more accepting of reforms, stimulating mundane processes of institutional change and making change "from below" more likely. For instance, Caiden (1984: 264) argues that, compared with other change proposals, administrative reform looks quite moderate and acceptable to rival interest groups. Internal resistance to reorganization is likely to diminish when threatened with drastic economies and the termination of programs. In such a case, the key to comprehensive administrative reform may be to keep the theme of privatization alive and reform on the political agenda.

These advantages of stimulating political conflict and confrontation through radical shocks and political persistence are easily recognized, but the idea of imposing major institutional change and creating political confrontation violated the postwar Nordic tradition of establishing widespread consensus before major reforms were implemented. Thus, abrupt reform would have threatened not only established administrative institutions of the Nordic countries but also their sense of proper political procedure. During the 1980s, the institutional strength of a Nordic welfare state lay particularly in its ability to cope in a pragmatic way with immediate problems and in its long-run capability for molding public values. Practical solutions and broad social agreement, rather than the discussion of principles and the construction of theories and ideologies, were its trademarks.

In many ways, the lack of ideological discussions and the use of consensus to solve specific problems were preconditions for the successes of the model Nordic state (Olsen, 1981). Within Nordic traditions, the most likely way to achieve comprehensive administrative change was to use the time necessary to create a new, shared understanding and to mobilize commitment, support, and consensus around reforms. The apolitical approach with modest attempts to introduce debates over competing institutional principles, the slow development of special agencies with a responsibility for change, the emphasis on professional competence rather than hierarchical authority, and the modest initial results can be interpreted as reflecting an application of Nordic political styles to a new situation. Those styles emphasized the gradual molding of attitudes about the public sector, exploring the political and institutional possibilities for reform, and searching for new visions of the role of the public sector in future society.

To some degree the Nordic reform programs focused competing institutional principles and values, but at least up to 1988 they had not led to new concepts or visions of democratic governance. Old visions of the benefits of the market, the *Rechtsstaat,* majority government, governmental hierarchies, voluntary associations and community initiatives were activated, but in general it appeared difficult to formulate a shared vision or an ideological superstructure for reforms in the public sector. As observed by the Swedish Federation of Trade Unions (LO) in 1986 (1986: 175): "Today it is perhaps less self-evident what our dreams look like." If a prerequisite for reform in the face of institutional frictions is the reformulation of a political vision, Nordic states in the 1980s were ill-equipped to achieve it. It seemed likely that a major reorientation would depend on ideological political conflict, political parties, and public opinion becoming more important in the political life of the Nordic states.

The second institutional friction interpretation of differences in approaches to institutional reform emphasizes variations in institutional capacities for comprehensive change. In Great Britain, as we have seen, reform was directed and coordinated from the highest levels of political authority. In the United States, President Reagan wanted to ensure a continued, organized emphasis on management improvement (Benda and Levine, 1986: 387), and in 1982 he established a Cabinet Council on Management and Administration that provided an official unit in the White House responsible for overall coordination and direction of management reform efforts, including those taken by the Office of Management and Budget. The initiative, however, ran counter to the American political-administrative traditions we have described in Chapter 5, and the Council had relatively little effect. The president shied away from centralizing management improvement responsibility (Benda and Levine, 1986). Efforts were carried out through multiagency channels (Hansen, 1985), and the president turned to a common vehicle for presidential policy development by appointing the Grace Commission which involved more than 2000 participants (Salamon and Lund, 1987).

In the Nordic countries, ministries and ministerial departments, as well as the committees in the parliaments, responsible for administrative reforms, have traditionally been weak politically and of low status. Moreover, Nordic governments have been reluctant to invest major resources in institutional reform and have spread control over the change in interinstitutional networks rather than concentrate it in a permanent central change agency. Since many of the resources critical to the success of an administrative policy were controlled by other agencies than those responsible for the reform programs, administrative policies had to be directed toward influencing those institutions. The role of central agencies with special responsibility for administrative policy making was to facilitate, stimulate, motivate, and help, rather than to control the change process. They were supposed to act on the basis of distinct technical competence rather than formal position. A prevailing attitude in the reform programs was that each institution was responsible for developing itself. Formal authority and political power may be sufficient when one is to make cuts and abolish administrative units. When reforms aim at changing administrative culture, concepts of meaning, norms, and identities, the resources necessary to mobilize support and commitment for change among civil servants and others directly affected appear to be considerably larger.

These restrictions on institutional capabilities made it difficult to focus attention and energy, to create motivation and commitment, and to set priorities and review experiences. For example, the failure of administrative policies in Sweden has been explained partly by the fact that the high ambitions of comprehensive administrative policies were not reflected in the organization of the reform process. Mellbourn (1986) described the minister of civil affairs as a general without troops, and argued that the failure of the reform process was a clear demarcation of the political limits of administrative policy making. Mellbourn also argued that the lack of coordination between the Ministry of Finance and the Ministry of Civil Affairs, and the weak position of the latter, contributed to the failure of Swedish policies. Such coordination problems seemed to exist, whether the responsibility of administrative policy making was located in a separate ministry (as in Norway and Sweden) or in a department of the Ministry of Finance (as in Denmark and Finland).

An active policy focused upon reforming the public bureaucracy, rather than simply adding or eliminating agencies and programs, may also be hindered by a lack of appropriate information and by the absence of a legitimate profession with recognized expertise for dealing with that information. The modern welfare state has to a large extent assumed a shared information base and a rational, fact-oriented style (Ruin, 1982). However, the information base developed has been linked primarily to economic models and data and to substantive social policies. Administrative reform has proceeded without serious efforts to build an inventory of information on which it might be based. Explicit theoretical models have been less important than practical, institution-specific knowledge and political pressure (Sjöblom and Ståhlberg, 1987). Often neither the objectives nor the effects of organizational changes have been clear (Gjerde, 1983; Christensen, 1985). Typically, governments have been accused of ill-considered reorganization proposals and decisions. Problems, goals, alternative organizational forms, and their consequences have been badly specified and analyzed. Little has been done afterwards to collect data about actual effects.

INSTITUTIONAL REFORM AS CONSTITUTIONAL CHANGE

Lurking behind the institutional frictions we have identified above is a grander issue of constitutionalism. When the apparently mundane and nonpolitical concerns of administrative efficiency become central concerns of the political process, the polity is likely to be led to issues of the constitutional principles upon which the political organization of society should be based, and thus of the moral dilemmas of democratic governance. By constitutional principles we mean those aspects of a polity that are generally viewed as not subject to routine political determination through various forms of majority rule.

The proper balance between majority rule and constitutional principles is an ancient, and perpetually controversial, one (Walzer, 1983; Slagstad, 1987). Democratic ideology assumes that elected leaders may design or choose the institutional forms so that they contribute to the achievement of political goals in the most effective and efficient way. Developing political institutions that reflect popular sovereignty is seen as a first-order political process and the struggle over institutional forms is at the heart of politics (Wheeler, 1968). The winners of the political competition have the authority and power to mold political institutions. When the focus is on constitutional principles, however, democratic ideology emphasizes the constraints placed by constitutional rules and established institutions on deliberate institutional design and choice.

Different polities define different things as being part of what is "taken as given," and the distinction between "constitutional" issues and those that are not is often elusive. Most political systems make more refined distinctions than the dichotomy permits. Nevertheless, it is clear that the comprehensive reform of political institutions is often classified as being toward the constitutional end of the scale, and so requires something closer to consensus than do other kinds of political actions. Such a program affects the political order regulating the exercise of public authority and power. A change in this order may alter the values of the state, the purpose and meaning of state actions, the rationale and legitimacy of institutional boundaries, the regulation of conflict, and the conditions under which different interests may be pursued (Poggi, 1978: 97; Dyson, 1980: 206).

From such a perspective, changes in administrative structure or procedures can be seen as challenging elements of the core system of meaning, belief, interpretation, status, power, and alliances in politics (Goodman and Kurke, 1982). Institutional reform involves issues of the proper role of the state and politics in society, the ethical base and legitimacy of government, and the appropriate priorities for the public agenda. In a modern era of administrative institutions, therefore, we should not be surprised if comprehensive administrative reorganization is treated by some political systems as a fundamental change for which substantial consensus is required. In an increasingly administrative structure of governance, however, such a treatment places much of the apparatus of effective popular control beyond the reach of elected officials.

The constitutional history of Western democracies varies from country to country, but the transformation of many countries from liberal-democratic states with modest public agendas to welfare states created a model of constitutional governance that can be described as a *corporate-bargaining* state. The corporate-bargaining state has a stable, institutionalized political process characterized by: a reduced role given to parliaments, ideological parties, and the public; the delegation of authority to a network of boards and committees where bureaucrats and organized interests are the main participants; a political agenda dominated by technical issues rather than broad ideological ones; a low level of conflict; and an emphasis on compromise. That model has been widely used, particularly to describe the governments of Western Europe (Heisler and Kvavik, 1974).

In the corporate-bargaining state, parliamentary governance based on electoral victory recedes in importance. In Rokkan's (1966) words—votes count but resources decide. Winning elections gives a place at the bargaining table, but the formal hierarchy is only a part of the real structure of control. Organized interests have direct, integrated participation in the formation of public policy and the administration of public programs (Egeberg, 1981; Olsen, 1981). Bureaucratic agencies are unlikely to be neutral instruments for elected leaders. Civil servants become key players in public policy making—as defenders of different institutions, agencies, values, and clients. Their views and behavior are formed by the tasks for which they are responsible, by the agencies and professions to which they belong, and by the parts of the environment with which they interact. They usually perceive their roles as negotiators or mediators—not impartial judges (Lægreid and Olsen, 1978; 1984; Olsen, 1983). As ideas about workplace democracy and codetermination spread from the private to the public sector, the associations of civil servants also become major participants (Lægreid, 1983).

In a corporate-bargaining state, political leaders are unable arbitrarily to design or reform the public bureaucracy. Reorganizations result from struggles over the control of organizations, and organizational structures are the results of previous political fights. To be effective, the reorganization process must reflect the heterogeneity of interests, beliefs, and power that surround public policy making (Rourke, 1957; March, 1962). Changes in the organization of the bureaucracy are a result of changes in constellations of interests, resources, and alliances. Elections and renegotiation of government coalitions have an impact, as do changes in the relative position of agencies, professional groups, experts, and organized interests in society.

The principles of the corporate-bargaining state are at odds with the principles of other contending visions of politics (Olsen, 1988a). Compare, for example, the *sovereign* state. Here the role of the state is to shape society to the political preferences, plans, and visions of a good society. Winning public elections gives political leaders the necessary authority, legitimacy, and power to act as the architects of society. Citizens are voters and subordinates of the state. The bureaucracy is a neutral instrument and its task is to implement political goals and programs. Political leaders design the administrative apparatus to make it more effective and efficient. The standard organizational model is the departmental agency, embedded in a hierarchy of influence, responsibility, and control, and insulated from other influences. Leaders may be ignorant about causal effects, but they have the authority or power to make choices. Thus, changes in organizations primarily follow changes in political leadership, such as when a government loses an election, or when coalitions break down and new ones are formed.

Similarly, the principles of the corporate-bargaining state are at odds with the *institutional* state. The institutional state is viewed as a political and moral order, and as a collection of long-lasting standard operating procedures reflecting values, principles, and beliefs that are shared by most of the population. The primary task of the state is to guarantee the political order and the autonomy of various institutional spheres of society. Political leaders are obliged to defend uniform and collective standards of appropriateness and justice, with a reference to what is best for society as a whole. Such standards rank higher than numerical democracy and cannot be changed arbitrarily through majority decisions. Rules of law are constraints on governmental actions rather than instruments of majority governance or vehicles for bargaining. Decision-making agencies act within clear regulations and standards. The public is viewed as consisting of citizens with system-defined rights and duties.

In the institutional state, governmental agencies are not neutral instru-

113

ments. They are carriers of cultures, missions, values, and identities. They are unlikely to adapt automatically to any attempts at influence, including those of political leaders (March, 1981b). Organizations are not designed, they develop slowly and imperceptibly over time through a "natural," historical process (Sait, 1938). Their long-run development reflects a gradual accommodation of practices and structures to changing conceptions of solutions, problems, and meaning. Rather than being transformed as a result of prior intentions, they evolve. Reorganizations formalize developments that have already taken place. They are symbolic and rhetorical events that educate the public and change the climate of opinion. Reorganization processes facilitate the maintenance, development, and transmission of cultural norms and beliefs, and they keep concepts, theories, and proposals alive (March and Olsen, 1983). Agency autonomy is based not upon leaders' choice, but upon a shared norm of noninterference and an appeal to higher and more stable values than numerical democracy, majority decision, ministerial responsibility, or interest group bargaining.

The prototypic organization in the institutional state is the independent court embedded in a political and moral order. The term of the major actors is indefinite. They exercise authority in a way that reconciles the history and the future of the institution, without necessarily reflecting or adjusting to the demands of a current set of elected political leaders, voters, consumers, employees, or owners. There may be substantial conflict between the immediate self-interest of current constituencies and the long-run interest of future constituencies. The idea of independence in courts or bureaus assumes that it is possible to identify or train incorruptible judges capable of perceiving the long-run logic of the institution. It also assumes that it is possible to induce the public to accept, a posteriori, actions in the name of the institution that they would not necessarily have chosen a priori (Hayes and March, 1970). Like Ulysses, they are willing to tie themselves to the mast in order to avoid the Sirens' song about short-term interests and benefits (Elster, 1979).

Finally, the corporate-bargaining state, with its focus on the bargaining table rather than the market (Hernes, 1978) is inconsistent with a view of politics as a free market system for providing services. In the *supermarket state* model, the state enters the market as one of several providers of a great variety of goods and services. Political leaders are the "bookkeepers of the great necessities" (Seip, 1958), but the market is the principal allocative mechanism. Agencies are supposed to perform services in the most efficient way and to adapt to changing needs and circumstances. The public is viewed as sovereign consumers or clients.

Survival, flexibility, economy, and efficiency become the key values for assessing organizational forms. Competition is the main factor in assuring flexibility, adaptability, and innovation. The flexibility of any particular organization depends on acquiring good intelligence about external changes and upon its capacity to process this information and respond appropriately. This implies a need for delegating decisions to those who have the necessary information and expertise (Child and Kieser, 1981).

The standard organizational model in the supermarket state is the corporation embedded in a competitive market. A government agency is just one among many market actors. Within this model, a common demand has been that public administration has to change from an "administrative culture" to a "service culture." Although such attitudes have not been universally accepted in political life, claims that the private sector is clearly better organized than the public are fairly well established as folk wisdom in countries such as the United States (Downs and Larkey, 1986). Where the private sector has been established as a model for the public sector, the villain is the bureaucratic organizational form. Modernization of public administration is often portrayed as the substitution of up-to-date business management methods for the old-fashioned administrative practices of public agencies (Metcalfe and Richards, 1987). The thrust of many recent reorganization efforts in the public sector has been to solve organizational problems of the public sector by using the private sector as a role model (Czarniawska, 1985).

These contending visions of the state are part of the current debate within which comprehensive administrative reform occurs. They suggest that some of the more profound issues of democratic governance can arise in the context of thinking about political institutions and their reform. As we saw in Chapter 5, the political process is not always a debate of first principles. But where administrative changes are seen as raising constitutional issues, administrative reform is likely to become a domain for shaping the way people in general think and talk about the state, including the values on which the state should be based (Mill, [1862] 1950; Goodin, 1986; Sunstein, 1988). Under such conditions, institutional changes in a democratic polity can not be imposed by government, by a majority in parliament, or be settled within the conventional corporate-bargaining procedures. As Lipson wrote about an earlier period of constitutional ferment, "When traditional modes of government are rejected, and men apply their reason to the deliberate formation of something new, they necessarily confront the issues that are fundamental. The organization of the state and the power of its agents, the rights of citizens and their duties, all have to be examined" (Lipson, 1964: 396).

So, we come to a discussion of the ways in which we might think about reforming political institutions in a democratic context. It is a classic question. In the tradition of cooperative games, most recent evaluations of constitutional systems of government have focused on their maintenance as contracts in repeated interactions. The interpretation is insightful and has proven productive in generating theorems within game theory, but it is hard to see that it can be a general explanation. Our intent is more in the tradition of classical questions of political philosophy. In the next two chapters we try, in such a spirit, to identify some criteria for evaluating institutions in politics.

7

The Search for
Appropriate Institutions

In chapters 4, 5, and 6, we examined the intentional reform of political institutions as it has been observed in several contemporary democracies. The analysis suggests that although the implementation of intention is complicated and uncertain, the process of institutional change is important to the development of polities, particularly since the process is relatively slow and the outcomes relatively indeterminate. In this chapter and the next one, we turn to questions of institutional design. We ask how we might think of political institutions as instruments of democracy.

We consider current issues of institutional reform on the basis of strands drawn from three rather distinct traditions. The first tradition is that of classical political theory and modern democratic theory. It attempts to specify the bases for evaluating alternative forms of political, social, or economic organization (Dahl and Lindblom, 1953; Pitkin, 1967). The second tradition is that of modern economics. It attempts to determine the conditions for beneficial use of alternative forms of economic and political institutions, particularly systems of voluntary exchange (Arrow, 1974; Williamson, 1975; 1985). The third tradition is that of behavioral research on organizations. It attempts to understand how social institutions actually function (Pfeffer, 1982; Scott, 1987a).

THE INSTITUTIONS OF POPULAR SOVEREIGNTY

The core idea of theories of popular sovereignty is that the will of the people should ultimately prevail (Pitkin, 1967). The theories differ in their conceptions of who "the people" are (is), how "the will of the people" is discovered, how long "ultimately" is, and what it means to "prevail." The differences are enacted into differences between the traditions of what we will call *aggregative* political processes, on the one hand, and *integrative* political processes, on the other. The distinctions are found in political theory, where they are linked to the contrast between contractual and communal perspectives on social organization (Birnbaum, Lively, and Parry, 1978; Dallmayr, 1978). They are also found in classical organization theory (Follett, 1918), in modern sociological treatments of institutions (DiMaggio, 1985), and in discussions of the role of psychology in public policy (Sarason, 1986). The differences between aggregation and integration are important for assessing real political institutions, which tend to involve a mixture of both.

The traditions of aggregation define "the people" as a collection of individuals currently qualified to be treated as citizens; the traditions of integration define "the people" as a group extending backward through history and forward into the future. In an aggregative process, the will of the people is discovered through political campaigns and bargaining among rational citizens each pursuing self-interest within a set of rules for governance through majority rule. In an integrative process, the will of the people is discovered through deliberation by reasoning citizens and rulers seeking to find the general welfare within a context of shared social values (Mashaw, 1985). Aggregative theories commonly presume an order based on rationality and exchange. Integrative theories commonly presume an order based on history, obligation, and reason.

Leadership in aggregative processes involves the brokerage of coalitions among interests. Leadership in an integrative process involves a trusteeship for social traditions and future needs, and an educational role. Theories of aggregative processes emphasize the instantaneous response to current interests of the people. Integrative processes assume a slower adaptation of the system and protections against momentary passions and rationalities. Aggregative theories emphasize the supremacy of majority rule. Integrative theories put majority rule within a framework of rights and institutional norms. Theories of aggregation see public policies and the allocation of resources as the primary outcome of a political process. Theories of integration see the development of a polity with shared purpose and trust as the primary outcome.

These differences lead to differences in approaches to some fundamental issues in governance. Consider, for example, the problem of agency. Political institutions involve the use of agents to prepare agenda, provide information, and make and implement decisions. Since agents cannot be presumed to share the value and knowledge premises of the people for whom they serve as agents, there is a problem of coordination. This problem is usually pictured as a problem of securing compliance, of assuring that the agent acts in the service of the principal (Ross, 1973; Fama, 1980; Levinthal, 1988).

Within aggregative theories of rational exchange, the problem of agency is defined as a problem of incentive compatibility. Bureaucrats are pictured as having private agendas and preferences that they seek to further through their official positions. Solutions to the problem are found in the design of incentives and controls, such that an agent acting rationally in his own self-interest will further the interests of the people. Classical systems of "spoils" in politics have been justified as ways of making the actions of administrative agents compatible with the desires of their constituencies, partly by favoritism for agents from the right family, cultural, gender, and ethnic background and partly by making access to rewards conditional on political reliability (Kingsley, 1944; Krislov, 1974). Similarly, systems of representative bureaucracies with short tenure or mixed (corporate) systems intertwine the fates of clients and bureaucrats through mutual co-optation (Krislov and Rosenbloom, 1981).

Within integrative theories of reasoned obligation, on the other hand, the problem of agency is one of official or professional integrity. Solutions are found in the socialization of agents to an ethic of administrative duty and autonomy. The classical bureaucrat acts in a manner appropriate to a position rather than in accord with personal preferences and can be trusted to do so, even in the face of considerable temptation to do something else (Weber, [1924] 1978; Lægreid and Olsen, 1978; Thompson, 1980). The issue is trust, and the appeal is to values that transcend self.

CRITERIA FOR ASSESSING AGGREGATIVE INSTITUTIONS

In most modern theories of popular sovereignty, political systems are seen as aggregating diverse individual and group interests into collective choices. They assume that the "people" who are to be represented are individuals, that those individuals have interests (preferences, wants, desires), and that the interests are jointly inconsistent (Sen, 1970; Pattanaik, 1971). That is, it is assumed that everyone cannot be simultaneously completely satisfied. The political problem is to specify a procedure that allocates scarce resources in a way that is satisfactory, without eliminating the pluralism of interests and values. In that respect, political systems are similar to economic systems built around competitive markets and prices.

Political processes of aggregation are fundamentally processes of interests, power, and exchange, and the study of such processes occupies much of the study of political institutions. Early discussions of political aggregation emphasized the role of electoral campaigns and voting as a way of recording individual preferences (Downs, 1957; Black, 1958). More recent portrayals picture the vote as one of many resources used in the formation of political coalitions. Political participants are seen as entering with certain resources (power) and interests. Candidates for office (or policies) seek the support of individuals whose combined power is adequate to win the election or establish the policy. The process is one of coalition formation, trades, and promises through which each participant seeks to achieve the best possible outcome for himself or herself, recognizing that not everything is possible. The prototypic instrument is the construction of a party platform or a legislative logroll, but the process extends through the entire course of decision making, from the formulation of alternatives, to the gathering of information about them, the formal choice, and the implementation of the decision.

Evaluations of alternative political institutions as instruments for aggregating private preferences emphasize questions of allocative efficiency subject to initial endowments or resources of participants and their preferences. The question of *efficiency* is: Does the institution find all mutually satisfactory voluntary exchanges that exist, that is, can it find Pareto-optimal solutions reliably and inexpensively? This idea of trading or market efficiency, taken from economics, is both more precise and somewhat narrower than the idea of efficiency in ordinary discourse, though many "inefficiencies" noted in common discourse could probably also be shown to be "inefficiencies" in these terms (Ordeshook, 1986).

The question of *preferences* is: Do the participants have preferences suitable for an aggregative process? The issues are threefold: First, do the participants agree on a set of constitutional constraints governing the aggregation process? These constraints include the rules of the game by which exchange takes place. For example, the rules underlying many political aggregative processes exclude the use of physical force to control the process of aggregation. In addition, they make, or seek to make, exchange agreements enforceable. And they may require certain kinds of disclosures and forbid others. In particular, they may seek to regulate the falsification of preferences.

Second, are the preferences of participants suitably precise for aggregation through voluntary exchange? Specifically, preferences are normally assumed to be consistent, stable, and exogenous, or convertible to some that are (March, 1978; 1981a; Elster, 1983b). Consistency assures that the process of interpersonal exchange is not confounded by intrapersonal confusion. Stability assures that agreements sensible in terms of the preferences of today can be expected to be sensible later. Exogeneity assures that preferences determine choices, rather than the converse.

Third, are the preferences of participants tolerable? Theories of aggregation assume that choices should reflect the preferences of participants, and hence that those preferences are within a range of acceptability. The reality of evil and the possibility of evil being reflected in the subjective preferences of participants is recognized in most systems by restrictions on admission to the rights of participation. It is shelved, but not eliminated, in formal discussions by presumptions of moral relativism. Nevertheless, it must be recognized that the appropriateness of an exchange system built on individual action in the name of personal preferences depends on the quality of the preferences. If the tastes of some participants are immoral, an efficient exchange system will reflect that immorality.

The question of initial *endowments* is: Are initial endowments, including rights, resources, and authority, distributed appropriately? The main claim of an efficient exchange system is that it finds Pareto-optimal solutions, but the particular Pareto-optimal solution discovered is extremely sensitive to the distribution of initial endowments. Thus, the attractiveness of outcomes generated by a system of voluntary exchange is heavily dependent on the attractiveness of the initial endowments. Recognition of the dependence of the outcome of any efficient market on the initial distribution of endowments is standard in economic evaluations of alternative institutions, but discussion of appropriate distributions is normally treated as being outside the realm of the discipline (Arrow, 1974). Without a proper specification of initial endowments, the moral position of efficient voluntary exchange is approximately equivalent to the moral position of an efficient system of threat and acquiescence.

These three sets of questions compose a classical frame for assessing alternative aggregative institutions in political science. Despite the traditions of Aristotle, Rousseau, and Mill, and the pioneering work of Dahl and Lindblom (1953), however, the primary intellectual locus for considering the design of appropriate political institutions in recent years has not been in political science but in economics. Contemporary economic discussions of markets and other institutions as instruments of aggregation are preeminently discussions of their efficiency in arranging voluntary exchanges of resources, or in other words, in locating Pareto-optimal solutions. Problems in efficiency are seen as partly structural (e.g., problems of externalities) and partly behavioral (e.g., problems of information, limited rationality, agency, concentration). The efficiency of markets is seriously compromised by such problems (Williamson, 1975; 1985), and criticism of market institutions within this tradition is addressed to such imperfections. Except for an occasional formal acknowledgment of their importance, the issues of preferences and endowments are ignored.

Politics can be viewed as a system for aggregating individual preferences through voluntary exchanges. From this perspective, the outcomes of politics are the consequences of the simultaneous pursuit of individual interests by individuals who possess exogenously determined positions and resources and who make exchanges, threats, promises, coalitions, and agreements within a constitutional structure until a policy is adopted (Riker, 1962; Tullock, 1967). Since different individuals have different positions and resources in different arenas of politics, the various arenas do not reliably yield the same outcomes; and individuals have preferences for which arenas should decide which policies. At all times, individuals have the option of trying to win within the rules of the political game (i.e., accepting the resources and positions as given) or of trying to change the rules in the metapolitical game that sets the rules, and in which—at another level—the same basic process proceeds. Because there are costs to engaging in politics, individuals are prepared to allow the policy outcomes and the rules of the game to deviate somewhat from what they might be able to achieve if they were fully engaged.

This view of politics is a useful and normatively rather attractive view. It assumes a decentralized exchange system that, subject to constitutional constraints and the distribution of endowments (i.e., positions and resources), locates acceptable solutions, acceptable presumably because none (or at least not many) of the actors can improve on things from a personal self-interested point of view by acting unilaterally or in combination with known allies who would also thereby improve themselves. Although the theorems about the efficiency of hypothetical democratic systems are less well developed than comparable theorems about hypothetical market systems, they have some of the same flavor (Taylor, 1975; Ordeshook, 1986). They point to imperfections due to the difficulties of assuring that the system finds Pareto-optimal policies within the constraints of citizen rights, resources, and interests. These imperfections

122

revolve around problems of locating, negotiating, and enforcing mutually attractive coalitions of interests, that is, problems of information and organization.

The question of endowments in politics is a question of the distribution of political rights and resources, and discussions of proper distributions are at the core of theories of popular sovereignty, including theories of representation (Pitkin, 1967), as well as many discussions of power and authority (Crick, 1982; Przeworski, 1986). In treatments of politics as an aggregative process, political rights and resources are most often seen as properly allocated to political participants in proportion to the extent to which political decisions impinge on them (i.e., the costs), the extent to which they make contributions to the political system, and the extent to which they share tolerable preferences. In democratic theory, these considerations, at the minimum, normally lead to rules that divide people into two groups. The first group (citizens) shares power equally among its members; the second group (noncitizens) has no power. In addition, the same considerations justify (under certain circumstances) special rights of participation or power for leaders and experts, for individuals or groups specially affected by a particular proposed public policy, or for individuals or groups prepared to devote more energy or time to the process. Under extreme circumstances, they justify the exclusion of certain individuals from participation because of their noxious preferences.

Those modern political theorists of institutions who have drawn their inspiration from economics tend to treat questions of preferences and endowments in much the same way as they are treated by economists— as important but outside the realm of technical analysis (Anderson, 1979), which is neutral with respect to such issues. There are some anomalies, however. For example, normative theories of aggregation in the name of popular sovereignty are often ambivalent about relations between the economic and political systems that convert political rights (or power) into goods exchangeable for other resources, especially money (Merton, 1957; Walzer, 1983). Despite the possible argument that restrictions on trading between the private and public sectors prevent mutually beneficial trades between those with political resources, such as votes or official position, and those with economic resources, such as money or control over economic interest groups (Nas, Price, and Weber, 1986), many such trades are defined as graft and treated as illegitimate. If citizens can trade their political rights, the system is seen as changed in a fundamental way that is repugnant to many visions of popular sovereignty. But the resulting contradiction between a vision of political rights as inalienable and a conception of political resources as a basis for exchange is left substantially unresolved.

CRITERIA FOR ASSESSING INTEGRATIVE INSTITUTIONS

Concern about the political and technical qualities of aggregation in institutions is frequently paired in political science with concern about the integrative role of institutions, including concern about the way different institutions tend to develop different citizens and different societies (Mill, [1862] 1950; Pateman, 1970; Pitkin, 1981). In fact, sentiments about the limitations of aggregative politics are found throughout modern democratic societies. Many areas of social choice are excluded from an aggregative political process. Trades, coalitions, and logrolls are viewed as inimical to good sense, justice, efficiency, and appropriate policy. It is routinely argued that the professional judgments of attorneys, physicians, scientists, theologians, historians, engineers, and beauticians should be buffered from hasty opinions and short-term political considerations. Officials are enjoined to act without regard to political considerations. Political intrusions in the courts or the bureaucracy are viewed as regrettably frequent, rather than regrettably infrequent.

The politics of aggregation is viewed as a significant part of any democratic political process, but theories of jurisprudence and administration tend to see social institutions not only as aggregating individual interests but also as shaping them and providing opportunities for their development (Selznick, 1957). Attention to issues associated with the development of meaning and the construction of preferences has become an important part of theories of organizational decision making (Olsen, 1970; March and Olsen, 1976; Cohen and March, 1986; March, 1988c), as well as of modern institutionalist perspectives on social organization (Meyer and Rowan, 1977; March and Olsen, 1984). These integrative political processes in the name of popular sovereignty are distinguished by two major features that are potentially quite inconsistent with the perspectives of aggregation outlined above. The first is the concept of rights. The second is the idea of reasoned deliberation in search of the common good.

Since it subordinates the principles of exchange to principles of human dignity and integrity, the concept of human rights has been a persistent problem for aggregative theories of popular sovereignty (Dahl, 1977;

124

1980b). The whole idea was described as "nonsense upon stilts" by Bentham (Crespigny and Wertheimer, 1970: 221), but later writers have attempted to provide utilitarian justifications for political rights in a democratic political system. The most common route to the rationalization of human rights in utilitarian theories of popular sovereignty is to treat certain rights as facilitating the functioning of a democratic system (Dahl, 1980b). For example, rights to free speech and free press can, within such an argument, be seen as instruments contributing to the efficient discovery and implementation of political trades. This instrumental justification of human rights fits them into an idea of aggregative popular sovereignty, but at the cost of removing the core of their traditional significance. To the extent to which a right is rationalized in terms of its contribution to a political process, it is not a right but an instrumentality. Like virtue and love, it loses its essential character as an entitlement when justified in terms of its contribution to values other than itself.

Alternatively, it is possible to see political rights as part of the value environment of a political system, existing as precepts prior to and independent of politics. They can be described as "natural" rights, as part of a social contract, or as part of the shared culture from which a political system springs. This value environment gives standards for evaluating and justifying institutions and their actions. At least for any foreseeable future, it is a binding commitment that constrains the realization of private interests and values, and gives meaning and order to the political system. The assertion of such a right is noninstrumental, in the sense that the individual making the claim is under no obligation to justify it in terms of other ends or values that it serves. And it is categorical in the sense that other ends and values may not be used legitimately to justify denying the right.

The distinction between political rights as instruments justified by their contribution to the efficient aggregation of individual preferences and human rights as inviolate and inalienable symbols of the integration of a political culture, as well as of the identities and commitments of citizens (Sen, 1982; 1985), permeates the distinctions between modern versions of aggregative and integrative institutions. Within an aggregative process, rights are either rules designed to ameliorate imperfections in the system of exchange, or they are resources distributed as initial endowments and available for barter. Within an integrative process, on the other hand, rights express key aspects of the structure of social belief. They are metaphors of human unity, symbolizing the common destiny and humanity of those who share them (Tribe, 1985: 13). One of the primary purposes of an integrative political process is to discover and elaborate the meaning of these fundamental values (Thompson and McEwen, 1958; Olsen, 1972).

The significance of the difference can be seen by considering recent extensions of the idea of right to include social and economic rights. Discussions of the rights of citizens have been extended from civic and political rights to entitlements to employment, medical care, housing, and a proper environment (Marshall, 1950). This extension of the terminology of rights to social and economic entitlements moves them from a domain of voluntary exchange to a domain of normative constraint. The nomenclature of "rights" evokes three special things about social and economic entitlements. First, a right is inviolate. It must be granted regardless of its cost to others. As a result, it is a friction on the exchanges involved in the implementation of popular sovereignty. The political power that is required to remove a right is orders of magnitude greater than the political power that would have been required to prevent its granting. Second, a right is inalienable. Once a right has been established, it cannot be voluntarily relinquished. The current beneficiaries of social and economic rights cannot authoritatively give them up, regardless of the price offered for their surrender (Fried, 1978; Dan-Cohen, 1986). Third, a right changes through interpretation, more than through legislative revision. It is part of the fundamental law. As a result, insofar as we have folded social and economic outcomes into a terminology of rights, we have moved the institutions of popular sovereignty a bit away from aggregative processes and a bit toward integrative processes.

The second major way in which integrative traditions differ from aggregative traditions is in the role of reasoned deliberation in search of the common good by which the system is to be guided. Integrative processes treat conflict of interest as the basis for deliberation and authoritative decision rather than bargaining. They are directed by a logic of unity, rather than a logic of exchange. They presume a process from which emerges mutual understanding, a collective will, trust, and sympathy (Follett, 1918; Habermas, 1975; March, 1988c). They seek synthesis and conversions rather than antithesis and concessions. The key integrative processes of politics seek the creation, identification, and implementation of shared preferences. They involve the classic political activities of thought, discussion, debate, education, coercion, and the exploitation of accumulated social experience encoded in expertise and conventional rules (Wolin, 1960; Berki, 1979; Sejersted, 1984; Wilson, 1985).

The idea of an institution as an embodiment and instrument of the community, or of the democratic order as a constitutional system, is an important aspect of institutional thought. It is captured in both ancient and contemporary discussions of common cultures, collective identities, belonging, bonds, mutual affection, shared visions, symbols, history, mutual trust, and solidarity (Arendt, 1958; Wolin, 1960; Dyson, 1980). These discussions have often been dismissed as reflecting a denial of the reality of conflict in a society, or as a way in which the weak are lulled into passivity (Edelman, 1964); and the idea of a common good has certainly been involved in both. But the persistence of the idea and its place in classical political thought may perhaps signal that politics and political institutions ought properly to be evaluated in terms of their contribution to the integration of a society, as well as their contribution to the aggregation of diverse interests. As numerous writers on political systems have observed, democratic institutions presume and develop a shared sense of citizenship, that is, a sense of a common heritage, a valued way of life, and a collective destiny. And one of the criteria for assessing alternative democratic arrangements is the extent to which they facilitate such a sense of community.

Within a framework of historically developed institutional forms and culturally ingrained standards of conduct, members of a political community evolve criteria for judging institutions with respect to their fairness and conformity to the spirit of the political community. There is a tension between the ideals described by the standards of assessment and the achievement of institutions—a continuous but not hopeless challenge to reform institutions and to train and cultivate individuals so that they look after the interests of others and the public interest (Pitkin, 1967: 239–40). For such individuals the public interest becomes an ethical criterion and a spur to conscience and deliberation, a stimulus to a process for imagining a sense of public purpose and public morality, rather than negotiating a bargain in the name of self-interest (Dyson, 1980: 274). The key assumption is that even in situations in which there is *ex ante* disagreement about values, there are processes of public discussion and private thought that arrive at better *ex post* social solutions than does bargaining, exchange, or coalition formation in the service of prior preferences.

The assessment of political institutions as instruments of integration involves two critical questions that are somewhat different from the questions of efficiency, preferences, and endowments familiar to problems of aggregation. The prime issues are questions of competence and integrity.

The question of *competence* is: Does the process develop and use genuine expertise of relevance to the problem? Does it strengthen the capabilities of citizens to understand and act on issues of public policy and to select competent representatives and advisors? Competence in this case includes both technical competence in areas of knowledge (e.g., science, history) that are relevant, and the competence of wisdom that comes from a deep appreciation of community needs and possibilities. The idea is that there is more to policy making than reflection of individual interests (Pitkin, 1967). The question of competence raises fundamental issues in the uses of selection and training, and rules of debate, to assure that those who make decisions become qualified to do so. The competence of the process includes considerations of the occasions on which deliberation does, or does not, clarify issues, exclude false directions, and discover correct alternatives (Taylor, 1984; Stinchcombe, 1986b).

The question of *integrity* is: Does the process ensure that participants act in a manner dedicated to the common good and uncorrupted by their personal ambitions or interests. Note that a person who acts with integrity is not a "neutral" person. Quite the contrary. Whereas neutrality confronts contending interests with a predilection to balance them, integrity puts interests aside. Actions of integrity are based on a set of publicly defined values, defended within a public order (Kalberg, 1980; Offerdal, 1986). Judges, bureaucrats, legislators, politicians, and citizens give meaning to the values they espouse.

Assuming that self-interest is not defined in a trivially tautological way to encompass any behavior, it seems obvious that human beings have a capacity to take actions on bases other than self-interest. Such actions are characteristic of religious and secular social movements, and are common in ordinary organizational life. Individuals in organizations routinely follow rules, partly perhaps because failure to do so is punishable, but also partly because they see themselves as rule-abiding members of an organization (DiMaggio, 1985). Weber ([1924] 1978) presumed that an official could, would, and should separate private sympathies and beliefs from public actions. Students of jurisprudence have long claimed and advocated similar behavior for judges. The professional ethics of many professions obligate their members to forego personal gain to serve their calling; and although those codes are not always followed, they frequently are.

Integrity can be seen as stemming partly from training and personal commitment, and partly from organizational arrangements, including accountability arrangements (Friedrich, 1940; Finer, 1941). An example of the former is found in training in professional standards and the Weberian ethic of bureaucratic behavior. The Weberian bureaucrat is a person of integrity, basing action on the demands of an official role and eschewing both personal aggrandizement and the private entreaties of relatives, friends, or clients. An example of organizational arrangements is found in the buffering of expertise from decision making, for example through rules of professional autonomy or through a knowledge system based on books and libraries (March, 1987).

THE EFFICACY OF INSTITUTIONS

Alternative institutions can be assessed by means of two quite different kinds of analyses. The first kind of analysis compares alternative institutional utopias—models of hypothetical institutions in hypothetical worlds. This is the world of theorems, philosophical demonstrations, and hope. The second kind of analysis compares the realized consequences of pursuing alternative utopian visions in a real political system. This is the world of experience and disappointment. The assessment of institutions is ultimately an evaluation of how real institutions interact with other real institutions and human behavior to produce real consequences. Since a common feature of political and economic debate is to compare the ugly reality of one institution with the utopian purity of the model of another, the distinction between theorems and consequences should be viewed with some caution. But it is important. It distinguishes the quality of a dream from the quality of a dream implemented and has been used to raise serious questions about utopian institutional arrangements as diverse as the French Revolution, Marxist-Leninist state socialism, anarchy, the free market, and liberal democracy.

We are driven to the question of *efficacy*—whether an institution produces in an imperfect world what it promises in an imaginary one and whether the failures can be remedied without undue costs. We ask whether pursuing a specific virtuous vision brings good citizens closer to, or more distant from, the good life—justice, a moral society, beauty, harmony. Asking such questions establishes a framework for evaluation that is both considerably broader than the usual one and a bit quaint, something out of Plato and Aquinas rather than recent models in economics and political science. It invites a reexamination of the dogma of simple moral relativism and invokes the reality of good and evil, while applying a pragmatic criterion to utopian design. Constitutional choices are practical ones. They involve judging and improving institutional utopias on the basis of their moral virtues in the real world (Pitkin, 1967: 238; Elster, 1983a: 29; Tribe, 1985), even though the effects of pursuing alternative visions of social institutions are not easy to specify in advance.

129

The Efficacy of Aggregation

The most conspicuous practical problems for modern aggregative institutions are connected to their inability to solve the problems of preferences and endowments. Ideas about efficient exchange presume that actors have consistent, stable, exogenous preferences. In practice, subjectively experienced political interests tend to be inconsistent, unstable, and endogenous. Such ambiguities pose relatively deep problems for systems of popular sovereignty. They have led to persistent debate as to whether information from the media or from political leaders can properly be viewed as modifying the expectations held by voters or as modifying their interests. And if the latter, what are the characteristics of an appropriate modification of preferences? They have also led to claims of disparities between the subjective interests of citizens and their "true" interests, the objective reality of their condition (Balbus, 1971). Aggregative institutions and theories have difficulty interpreting and improving the ways in which democratic institutions respond to ambiguous, changing interests on the part of citizens, or the ways the political system itself contributes to the creation and elaboration of citizen interests, including the ways citizens combine into groups and subcultures (Wildavsky, 1987; March 1988c).

Similarly, endowments are a problem. It has been argued that "procedural legitimation" is the emerging organizational principle of postmodern society: The state will regulate endowments, but individual actors will be free within such constraints, that is, outcomes will be affected but not stipulated (Nonet and Selznick, 1978; Mayntz, 1983; Teubner, 1983: 254; 1984; Dalberg-Larsen, 1984). The regulation of endowments is, however, not easy. There have been numerous attempts to correct endowment inequities in Western democracies. In addition to direct efforts at the redistribution of wealth, these include attempts to educate people in order to give them a better chance in the job market, to provide legal help in order to strengthen their position in courts, to help the unorganized organize in order to give them representation in public policy making, to give financial support to political groups in order to make political competition more equal, and to support newspapers in order to provide a more balanced information market. Despite these attempts, existing disparities in endowments continue to be widely viewed as unacceptable in Western democracies (Dahl, 1986).

The problems of endowments in aggregative politics go deeper than the distributional problems of wealth and other resources among current citizens, however. Democratic political systems have persistent ambiguities associated with the allocation of political rights. The formal rules habitually leave some relevant groups without political power, and allow well-organized groups to gain special access. Residents in one political jurisdiction cannot vote in another, even when the actions of the other clearly impinge on them. For example, the political institutions of Sweden do not give the inhabitants of Copenhagen participatory rights in decisions with respect to a nuclear power facility in Barseback that might require a total evacuation of the Danish city in the event of a serious disaster. Even more generally, future citizens (particularly the unborn) cannot vote, even though the actions taken today have clear consequences for them. The political disenfranchisement of the unborn is clear in the formation and execution of policies surrounding population, environment, and war. It is celebrated in Samuel Butler's insistence that newly born individuals in Erewhon admit their culpability in their own conception, thereby absolving their parents of responsibility for bringing them into the world (Butler, 1927; Hansot, 1974).

These difficulties have led to frequent appeals for the intervention of state authority in an aggregative system serving the interests of its current constituents. Such appeals involve claims that the state is a trustee for important segments of the community that are weak in, or excluded from, politics—the poor, the unborn, and the disorganized, for example. The proposition is that they have a right to be represented, that any aggregative political system deprives them of that right, and that therefore it is only through the intervention of their trustees, found in the institutions of the state, that they can be properly protected. The argument becomes more forceful as other institutions (e.g., the family) become less reliable trustees. The claim is generalized to the identification of the state as the carrier of a culture or civilization and the need to protect that tradition from momentary passions of contemporary majorities or powerful minorities.

The Efficacy of Integration

The most conspicuous practical problems for modern integrative institutions are connected to their inability to assure integrity, competence, and reasoned debate in political life. Integration requires commitment to the meaningfulness and openness of the pursuit of the common good. It requires a good faith attempt to examine public policy as an instrument of the community, to subordinate personal needs and private desires to a sense of the public interest as defined by the community, and to maintain confidence that similar commitments and subordinations can be expected from others. Thus, it demands public-spirited citizens with a concern for openness and the public good.

At least since Diogenes, the ability of political institutions to identify and sustain honest integrity in the pursuit of the public good has been in doubt. Skepticism about the possibility of integrity in life is a traditional theme in political and economic thought and has become dominant in recent years. It is axiomatic in much contemporary literature that individuals act in the name of their own self-interests. The proposition is conspicuous in economic theories of organization and agency. Ideas about the management of subordinates or agents are largely theories of incentive compatibility. The objective is to design employment contracts that induce self-interested employees (or other agents) to act in ways desired by self-interested employers. In a similar way, much of modern political theory presumes that individual actors use power in the service of their own interests, that public policy is the outcome of some bargaining process among self-interested actors, and that regulation of political institutions requires control over the incentives of political agents.

The problem is not that behavior is driven exclusively by self-interest, for we know that is not the case. There is considerable evidence that individuals are capable of behavior that is not, in a narrow sense at least, self-interested. For example, people act differently when acting on behalf of others (Pitkin, 1967: 118), when they are made responsible for outcomes rather than following rules (Eckhoff and Jacobsen, 1960), or when they are in public (Selznick, 1968; Rawls, 1971; Habermas, 1975). The problem is to sustain a suitably high level of such behavior, particularly among officials but also among those whom the officials serve.

One obvious solution is civic education. Many of the tools of democracy are directed toward socializing ordinary citizens into the responsibilities of citizenship, including the obligations of public servants. The institutions of subnational government, for example, are portrayed and defended as instruments of political socialization and training as often as they are seen as decentralized administrative/political agencies. Education in the principles of unity, selflessness, and possibilities of human development is a frequent objective of a society, but the political socialization of citizens to those ideals is not reliably successful.

Without such integrity, the pursuit of unity becomes a sham. Agreement is coerced or manipulated, rather than secured through honest discussion. Conflict in society is suppressed, and genuine differences in lifestyles and values are ignored (Øystese, 1980). Individual rights are twisted into claims of individual privilege. Thus, the challenge is not only to train, or select, selfless people of integrity. It is also to protect selflessness from the temptations of an integrative order. Authority, autonomy, and power are essential aspects of integrative institutions, but they all tend to undermine the integrity that is indispensable to their proper functioning. There are legitimate doubts about the ability of individuals to sustain their capabilities for selflessness in the face of the overwhelming temptations introduced by positions of power, and it is the capacity of power to corrupt that challenges the design of instruments of political integration.

The competence of reasoned debate is similarly difficult to maintain in practice. It is a fragile and easily corrupted process (Elster, 1983a: 22). There are problems of participation, of ensuring that effective participation is tied to competence and that competence is enhanced through participation. The issues seem to be fourfold: First, how do we arrange access to debate so that competence can enter judiciously? Balancing the rules of access and participation so that they are neither too exclusive nor too open is obviously difficult. Second, how do we make motivation to participate consistent with competence? There is no reason to believe that incentives and personal values will necessarily be arranged so that entry into debate will be differentially attractive to those whose contributions would be most valuable. Third, how do we use the process of debate in a way that broadens competence rather than narrows it? Debate is part of an educational process contributing to the long-run competence of the institution, as well as part of the current decision process. Fourth, how do we manage the process of discussion to produce a valid consensus, making the process of deliberation and argument specially attentive to competence? Rules of relevance, evidence, and logic are involved. How do we keep the process from corruption by those who do not contribute to the common good, yet possess resources of time, energy, or money?

Reasoned debate is particularly vulnerable to misuse and manipulation by individuals and groups with special talents at argumentation or rhetoric (Tarschys and Eduards, 1975: 91; March, 1978). In an integrative institution devoted to discussion, ability at discussion is a key endowment. There is no guarantee that that ability will be well correlated with virtue or other forms of competence. Moreover, just as aggregative institutions flounder on the bias against redistribution induced by their dependence on initial endowments and voluntarism, integrative institutions flounder on the bias against unreasoned sentiments induced by their dependence on processes of rational discourse. Reasoned debate is essential to integrative popular sovereignty as protection against the false integration produced by emotional hysteria or mass obsession. But by failing to recognize the legitimacy of unreasoned sentiments, integrative institutions become tied in practice to a mode of intelligence that excludes important parts of collective wisdom. Thus, even without the corruptions of self-interest masked as public concern, processes of debate are flawed by their suscepti- bility to well-intentioned individuals rich in eloquence or analysis but poor in judgment or feeling.

CONTRADICTIONS AND INSTITUTIONAL CHANGE

The Cycles of Cyclic Change

While the history of Western democracies can be written in terms of consistent change, such as democratization, bureaucratization, or growth of the public sector (Weber, [1924] 1978; de Jouvenal, 1949; Eckstein, 1982), it is also a history of cycles in institutional forms and theories. For example, administrative development in the United States has been described in terms of the inconsistencies among three sets of values: representativeness, neutral competence, and executive leadership. In our terms, the first leads to aggregativeness, the last two to integrativeness (of somewhat different forms). According to Kaufman, there are periods in which one or two of the three dominate without totally suppressing the others, which come to the fore again as "a consequence of the difficulties encountered in the period preceding the change" (Kaufman, 1956: 1057).

These cycles result from sequential attention to the unsolvable dilemmas of popular sovereignty (Eisenstadt, 1965). Values central to the democratic creed are difficult to accommodate simultaneously. Principles of majority rule conflict with equally strongly held principles of individual rights (Dan-Cohen, 1986). It is difficult to balance the need for autonomy on the part of political representatives (Dahl and Lindblom, 1953; Pitkin, 1967) or burcaucrats (Eisenstadt, 1958; Jacobsen, 1964) with the need to limit that autonomy in order to make representatives and bureaucrats responsive and accountable (Miller, 1982; Rueschemeyer and Evans, 1985). It is difficult to balance demands for making bureaucrats responsi- ble to changing political governments, to be neutral in terms of treating citizens equally and in terms of the law, and to represent rationality and expertise based on professional knowledge (Jacobsen, 1960; Salamon and Abramson, 1984; Levine and Hansen, 1985).

Institutional development is characterized by sequential attention to these mutually conflicting desires, rather than the reconciliation of them or the development of consistent trade-offs among them. Old solutions

134

do not go away but wait for new occasions on which they might be represented as answers to problems unresolved by current practice (Cohen, March, and Olsen, 1972; Kingdon, 1984; March and Olsen, 1986a). As a result, the mixes of aggregative and integrative processes in the institutions change over time, swinging from institutional structures and theories of popular sovereignty that emphasize aggregative functions to structures and theories that emphasize integrative functions. These changes in the mix may be reflected in a homogeneous shift across institutions, or in a change in the numbers of relatively pure aggregative, as opposed to relatively pure integrative, institutions.

The Expansion of Aggregative Processes and the Homogenization of Institutions

In recent decades, the cycle has been in an aggregative, homogenizing phase. Western democracies have tended to make institutions more aggregative and reduce the differences among them. Theories of institutional evaluation have also become strongly aggregative in form, emphasizing questions of allocative efficiency and deemphasizing questions of preferences, endowments, competence, integrity, and efficacy. Pateman (1985: 165, 183) observes that over the past two decades "assumptions of liberal individualism have permeated the whole of social life," at the same time as there has been an erosion of forces like love, friendship, solidarity, family, altruism, and remnants of religious and other established worldviews, which traditionally have constrained completely self-interested behavior. These assumptions are built into a conception of politics as aggregation. They lead to claims that "everything is politics," demands for direct participation, and reduced confidence in expertise, rights, or concepts of public interest.

Neocorporatist arrangements in the democracies of Scandinavia, Netherlands, Germany, and Austria (Schmitter and Lehmbruch, 1979; Olsen, 1981; Lehmbruch, 1985; Streeck and Schmitter, 1985), mark a high point in the expansion of aggregative institutions and processes. In particular this is true for sectorial corporatism (Lehmbruch 1984:61–62), while forms of corporatist concertation also include integrative features. The significance of organized interests is reflected in extensive interest group participation in governance and (as in the United States and Britain) the development of regions of interest group hegemony with their informal "iron triangles" and policy networks (Heclo, 1978; Jordan, 1981; Peters, 1984). The autonomous role of the state and administrative institutions as guardians of the public interest and common welfare has become

135

more problematic at the same time as the state has become involved more deeply and broadly in the social and economic systems. The intervention of elected leaders is sporadic rather than continuous, and often triggered by mass media, scandals, or disasters (Weinberg, 1977; Mayntz, 1979: 643; Olsen, 1983). And the growing necessity to bargain with affected interests (especially when the problem is to achieve some positive cooperation rather than to prevent some unwanted behavior), makes it more difficult for administrative agencies to operate solely on the basis of hierarchical command and rules. They enter into arrangements involving bargaining with organized interests in society as well as with other bureaucracies.

The Dynamics of Cyclic Change

Although aggregative political institutions and theories dominate the current scene, the natural processes of cyclic change seem likely to undermine their dominance over the next few years or decades. Aggregative forms are particularly characteristic of good times. An excess of resources over current demands is a buffer between conflicting forces in the society and a facilitator of the voluntary exchanges that are fundamental to aggregative processes (Cyert and March, 1963; March and Olsen, 1976). Identifying and implementing mutually acceptable trades are generally more feasible when resources are increasing than when they are decreasing. Reductions in resources tend to presage an increase in integrative structures (Canovan, 1985: 625–626). In addition, changes in slack affect the amplitude of current cycles. Increases in resources provide momentum for current trends and encourage a greater variety of mixtures of aggregative and integrative processes. Reductions in resources tend to slow or reverse the momentum, and to create a demand for purer forms.

The effects of changes in resources are accentuated by internal institutional processes. On the one hand, there are tendencies toward institutional purification. During periods of aggregative dominance, or in institutions that are primarily aggregative, the homogenizing forces of socialization and internal pressure accentuate self-interested action and exchange. During periods of integrative dominance, or in institutions that are primarily integrative, the same forces accentuate attention to rules and roles and to concerns of unity. These purifying tendencies are honored and strengthened by public postures. Institutions make ostentatious displays of their primary normative character. Legislatures display their internal differences and aggregative functions in public sessions; they perform their integrative activities in private, in closed committee meetings or in informal sessions. Executive and administrative institutions do the opposite, keeping internal struggles private and displaying unanimity in public.

Tendencies toward purification are, however, overshadowed by tendencies toward reconstitution. Institutions are sites for the same cyclic processes of internal contradiction that describe the political system more generally. Aggregative institutions and their ideologies create problems for integrative institutions and for themselves. The corruption of the integrity of public institutions through cross-sector exchanges is an example of the first. The short-term rationalities of election periods that create subsequent problems for rational exchanges is an example of the second. Similarly, integrative institutions create problems for aggregative institutions and for themselves. The resistance of ''men of principle'' to efficient logrolls is an example of the first. The loss of competence through insularity and the iron law of oligarchy are examples of the second. While integrative state builders aspire to design harmonious and unitary systems divided into organs, branches, and departments, the component elements in such designs fairly quickly become seats of interests struggling to increase their autonomy, their reciprocal standing, and their command over resources (Eisenstadt, 1964: 246; Poggi, 1978: 136).

Finally, institutions copy one another. Institutional forms tend to diffuse through a population of institutions in much the way that other fashions diffuse (Zucker, 1977; Tolbert and Zucker, 1983; DiMaggio and Powell, 1983). This includes diffusion within a particular society and diffusion from one society to another. For example, ideas about neocorporatist arrangements spread through OECD countries a few years ago with the same kind of enthusiasm and speed that neoclassical uses of the market are spreading currently (OECD, 1983).

Kings, Barons, and Popular Sovereignty

Cycles of change in political institutions are not new. Many Western democracies have histories reflecting a persistent tension between the forces for centralized power in a monarch or central regime and the forces for decentralization to regional or functional fiefdoms, with the masses of ordinary citizens alternately seeking refuge from the tyranny of each in the ambitions of the other (Poggi, 1978). These processes did not end with the creation of the neocorporate state and the rise to prominence of economic theories of institutional assessment. There has been no miraculous abatement of the fundamental contradictions of popular sovereignty, fluctuations in resources are obvious in the present world, and the internal processes of institutional change continue. The cycles

137

of countervailing tyrants that involved kings and barons in the Middle Ages have given way to cycles that involve the central authorities of elected leaders, courts, and bureaucracy, on the one hand, and the baronies of major organized interest groups, on the other.

Cyclic periods of integration have periodically strengthened the institutional instruments of the state capable of limiting baronial power. A prime example is the system of royal courts. When peasants appealed to the king's justice as the embodiment of the state, they solicited royal intervention in a baronial political system, evoking the claims of individual rights and the common good as represented in the spirit of the law. Historically, the institutions of integration have included national systems of law, economic exchange, military force, and administration. And it is around these systems that the battles over contemporary popular sovereignty are fought, for in the major Western democracies great inroads on integrative functions within each of these institutions have been made by the barons of modern life.

The movement toward baronial power is general. National armies are more tightly tied to the military-industrial complex than to national purposes (Galbraith, 1967). Courts protect the rights of the strong to ignore the common good, or have been supplanted as arenas for mediating major economic conflicts (Eckhoff, 1976; Andenæs, 1985). Markets are managed by large industrial and financial groups for their own benefit. And administrative bureaucracies have been captured by their special interest clients (Lowi, 1969; Wilson, 1980). The classic instruments of the state have been feudalized through a corporatist political system, and control has passed to the barons. Even institutions of national integration have taken on the character of interest groups in their own right, competing with other special interests for position and power in the glorification of "bureaucratic politics" (Allison, 1971; Peters, 1984).

THINKING ABOUT INSTITUTIONAL REFORM IN A CYCLIC WORLD

We seem to be at or near a new zenith of aggregative politics and theories about politics. Consequently, the usual cyclic forces have begun to produce complaints about current intellectual, ideological, and political regimes. For example, a major concern of contemporary "mixed" polities and economies, such as those in Scandinavia, is that the social, economic, and political interdependencies have become so complex that it has become difficult or even impossible for ordinary citizens as well as elected politicians to understand or influence the process (Study of Power and Democracy in Sweden, 1985: 36; SOU, 1985: 40; Olsen, 1988a). The different institutions of the political system have lost their distinctive characters. Elements of one type of decision process have been used to cope with or modify the difficulties of others (Dahl and Lindblom, 1953; Briggs, 1961; Lindblom, 1977; Hernes, 1978; Goodin, 1982; Streeck and Schmitter, 1985). And there has been a proliferation of organizational forms at the interface between the public and private sectors, as well as between "politics" and "administration" (Hague, Mackenzie, and Barker, 1975; Sharkansky, 1979; Barker, 1982; von Beyme, 1985; Hood, 1986; Hood and Schuppert, 1988).

A typical solution, found for example in the reform program of the Norwegian conservative-center government (Chapter 6), is to search for a new balance between institutions of integration and aggregation, and especially to restore clearer boundaries between the two types of institutions. Thus, it is proposed that elected leaders be more concerned with major decisions, major developments, and creating frameworks for other systems; administrative agencies should be made instruments for elected leaders, but should be strengthened as defenders of cultural values; business should go back to markets; organized interests should concentrate upon representing their members, but should be less involved in public policy making; and professions should act more in the interest of clients and less in self-interest.

Considering the cyclic history and these symptoms of discontent, it is easy to predict a shift over the next decade toward more integrative institutions and theories, and toward sharper differentiation among institutions in their roles (i.e., integrative or aggregative). The predictions are made even easier by the tendency toward reductions in slack in Western democracies. Such predictions are themselves, of course, a part of the cyclic process. They are manifestations of the relative ease scholars and participants have in perceiving the problems of current institutions and neglecting previous experience with alternatives.

We do not escape the cyclic process through an awareness of it, but understanding may provide a basis for more thoughtful approaches to the search for appropriate institutions within a political system dedicated to popular sovereignty. Such approaches depend on recognition of five fundamental points.

First, politics is not the residual category of an economic system. Modern conventions in market theories of economics picture a proper political system as foregoing most issues concerning the allocation of scarce resources. Within such a conception, politics may properly be involved in decisions about the distribution of wealth (and other initial resources) and in setting the rules of the game, but it is not properly involved in allocative decisions except to correct imperfections in the functioning of a free market, particularly externality problems and problems of concentration. Such a perspective has a certain charm to it. It allows one to define the problem of social engineering as that of modifying an admittedly imperfect actual market to make it conform to the ideal of a perfectly competitive market. To political philosophers, however, the strategy may seem more a form of disciplinary imperialism than either good history or good logic. An alternative would be to picture markets and other social institutions as technical adjustments, justifiable only when there are imperfections in politics. It is at least arguable that such a perspective has greater historical validity than the converse.

Second, although the ability of an institution to find Pareto-optimal solutions is an important asset, it is not an adequate basis for choice among institutions. Assessing the appropriateness of different institutions in a society committed to popular sovereignty involves an assortment of criteria associated with both aggregative and integrative processes. In addition to the issues of allocative efficiency, we have identified issues concerning preferences, endowments, competence, and integrity, as well as concerns about the relation between the hypothetical attractiveness of an institutional form and its efficacy in the real world of real people, groups, and experiences. These issues cannot be treated as peripheral to the debate. Although they do not deny the significance of allocative efficiency, they place that criterion in a broader context that leads to different institutional choices.

Third, the issues of institutional design or evaluation are not routinely decomposable into separable problems. As we have seen, the institutions and ideologies of aggregation and integration affect each other in ways that make it impossible to consider the solution of the problems of one without considering the other. Moreover, even if we could look at only one of the functions, the criteria cannot be considered separately. For example, it is not clear that a society can arbitrarily and independently choose a system of power and an allocative mechanism. Nor is it obvious that individual preferences are independent of institutional form. One of the oldest claims for democratic political processes is that they help develop an ethos of preferences that encourage cooperation and a sense of community. A parallel criticism is that they discourage individual initiative and reward passivity. One of the oldest claims for market processes is that they develop a commitment to individual freedom and a sense of international interdependence. The parallel criticism is that

140

they nurture greed, envy, and competitiveness. Where interests are shaped by the process, the choice of institutions is partly a choice of values and cannot be treated as simply an implementation of them.

Fourth, a society is probably better served by continual contradiction among contending concerns, demands, and values than by procedures requiring a permanent resolution of them. Conceptions of values and identity are elaborated through enduring tensions among values and models that recur and transform and recur again. Attempting to eliminate contradiction and inconsistency through reconciliation, resolution, and trade-offs may be less effective than struggling with conflicting pressures and ambiguities in order to establish a tolerable alternation (March, 1978; Winston, 1985). In such a spirit, any institution should have within it the seeds of its reconstruction. The cycles of enthusiasm for aggregative and integrative institutions, and the internal logics of transformation that bedevil both kinds, ensure this continual struggle.

The case for unresolved contradiction and dedication to alternation among incomplete principles depends on some assumptions about the moral consequences of ethical struggle as opposed to ethical clarity. The case for struggle lies in a calculation that it forces more or less continual awareness of moral dilemmas. This maintains a steadier reconsideration of decisions on the basis of new feelings and experiences, including the experience of guilt and doubt, than does making a firm resolution. The argument is analogous to one made frequently about the advantages of maintaining choices as conscious actions rather than relegating them to a routine. As a case in point, consider the classic distinction between "politics" and "administration." Everyone "knows" that policy making and administration should be kept distinct. At the same time, everyone "knows" that policy making and administration cannot be kept distinct and that the distinction itself is difficult to make precise. Still, the alternation between the realpolitik conception of administration as contending interests groups that permeate everything and the bureaucratic conception of administration as being distinct from policy making seems to allow both ideas to develop and to reflect the cycles of current enthusiasms (March and Olsen, 1983). The alternation reflects a sense that it is better to elicit richness from ambiguity than it is to purify principles (March, 1971; Jacobsson, 1984; Egeberg and Stigen, 1985; Christensen, 1985).

Fifth, many Western democracies and theories of them might appropriately be nudged somewhat in the direction of greater concern for integrative functions and institutions, and toward a greater differentiation of institutions. Students of organizations often show dampened enthusiasm for institutional reform (March, 1981b; March and Olsen, 1983; Scharpf, 1986), preferring to note the numerous complications in sustaining a sense of efficacy in a cyclic world; but those complications are not a bar to reform. In order to justify the appropriateness of more integration, we may have to persuade ourselves of the degeneracy of aggregative institutions and the glories of rights, reasoned debate, and administrative autonomy, while at the same time recognizing that within a few decades we will rediscover the evils of integration and will once again embrace exchange in the name of self-interest. We may have to recognize not only the advantages that lie in that seemingly endless oscillation, but the desirability of decisive action in a world without decisive consequences.

8

Preferences, Power, and Democratic Institutions

This chapter explores some implications of the democratic criterion of political equality for the design of political institutions. As in Chapter 7, we argue that meaningful political equality cannot be viewed simply as a problem of aggregating interests but requires attention to the shaping of citizen preferences. The argument depends, first, on some observations about the ways in which equality of power implies interpersonal and intertemporal comparisons of preferences, and second, on some observations about the ways in which the distribution of preferences in a society affects the distribution of power.

THE AMBIGUITIES OF POLITICAL EQUALITY

Political equality among an appropriately inclusive set of citizens is a necessary, though not sufficient, condition for democracy (Dahl, 1977; 1986). In traditional treatments of democracy, citizenship is assumed to depend on unquestioned historical distinctions (e.g., between nations, age groups, castes, and sexes), or some primordial contractual agreements. More recent discussions tend to base rights of participation on considerations of the costs inflicted on particular individuals or the benefits provided by them (Dahl, 1977), concerns also familiar to Plato and Aristotle. These justifications, however, are complicated in a modern era of choices with consequences extending beyond political boundaries and far into the future. The former raises profound questions about the geography of democracy; the latter dramatizes the difficulties democratic societies have in responding to the legitimate interests of future citizens. At the same time, assessing the distribution of power in a contemporary society has not been easy. Since ordinary political life provides inadequate data to resolve many uncertainties about relative power, the democratic criterion of equality tends to be empirically problematic.

Such ambiguities and complexities affect attempts to answer three classic questions about power in a democracy: What are the reasons for disparities of power in a democratic system? How can those disparities be reduced? What can be done to ameliorate the effects of irreducible disparities? These questions have been crucial to political theory at least since Plato. They are considered at some length by various contemporary political philosophers and theorists of social choice (Pitkin, 1967; Parenti, 1978; Elster, 1983b; Pateman, 1985).

Most modern treatments of political equality emphasize the major problems for democracy produced by economic inequality (Dahl, 1986). The problems are conspicuous and important. Contemporary experience suggests that sustaining political equality in the face of substantial economic inequalities is probably impossible. The difficulties for democracy posed by disparities in wealth are not, however, the focus of the present chapter. Rather, the chapter examines the relation between preferences and power in a democracy. It argues that political equality cannot be meaningfully achieved or assessed without a variety of political institutions concerned with the construction, elaboration, and empathic appreciation of individual preferences. To develop that argument, the essay observes that most theories of power, along with most other theories of choice, are based on a conception of preferences (or interests) that is inadequate for situations in which preferences are ambiguous, changing, and endogenous to the political system. Along the way, it explores some complications induced by the relation between assessments of relative power and interpersonal and intertemporal comparisons of interests, the relation between the distribution of preferences in a society and the distribution of power, and the role of integrative political institutions in generating the enlightened understanding, empathy, collective identity, and trust that create and sustain a system of equal political power.

MEASURING AND COMPARING INTERESTS

If we define power as something like the ability to induce others to act in a way that contributes to a power holder's interests, any measurement of power involves an assessment of individual interests (preferences) and of the value distances between alternative outcomes. And any comparison of the power held by different people involves the interpersonal and intertemporal comparison of those distances.

Interpersonal Comparison of Interests

To say that two people have equal power is to say that there exists a metric by which the extent to which one person has induced others to contribute to his or her interests can be compared with the extent to which others have done so. The dimensions of such a metric are the dimensions of individual interests or preferences. Since assessing disparities of power requires the interpersonal comparison of interests, a criterion of equal power cannot be given unambiguous interpersonal meaning within a conception of interest that treats interests (preferences) as individually subjective. For if preferences are seen as subjective, so also is their comparison; and if comparison is subjective, so also is relative power.

These difficulties suggest two quite different possibilities for the elaboration of the criterion of political equality. The first direction is to establish some basis for shared interpersonal comparisons, in effect some basis for assessing the gains and losses of different individuals conditional on a social outcome. Interpersonal comparisons of individual gains and losses stemming from alternative social choices are common within most systems of collective choice. By placing such comparisons outside the realm of permissible discourse, theories of social welfare that eschew interpersonal comparisons restrict considerably their relevance for thinking about political institutions. The problem is particularly acute in a democracy. If we wish to invoke a shared meaning for the criterion of political equality, it is hard to see how we can escape the necessity for interpersonal comparisons. The difficulty, of course, is in designing political institutions and processes that are able to make interpersonal and intertemporal comparisons of gains and losses in a way that sustains a democratic vision of popular sovereignty, rather than undermines it.

The second possibility within a theory of subjective preferences is the full acceptance of a subjective definition of relative power. That is, we might imagine that subjectively meaningful interpersonal comparison of interests can be made by each citizen. Thus, each individual citizen is presumed to be able to determine a distribution of power in the society. However, the interpersonal metrics imposed by different citizens are not guaranteed to be, and in general are not, the same; and the associated distributions of power differ. From this point of view, the criterion of

145

political equality is necessarily a citizen-specific criterion. Political equality would require that each citizen determine (subjectively) that power is distributed equally, or perhaps that his or her own power be perceived as at least equal to anyone else's power.

Intertemporal Comparison of Interests

Even an entirely subjective definition of power, however, poses intertemporal problems that are well known in the theory of choice (March, 1978; Elster, 1979; 1983b). Preferences are neither clear nor stable. They develop over time. They are shaped not only by forces exogenous to politics and decision making but also by the processes of politics themselves. Thus, the current interests of citizens are only a fraction of their interests as they unfold over their lifetimes, and that unfolding is affected by choices along the way. Since determining relative individual power at a particular point involves characterizing sentiments that are ambiguous, changing over time, and changing partly as a result of the processes and outcomes of politics, even intrapersonal subjective definitions of political equality are problematic. At a formal level, comparisons between preferences now and preferences later are hard to distinguish from interpersonal comparisons.

Additional intertemporal problems are generated as we try to make extra-individual comparisons. These problems occur in their most extreme form in the requirement to accommodate the interests of future citizens, those to be added to the society in the future through birth and immigration. Political equality in a renewing society cannot sensibly be restricted to current citizens. Current political actors must act, at least implicitly, in the name of the interests of others. The most obvious case is the large number of citizens who have not as yet been born. Unless a democratic system can solve the problem of representing the future, changing interests of the unborn, it violates a rather fundamental underlying premise of democracy—that those who bear the costs of decision should have their interests adequately reflected in the choice. The interests of such future citizens must be compared in a meaningful way with the interests of those currently present.

If aggregative democracy cannot be extended to the unborn, or to the future (changed) preferences of current citizens, or to a comparison among the preferences of citizens, the criterion of political equality is compromised as a foundation of democracy. Aggregative democracy based on subjective political equality among current citizens appears to be only a crude approximation to political equality (Arendt, 1958; Haber-

146

mas, 1975; Mansbridge, 1980). It is conceivable that it is the best practical solution to a complicated problem. But the assertion of practicality is a claim that the flaws of such a system as an instrument of the ideals of democracy are less than the flaws of procedures that seek to provide some kind of basis for interpersonal and intertemporal comparisons; and such a claim is not self-evidently justified.

Empathy, Trust, and the Extra-Individual Consciousness of Individual Interests

The classic alternative to subjective preferences in an aggregative system is to determine the interests of individual citizens in an extra-individual way. If we consider only present citizens, the terminology of ''interest'' invites a subordination of individual subjective preferences to some conception of objective interests derived from an external perspective and related to social or economic position (Balbus, 1971; Polsby, 1980). The possibility that an individual might, for various reasons, misperceive his or her own interest is hard to deny. Subjective judgments of self-interest may frequently be misguided in complicated ecologies of repeated interactions. There are issues of conflict between short-run and long-run interests. There are issues of false consciousness with respect to class, family, gender, ethnic, or national interests. There are problems of judgment and inference.

The efficacy of subordinating the subjective preferences of current citizens to an extra-individual determination of interests in the name of society is, however, not obvious. The difficulties associated with concepts of interest and the representation of the absent form a large part of traditional and contemporary debate in political theory (Dahl, 1978; Pateman, 1985; Pitkin, 1981). The remainder of the present chapter takes a particular position with respect to some of the key issues involved in political representation. The position is that political equality is impossible within a conception of politics based strictly on aggregating current preferences of current citizens. It will be argued that the extra-individual assessment of individual interests is not so much a bad vision as it is a vision without a reliable instrument within aggregative democratic institutions.

A primary concern of a political system dedicated to equality of power is to specify a set of institutions that encourages the estimation and comparison of preferences in a way that provides equal attention to the interests of each current and future citizen. The future interests of present and future citizens secure their voice, if they do, through the ability of current citizens to feel empathy with them, and through the willingness of current citizens to serve as trustees for the interests of the future (Pitkin, 1967; Elster, 1983b; Pateman, 1985). A perspective of empathy is also required for the evaluation of political equality through interpersonal and intertemporal comparisons. These ideas of empathy and trust should be distinguished from ideas of guardianship. Although it is possible to argue that a citizen's own interests might be better anticipated by others under some conditions, such a condition is not essential to the present argument. Empathy among current citizens is sought in order to develop the interpersonal comparisons required by political equality, not as a basis for guardianship.

Traditionally, conceptions of political trusteeship and the concomitant qualities of empathy have been implemented primarily through the social structure of the society, particularly in the relations among generations of parents and children, and through the arbitrary contacts and associations generated within an active community life. Through the various miracles of family and community identification, current citizens act consciously to preserve the heritages and legacies of future generations (Dahl, 1982). In an age in which families and communities have become more diffuse and ideologically less central, political equality becomes more difficult to sustain and perhaps a more direct responsibility of the political system.

The obligations of political actors to serve as trustees for the unrepresented has long been recognized as a part of democratic politics. It is an important part of political rhetoric and the rules of political propriety. Consider, for example, efforts to restrict the intersector exchange of resources. Restrictions on bribery of officials, on contributions to political campaigns, on postpolitical employment, and on the awarding of gifts or preferment are all attempts to place frictions on the free exchange of resources between the economic and political sectors. Presumably, we restrict bribery with respect to the action of officials because we feel official actions should not be exchanged for private gain, that officials should act in the service of interests broader than their own. It is a straightforward problem of agency (Ross, 1973; Levinthal, 1988), and exists independent of economic inequalities. Even if wealth were equally distributed among current citizens, the exchange of official action for private gain would corrupt a process of governance.

At first blush, the same kind of argument does not seem to hold with respect to the individual citizen acting as an individual citizen within an aggregative system. From the relatively narrow self-interest of individual actors in the system, or from the point of view of effective exchange, restrictions on the sale of individual political rights (e.g., the vote) reduce the opportunities for individual citizens to maximize their own subjective

148

utilities. Since that is, presumably, the purpose of an aggregative system, restrictions on selling political rights might be viewed as unfortunate interferences with individual freedom and exchange efficiency. As Dahl observes, "the essence of all competitive politics is bribery of the electorate by politicians" (Dahl, 1956).

Yet, our instincts are to condemn the exchange of individual rights for individual economic gain as inconsistent with political democracy. The instincts can be seen as stemming from many ways in which the selling of votes offends our sensibilities, in particular our concern that the distribution of economic endowments is unequal. But from the present point of view such sentiments are also an assertion that politics is not simply a matter of aggregating over the current preferences of current actors. Individual citizens in their capacities as citizens are officials, trustees for the present and future preferences of present and future citizens. They cannot legitimately alienate their political rights because they hold those rights in trust.

Neither empathy nor trust are necessarily fostered by political institutions, but they are not unknown to them. Despite acrimonious interactions involving substantial differences in opinion and genuine conflict of interest among members of the Congress of the United States, almost every observer of the institution comments on the extent to which members come to identify with the collectivity and to have sympathy with the problems of their colleagues. Members with no direct interest, and without explicit instruction, can be trusted to protect the interests of others. It may reasonably be questioned whether that empathy extends to the constituents of colleagues, or whether the trust reflects sentiments beyond well-defined expectations of reciprocity, but the legislative process frequently brings elements of empathy and trust to the political process. Similar phenomena can be observed in other institutions that involve face-to-face contact and mutual dependence. Indeed, this is one of the more important claims for a system of local government based upon political representation.

To speak of trust and empathy as instruments of politics is to conjure up ancient traditions of humanistic thought. The argument, however, is not one based on the beauty and richness of a life built around such elements, but a much more pragmatic one based on the realism between the construction of preferences and the most realistic concerns about political systems—concern with the distribution of power and the equal power imperative of democracy. Without empathy and trust, political equality cannot be achieved, nor can the degree of its attainment be determined.

149

PREFERENCES AND POLITICAL EQUALITY

When the power of an individual citizen is defined in terms of the ability to induce collective actions that conform to his or her interests, it is natural to think of preferences (interests) as developing through one process, and power through a different one. Their interaction produces policy, but they are perceived as independent. Thus, the democratic criterion of political equality is generally seen as separable from any additional criteria with respect to the distribution of preferences. The separation is, however, not as obvious as such a formulation might suggest. In any political system that considers individual preferences in making a collective choice, the extent to which citizens believe they have, are seen to have, and do in fact have power will depend importantly on the distribution of preferences in the society.

Preference Heterogeneity and Voluntary Exchange

Politics can be portrayed as a system of voluntary exchange, a search for Pareto-optimal accommodations to prior preferences. Such a political system thrives on a certain kind of heterogeneity in preferences. In order for voluntary exchange to take place, each trading partner must believe that the exchange increases the utility of his or her position. In the absence of erroneous expectations, this means that two trading partners must value the goods exchanged differently. These differences in marginal rates of substitution can be seen as arising either from differences in preferences, or from differences in endowments, or from both.

Thus, in voluntary exchange, trading advantage comes from two things: The first is possession of resources desired by others. Inequalities in such endowments are generally recognized as a primary source of political inequality. Concern over the extent to which differences in the possession of economic resources dominate political exchange is a conspicuous feature of contemporary writing on democracy (Dahl, 1977). Insofar as the basis for political exchange is a difference in marginal rates of substitution attributable to disparities in initial economic resources, the political system is basically an arena in which the resources of politics are bartered for the resources of the economic system.

The second source of advantage in voluntary trading comes from desiring things undesired by others. This advantage is less commonly noted in discussions of power, but it is an important aspect of modern democratic systems. Voluntary exchange in politics often involves the crafting of policies linking coalition members who are mutually indifferent about

150

the demands of their partners, the classical form being the logroll. In general, the making of public policy through logrolls is facilitated by interests that are different but not conflicting. In such a world, it is possible for individual citizens of a society to be quite distant from each other in values, yet able to induce others to act to advance their self-interest—in short to be powerful. Indeed, being indifferent to the preferences of others makes one an attractive coalition member in a logroll, thus augmenting one's power. As a result, it is possible, in principle, for all citizens to assess themselves as more powerful than others, a result that not only might be viewed as favorable by some democratic criteria but also allows aspirations for domination to be fulfilled. It is, of course, also possible for all citizens to assess themselves as less powerful than others, a less attractive result.

Some of the buffers that produce mutual indifference are excess social resources, ignorance of opportunities, heterogeneity in cultural traditions, physical and social distance, and ideologies of cooperation and affiliation. For the most part, modernism, the rise of nationalism and internationalism, rapid changes in the ease of communication and travel, the development of modern weapons of trade and war, and ideological emphases on domination and subordination all reduce such buffers and make widespread mutual indifference a less characteristic feature of national political systems. From this point of view, many of the social, economic, and ideological changes of the past century have made a democratic process based on voluntary exchange and the discovery of mutually beneficial trades less, rather than more, feasible. This appears to be true even if we concede that technological change has made the discovery of trading possibilities more feasible.

Heterogeneity of Preferences and Preference Pooling

Politics can also be portrayed as preference pooling. Preference pooling is a process that produces a collective choice as the weighted average of individual preferences. The weight assigned to each individual preference is some measure of that individual's resources or power. In the politics of preference pooling, heterogeneity in preferences seems less favorable for political equality. As has been noted frequently in the context of trying to develop a satisfactory measure of power, the success of any citizen in achieving his or her interests in such a system depends on the relation between the individual interests and the distribution of interests in the society.

Citizens with preferences close to the preference center of the society are more successful in pooling processes than are citizens who are more deviant. The proposition is easiest to see in a single-dimension policy space. With multiple dimensions, the "center" for any particular policy is less well defined; but the basic principle that success will depend on the relation between the individual's preferences and the preferences of others remains. This feature of pooling processes has often been pictured as a complication in measurement since it tends to confound the independent "powers" of citizens who share policy preferences. But it can alternatively be seen as a form of political advantage. Just as indifference to the demands of others provides an advantage in a system of voluntary exchange, agreement with the preference of others provides an advantage in preference pooling.

Such a characterization has been overlooked or resisted traditionally for at least two major reasons: On the one hand, because most definitions of power are tightly tied to ideas of causality, we seek to maintain a distinction between achieving one's desires by one's own actions and achieving one's desires by the possibly fortuitous consequence of sharing those desires with others. And, on the other hand, we are reluctant to legitimize any conception of power that treats the power implications of changes in preferences as equivalent to those produced by changes in resources. Such concerns are important, but they lead us away from some conspicuous ways in which the relation between one's own preferences and those of others is a vital aspect of one's capability for inducing a society to do what one wants.

It is an obvious and important feature of democratic debate that citizens whose preferences are distant from the preference center in a society tend to see the political system as functioning poorly as an aggregative system, and to see themselves and their allies as lacking power. One clear example of this in modern discussions is the treatment of the persistent failure of Western "democratic" countries, and particularly the United States, to achieve comprehensive redistributions of wealth and income. Even when these outcomes appear to be consistent with current popular sentiment (Dahl, 1986), they are experienced by citizens with contrary views as a lack of power. Such disparities in the ability to induce collective choices consistent with one's own interests do not depend on inequalities in the resources of power. They are implicit in the heterogeneity of preferences within a society, and would not be removed by making resources equal.

From the point of view of the individual citizen in a preference pooling political system, the distinction between powerlessness (or power) due to the distribution of preferences and powerlessness (or power) due to the distribution of political resources is not a compelling one. Nor is it obvious that the distinction is compelling for a democratic society. Preference heterogeneity in a preference pooling system places some citizens in positions comparable to those that in other contexts yield learned helplessness (Wortman and Brehm, 1975; Abrahamson, Seligman, and Teasdale, 1978). In this case, however, it is not only a psychological pathology; it reflects a palpable political disadvantage, and cries of "inequality" stem from a genuinely experienced powerlessness.

Reputations for Power in a Preference Pooling Process

The effect of heterogeneity of preferences on power disparities is not limited to issues of perceived disadvantages or subjective definitions of power. For example, it is frequently observed that power (in the sense of the power weight associated with an individual in a preference pooling process) depends, in part, on a reputation for power generated from past success in achieving favorable outcomes. Consider a decision process in which collective outcomes are determined by the distribution of power among individuals, and an individual's relative power changes as a consequence of social choices, increasing when outcomes are relatively close to that individual's preferences and decreasing when outcomes are relatively distant. One obvious speculation about such a process is that the accumulation of power reputations will accentuate disparities in power. That is, the updating of power by observation of collective outcomes will tend to convert small differences in power into large differences. The speculation is plausible, but it is wrong.

The equilibrium distribution of power stemming from this process is independent of the initial distribution of power. It depends only on the distribution of attitudes, not on the (exogenous) initial power distribution. Individuals with attitudes near the center of the group will come to have more power than those with attitudes that are relatively distant from the center, independent of the initial distribution of power. And the magnitude of disparities in power at equilibrium depends only on the disparities in preferences. Put most starkly, insofar as the distribution of power in a society depends on reputations for power developed over time by observing the extent to which collective outcomes deviate from an individual's preferences, the extent to which a society can approximate equality of power among citizens will depend on the extent to which it has, or can produce, either homogeneity of preferences or a distribution of policy issues and preferences that eliminates pervasive preference disadvantages.

153

The result is certainly not surprising, given the assumptions of the model. Nor would it be imagined that the model is more than a rough metaphor for the ways in which power reputations develop and affect collective decision outcomes. It is a reminder, however, of a feature of power and powerlessness that is easily overlooked. A primary factor in a reputation for power as well as a personal sense of power is the closeness of collective outcomes to one's own preferences. From this point of view, equality of power can be achieved in a democracy only in situations in which it is largely irrelevant in an aggregative sense.

As many students of democracy have observed, the prerequisites of democracy, and particularly the equal power and enlightened understanding requirements, seem very difficult to achieve in large heterogeneous nation-states. The standard comparisons are between the sizes of contemporary nations and the size of the Greek polis. The usual explanation emphasizes the complications faced by large political units in producing political institutions through which citizens participate equally, or have the opportunity to do so. For example, the number of local governments increases with total national population, but not proportionately. As a result, the proportion of the population participating directly in government is negatively related to total population. This has consequences for integrative processes in politics.

Population size is also associated with another factor that seems to complicate equality—the degree of social homogeneity (Dahl and Tufte, 1973; Dahl, 1984a). Disparities between the potential for democratic processes within relatively heterogeneous societies or societies with linguistic, ethnic, or religious cleavages, on the one hand, and relatively homogeneous societies, on the other, seem important to modern students of democracy. As preferences become more homogeneous, political power—whether based on possession of resources, formal position, or reputation—loses its instrumental value for the individual (Mansbridge, 1980). As preferences become more heterogeneous, opportunities for empathic interaction and mutual education become more critical. From this point of view, the relative inattention by modern students of politics to local government and politics is unfortunate.

Power and the Molding of Preferences

There are numerous reasons for lamenting the tendency to treat preferences as given in theories of choice. Where preferences are ambiguous and changing endogenously, treating them as consistent, clear, stable, and exogenous leads to predictive theories that are wrong and normative theories that are misleading (Mill, [1862] 1950; March, 1978; Elster, 1983b; Wildavsky, 1987). In fact, the convention of treating interests as inviolate is a modern one. It became part of the received doctrine of decision theory, economic theory, and political theory only within the last hundred years or so. It was central to many older theories of politics that the processes by which interests are created, nurtured, and transformed are a critical part of a political (or economic, or decision) process (Machiavelli, [1513] 1940; Marx, [1838] 1961; Durkheim, [1893] 1933).

Students of democracy have often argued that democratic political systems, like other kinds of political systems, require integrative institutions (Pye and Verba, 1965; March and Olsen, 1986b). On the one hand, it seems clear that no system can function without general acceptance of the rules of the game, in this case an acceptance of the legitimacy of legitimately elected rulers and the decisions they make. Integrative institutions designed to foster such legitimacy are an important part of democratic governance. Thus, the emphasis on the ideologies and rituals surrounding democratic processes of debate and elections, and on the sanctity of the vote. In addition, it is often seen as essential to a democracy that it proceed on the basis of reasoned debate and enlightened understanding. The usual argument is that the process must be such that citizens have the opportunity to be fully informed of the implications of alternative policies, so that subjective conceptions of interests coincide with true interests, and so that unreasoned positions and unenlightened preferences can be recognized and discounted. Dahl proposed that one of the criteria for evaluating Congress be the extent to which it facilitated "discussion directed toward clarification of ends, the means to those ends, and the possibility of agreement on means and ends" (Dahl, 1950). The focus on ends as well as means differentiates such a criterion from most ideas of complete information in aggregative institutions. As already discussed, political equality is threatened by heterogeneity of interests among citizens. As a result, political institutions for discovering, comprehending, and shaping the sharing of citizen interests are vital to political equality. Interests and preferences develop through social processes of identity (Gecas, 1982; Wildavsky, 1987), learning (Cohen and Axelrod, 1984), and discussion (Elster, 1983b). The routes to preferences that make power widely shared rather than concentrated in the hands of a few involve institutions that foster collective identity and openness with respect to the development of interests.

What is less clear is how to design political institutions that foster collective identity and power-producing preferences without corrupting citizens into slaves (Dahrendorf, 1959), institutions that promote prefer-

155

ence agreement, but at the same time support the exploration of alternative visions and possible new preferences, institutions that sustain the heterogeneity desired on other grounds with minimum cost to political equality. This is, of course, the vision of polyarchy (Dahl, 1971; 1978; 1986). The essential idea is to develop a structure of preferences and a process of political competition and coalition formation that prevents any group from being permanently disadvantaged (Miller, 1983). It is possible, for example, to imagine developing heterogeneous preferences that vary independently on different policy issues, so that the positions of individuals similarly vary across different issues. This would produce disparities in power in any one policy domain, but a tendency to equalize power on the average. Such an effort would require some attention to how tendencies toward intrapersonal and interpersonal inconsistency in preferences can be supported and extended.

Even in a world of consistent preferences (or at least intercorrelated preferences), it is possible to sustain political equality if the political process is designed to assure instability in winning coalitions (Riker, 1982; Miller, 1983), either across time or across political jurisdictions. Instabilities are produced by fluctuations in political mobilization and by institutions that partition society into internally homogeneous subgroups. Organizational and geographic partitioning may produce serious problems in reconciling the various claims of different subgroups, of course. It is not an accident that issues of mobilization, federalism, and democratic centralism are frequent refrains in the analysis of democratic systems (Dahl, 1971; 1983). But systems vulnerable to variations in political activation, and systems of local autonomy, including local governments and political parties, allow many individuals to experience power even when their preferences deviate from those of the rest of society.

CONCLUSION

Although there are exceptions, contemporary social welfare theorists in both political science and economics are inclined to define the problem of politics as one of aggregating prior and exogenous individual preferences into a collective choice. Individual interests are converted to collective decisions through bargaining, coalition formation, exchange, and the exercise of power. Preferences (interests) are taken as given. The main thrust of the present chapter is that such a conception of politics and preferences leads to an incomplete understanding of power in a

156

democracy, and consequently to an incomplete specification of the problems involved in designing democratic institutions.

The incompleteness is implicit in two conclusions of our discussion: First, within conventional definitions of power, the assessment of the distribution of power in a political system requires estimating and comparing the present and future interests (preferences) of present and future citizens. Second, the extent to which equality of power is achieved within a political system will depend not only on the distribution of resources but also on the distribution of preferences (interests) in the society. Each of these conclusions indicates serious limitations in an aggregative conception of political equality and democracy.

It is precisely an awareness of such difficulties that drove many classical philosophers of politics toward a conception of politics somewhat different from that underlying modern treatments and toward a consideration of the role of political institutions in integrating and shaping interests as well as aggregating them. In a related spirit, Dahl has suggested that both political equality and enlightened understanding are essential features of democracy (Dahl, 1979; 1982; 1984a; 1984b; 1986). By enlightened understanding, he means:

> each citizen ought to have adequate and equal opportunities for
> discovering and validating, in the time permitted by the need for a
> decision, what his or her preferences are on the matter to be
> decided . . . ; alternative procedures for making decisions
> ought to be evaluated according to the opportunities they furnish
> citizens for acquiring an understanding of means and ends, and of
> oneself and other relevant selves. (Dahl, 1979)

In such a conception, enlightened understanding is seen as necessary to make the preferences that are weighted equally by political equality a true expression of the individual citizen's desires. Political equality and enlightened understanding are each required to satisfy Dahl's criteria for democracy, but one could imagine a political system having one without the other.

The present analysis suggests that political aggregation based on equality of power among citizens and political integration based on trust, empathy, collective identity, and enlightened understanding are not parallel criteria, separately important. Aggregative political equality has meaning only within an understanding of the empathic comparison and development of interests. In this sense, contemporary theories emphasizing the aggregative aspects of political equality are incomplete, and contemporary treatments of the integrative aspects of politics underestimate their significance for political equality.

It is possible that the various risks associated with integrative institutions, the threats of their corruption, the dangers of their perversion by willful, self-interested actors, and the accumulated inertia of institutional structures, make their design and maintenance a study in frustration and disappointment. But achieving political equality is not simply a matter of perfecting institutions for mediating among conflicting interests. It requires significant attention to what those interests are and how they can be compared, shared, and molded in a way that sustains, rather than undermines, democracy. If we wish to pursue political equality, we may have to run the risk of attending to theories of endogenous preferences somewhat more and to theories based on notions of exogenous interests and power somewhat less.

9

The Role
of Political Institutions

Traditionally, students of politics have been interested in how political institutions work, and how the political organization of society contributes to the well-being of citizens and to their enslavement. Political institutions have frequently been seen as preconditions for a civilized society, frequently as symptoms of its decay. Political institutions have been described and analyzed in terms of perspectives as varied as that of a formal, legal style concentrating on constitutions, laws, and rules, of a purely descriptive style focusing on the origins and developments of specific institutions, of a great man tradition portraying political institutions as arenas for charismatic leaders, and of a realpolitik style emphasizing political institutions as arenas for rival, external groups with different resources and interests (Neumann, 1957; Wolin, 1960).

Although it lies within this heterogeneous tradition, this book reflects a specific perspective on institutional analysis. Within that perspective, political actors are driven by institutional duties and roles as well as, or instead of, by calculated self-interest; politics is organized around the construction and interpretation of meaning as well as, or instead of, the making of choices; routines, rules, and forms evolve through history-dependent processes that do not reliably and quickly reach unique equilibria; the institutions of politics are not simple echoes of social forces; and the polity is something different from, or more than, an arena for competition among rival interests.

In short, the organization of political life makes a difference, and institutions affect the flow of history. We have been particularly concerned

159

with two aspects of such a view: the way in which an appreciation of the role of political institutions contributes to a positive theory of politics; and the way in which understanding political institutions contributes to the normative evaluation and design of them. Understanding involves a theory of how the polity comprehends, changes, and maintains a relationship with its environment through its institutions. Evaluation involves assessing the extent to which political institutions contribute to a meaningful sovereignty of the people.

As a preface to a theory of political institutions, we have identified three broad clusters of ideas. The first emphasizes the way in which political life is ordered by rules and organizational forms that transcend individuals and buffer or transform social forces. The second emphasizes the endogenous nature of reality, interests, and roles, and so a constructive vision of political actors, meaning, and preferences. The third emphasizes the history-dependent intertwining of stability and change. In this chapter we take a brief look at these ideas and their significance for interpreting and assessing political institutions and processes.

THE LOGIC OF APPROPRIATENESS

Politics is organized by a logic of appropriateness. Political institutions are collections of interrelated rules and routines that define appropriate actions in terms of relations between roles and situations. The process involves determining what the situation is, what role is being fulfilled, and what the obligations of that role in that situation are. When individuals enter an institution, they try to discover, and are taught, the rules. When they encounter a new situation, they try to associate it with a situation for which rules already exist. Through rules and a logic of appropriateness, political institutions realize both order, stability, and predictability, on the one hand, and flexibility and adaptiveness, on the other.

A logic of appropriateness can be contrasted with a logic of consequentiality. In a logic of consequentiality, behaviors are driven by preferences and expectations about consequences. Behavior is willful, reflecting an attempt to make outcomes fulfill subjective desires, to the extent possible. Within such a logic, a sane person is one who is ''in touch with reality'' in the sense of maintaining consistency between behavior and realistic expectations of its consequences. The sacred texts are Bentham and classical decision theory.

In a logic of appropriateness, on the other hand, behaviors (beliefs as well as actions) are intentional but not willful. They involve fulfilling the obligations of a role in a situation, and so of trying to determine the imperatives of holding a position. Action stems from a conception of necessity, rather than preference. Within a logic of appropriateness, a sane person is one who is "in touch with identity" in the sense of maintaining consistency between behavior and a conception of self in a social role. Ambiguity or conflict in rules is typically resolved not by shifting to a logic of consequentiality and rational calculation, but by trying to clarify the rules, make distinctions, determine what the situation is and what definition "fits." The sacred texts are Homer and classical jurisprudence.

From this perspective, the polity embodies a political community and the identities and capabilities of individuals cannot be seen as established apart from, or prior to, their membership and position in the community. For instance, the role of civil servant is defined by shared assumptions about what is due to occupants of other roles, like those of an elected leader or a citizen. The political community is based on a shared history, a valued way of life, a shared definition of the common good, and a shared interpretation and common understanding embodied in rules for appropriate behavior. The rules provide criteria for what is worth striving for, and for what is accounted as good reasons for action. Citizens give their allegiance to a set of norms, beliefs, and practices embodied in political institutions. The language is one of the duties and rights associated with specific role relationships.

A major activity of political institutions is educating individuals into knowledgeable citizens. A knowledgeable citizen is one who is familiar with the rules of appropriate behavior and with the moral and intellectual virtues of the polity, and who thus knows the institutional reasons for behaviors, and can justify them by reference to the requirements of a larger order (MacIntyre, 1988). Individuals are seen as having a potential for a great variety of behavior. They may act ethically or nonethically; behave in a goal-oriented way or follow institutionally defined rules and obligations; pursue self-chosen goals or act to achieve institutional ends; and they may identify with a variety of smaller or larger collectivities, organizations, professions, or interest groups. Institutional contexts influence which of these potentials are actually realized.

We have argued that most behavior in politics follows such a logic of appropriateness, that rules are followed and roles are fulfilled. The logic of appropriateness, however, is ideologically beleaguered. The same structure of appropriateness that establishes rules for other behavior also establishes rules for justificatory behavior. And in discourse about action and in the justification of action, Homer has given way to Bentham.

In political institutions, as elsewhere, behavior is justified by a logic of rationality, consequentiality, and individual will. The question "Why did you do that?" elicits an answer of the form "I did it because I expected it to have consequences that I value."

Having determined what action to take by a logic of appropriateness, in our culture we justify the action (appropriately) by a logic of consequentiality. This structure of action and justification results in one of the more frequently observed regularities in decision-making behavior—the elaboration of reasons for action after the decision has been made (Feldman and March, 1981; Brunsson, 1985). Reasons are important. It is clear they must be expressed, but their role in affecting outcomes is more obscure. The explicit processes of choice often seem more designed to justify or legitimize a choice than to make it.

This tension between action based on a logic of appropriateness and justification based on a logic of consequentiality is not a necessary one. It is entirely possible for action to be justified by appeal to identity, to what a role demands, and such justifications are common. For instance, appeals to national identities and the appropriateness of personal sacrifices are common in situations of national disaster and war. Similarly, it is entirely possible for action actually to be based on rational calculation of its consequences as well as justified that way, and such actions are also common. The tension is, however, characteristic of political institutions. It can be seen as resulting in a kind of healthy charade of hypocrisy in which reasons and actions are not tightly linked but place pressure on each other in a way that strengthens each (March, 1978).

THE CONSTRUCTION OF ACTORS, MEANING, AND INTERESTS

Political institutions not only respond to their environments but create those environments at the same time. Such phenomena are not routinely accommodated by modern political theory, which makes political outcomes a function of three primary factors: the distribution of preferences (interests) among political actors, the distribution of resources (powers), and the constraints imposed by the rules of the game (constitutions). Each of these is treated as exogenous to the political system. That is, preferences are developed within a society and transmitted through socialization, resources are distributed among political actors by some broad social processes, and rules of the game are either stable or change by a revolutionary intervention exogenous to ordinary political activities.

The idea that preferences are produced and changed by a process that is exogenous to the processes of choice is fundamental to modern decision theory. In the "revealed preference" version of the theory, preferences must be stable in order for the theory to be testable. In other versions, preferences can change, but choice itself does not produce a change in preferences. Conventional theories of markets, for example, picture advertising and experience as providing information about alternatives and their properties, not as affecting tastes. Similarly, conventional theories of politics assume that a voter's exposure to and choice of a candidate do not change that voter's preferences for various attributes that a candidate might possess, although they may change a voter's beliefs about which candidates possess which attributes.

Most research on preferences, on the other hand, indicates that preferences and meanings develop in politics, as in the rest of life, through a combination of education, indoctrination, and experience. They are neither stable, nor precise, nor exogenous (March, 1978; Fischhoff, Slovic, and Lichtenstein, 1980). If political preferences are molded through political experiences, or by political institutions, it is awkward to have a theory that presumes preferences are exogenous to the political process. And if preferences are not exogenous to the political process, it is awkward to picture the political system as strictly dependent on the society associated with it (Witt, 1985).

The contrast between the two kinds of notions is found most starkly in theories of political leadership. One classic idea of political leadership emphasizes the creation of winning political coalitions among participants with given demands (March, 1970; Schofield, 1982). The leadership role is that of a broker: providing information, identifying possible coalitions, and facilitating side payments and the development of logrolling. Such a view of leadership is implicit in the theory of the political process that has been developed in political science in recent decades. A second conception of leadership emphasizes the transformation of preferences, both those of the leader and those of followers (Selznick, 1957; Burns, 1978). Leaders interact with other leaders and are co-opted into new beliefs and commitments. The leadership role is that of educator, stimulating and accepting changing worldviews, redefining meanings, and exciting commitments. Such a view is more conspicuous in theories that assume a more autonomous role for political institutions.

The distribution of political resources is also partly determined endogenously. Political institutions affect the distribution of resources, which in turn affects the power of political actors, and thereby affects political institutions. Wealth, social standing, reputation for power, knowledge of alternatives, and attention are not easily described as exogenous to the political process and political institutions. Holding office provides legitimacy and participation rights, and alters the distribution of power and access (Egeberg, 1981; Lægreid and Olsen, 1978; Olsen, 1983). The policy alternatives of leaders are not defined completely by exogenous forces, but are shaped by existing administrative agencies (Skocpol, 1980; Skocpol and Finegold, 1982; Skowronek, 1982). The outcomes of the political process modify reputations for power, which in turn modify political outcomes (Enderud, 1976; March, 1966).

Finally, the third exogenous factor in conventional theories of politics, the rules of the game, is not really exogenous either. Constitutions, laws, contracts, and customary rules of politics make many potential actions or considerations illegitimate or unnoticed. Some alternatives are excluded from the agenda before politics begins (Bachrach and Baratz, 1962). The deadlines of political processes, the timing of elections, budgets, and political events, and thus the temporal ordering of choice opportunities, are specified. These constraints are not imposed full-blown by an external social system; they develop within the context of political institutions. Public agencies create rules and have them sanctioned by politicians (Eckhoff and Jacobsen, 1960), and revolutionary changes are initiated and pursued by military bureaucrats (Trimberger, 1978).

Actions taken within and by political institutions change the distribution of political interests, resources, and rules by creating new actors and identities, by providing actors with criteria of success and failure, by constructing rules for appropriate behavior, and by endowing some individuals, rather than others, with authority and other types of resources. Institutions affect the ways in which individuals and groups become activated within and outside established institutions, the level of trust among citizens and leaders, the common aspirations of a political community, the shared language, understanding, and norms of the community, and the meaning of concepts like democracy, justice, liberty, and equality.

As a result, arbitrary institutional change can change the political environment. Two striking examples of how a relatively arbitrary change in an institution can become a relatively permanent change in the political landscape were found by Brady (1988) and Olson (Bergevärn and Olson, 1987; Olson, 1987). Brady studied the transformation of American politics in the last quarter of the nineteenth century. Changes in the Congress attributable more to the special features of a single-member, plurality election system than to changes in public attitudes led to subsequent shifts in political interests. Olson studied the impact of changes in public accounting procedures in Norwegian municipalities as a result of the German occupation during the Second World War. Changes introduced by occupation authorities became institutionalized in Norwegian practice

164

and persisted subsequently, even in the face of the postoccupation rejection of German influence. As a result, Norwegian and Swedish routines, which were similar before the war, diverged substantially.

The autonomous role of institutions in the molding of political community and meaning has long been seen as an welcome part of a democratic system. It is the base of theories of democratic leadership (Selznick, 1957; Burns, 1978), as well as many conceptions of jurisprudence (Levi, 1949; Stone, 1950) and political development (Pye and Verba, 1965). Institutional capability for transforming political interests is also, as we have seen in chapters 7 and 8, an important aspect of integrative, as contrasted with aggregative, conceptions of politics. If we see politics as building community and a sense of common identity within which decisions are made, we welcome the role of political institutions as agents in the construction of political interests and beliefs. They are a source of vitality in political life and coherence in political identity.

There is, however, no guarantee that institutional development will necessarily further the integration of a polity. The development of the post–World War II welfare state provides an example of how institutional processes can move the polity in an opposite direction. The expanding agenda and social policies of the welfare state were responses to major shifts in power, resources, and beliefs within the society. Those shifts propelled social democratic parties into political power in many Western democracies. Social democratic policies were dedicated to providing services to all citizens, independent of their social and economic status, and thus to create a political community—*folkhemmet* (the people's home), in Swedish terminology.

The implementation of that vision through specific political institutions, however, tended to move the polity away from an integrated vision of the *folkhemm* and toward a more fragmented system. New institutions were created to implement new conceptions of justice and equity, to solve immediate social problems, and to resolve social conflict. The internal dynamics of these institutions contributed to the creation of new political actors—new agencies, professions, unions, and client groups. In particular, many of the policies of the welfare state created highly specialized categories of clients, for example, farmers receiving state subsidies, single parents receiving welfare benefits, and homeowners with state loans. For such client groups, the rights and interests linked to the statuses created by public policies tended to become more important for their welfare, and for their political behavior, than their traditional ties to social classes, religions, or geographical regions.

The result was a significant transformation of the social basis of politics, as illustrated for instance by voting studies (Valen, 1981). The process created new personal and group identities. Specialized agencies, professions, unions, legislators, and organized client groups acted as political interest groups, developing alliances, mobilizing citizens for political action, and even demanding political action. This development contributed to a segmentation of the welfare state (Olsen, 1983). Efforts to achieve universality through detailed justice (millimeter-justice) tended to fragment the political community into small constituencies, and thus weakened integrative aspects of public policy making.

Institutional autonomy is, therefore, an important factor in the development of political integration, but it does not guarantee it. Similarly, the molding of public sentiment through political institutions is in many ways a necessity for political equality, but the capabilities of institutions to affect interests as well as respond to them is an obvious threat both to popular sovereignty and to the power of organized interests. If a wide range of institutional actions can secure post hoc popular approval, the mechanisms of popular control are compromised. The extreme case is a government that seeks mass plebiscitary approval of actions already taken. Experience suggests that such approval is readily, but not always, obtained for quite a wide range of possible policies.

Thus, every democratic system faces a difficult problem of balancing the undoubted advantages, even necessity, of institutional autonomy with the risks that such autonomy will make popular control difficult or impossible. Ultimately, the system works only because of institutionalized limits and mutual trust. Institutional actors refuse to exploit opportunities for autonomous action that might compromise the system. Interest groups grant a reasonable range of independence to political institutions. Sustaining the limits and encouraging the trust, therefore, become an essential part of institution building.

STABILITY AND CHANGE

Although they provide important elements of order in the changing scene of politics, political institutions themselves also change. The processes of change include the mundane, incremental transformations of everyday life as well as the rarer metamorphoses at breaking points of history—when a society's values and institutions are challenged or shattered. These are situations where citizens are more likely to become aware of the values, concepts, beliefs, and institutions by which they live. Typically, in such situations the political institutions and the ways in which

166

they organize the relations between citizens, elected representatives, bureaucrats and experts, and organized interests are reexamined, and possibly modified, transformed, or replaced.

In general, changes are produced through some kind of encounter between the rules (or action based on them) and an environment, partly consisting of other rules. The dramatic version is war or civil war which may replace one definition of appropriateness with another. The less dramatic version is an ongoing tension among alternative institutional rules—and an ongoing debate or struggle over the matching of institutional principles and actual situations and spheres of activities. The constitution of a polity defines the major institutional spheres in terms of the appropriate times and places for different types of decisions, and in terms of appropriate participants, problems, solutions, and decision rules, but political orders are never complete. Polities go through periods where a sphere of action is regulated by a single institution, to periods where several institutions make claims upon an individual's allegiance. Some spheres of social life may not be organized by any political institution, or very weakly organized (e.g., the open structures of garbage can situations). Such spheres may become institutionalized, and infused with conflict and debate over the adequacy of different principles.

Contemporary welfare states appear to be in the process of redefining the appropriateness of different institutions, for instance the boundary between a sphere of solidarity based on universal citizens rights implemented through state bureaucracies, a sphere of self-interest and competition implemented through a price system, a sphere of organized interests and bargaining through a "corporatist" system, and a sphere of community values implemented through voluntary associations and citizens initiatives (Olsen, 1988b; Eriksen, 1987). They appear to be developing an interpretation of history by which to explain the expanded agenda of the welfare state. But whether that interpretation will picture the welfare state as resulting from a coalition of self-interested beneficiaries, or as resulting from acceptance of ideals of justice, is not clear. Thus, they may be testing the boundaries of solidarity and community (Martinussen, 1988). The outcome of that process of interpretation may affect the extent to which the next historical period will see cooperation as based on communities or as based on contracts.

Institutions change, but the changes are not predicted simply by institutional environments. Thus, to portray political institutions simply as an equilibrium solution to the conflicting interests of current actors is probably a mistake. Institutions are not simple reflections of current exogenous forces or micro-behavior and motives. They embed historical experience

167

into rules, routines, and forms that persist beyond the historical moment and condition. If the institutions of the polity were instantaneously and precisely controlled by the balance of exogenous political and social forces in a society, governance would be different from what it is. For example, Lipset has argued that although Canadians and Americans "probably resemble each other more than any other two nations on earth," they differ consistently and substantially as a result of a different historical development beginning at the time of the American Revolution. Despite considerable cultural and economic interpenetration of the two countries, the events culminating in American independence have organized the development of the two countries to produce two distinct political cultures (Lipset, 1986).

Unless we assume that a political environment is stable, it is likely that the rate of change in the environment will exceed the rate of adjustment to it. The institutions at a particular moment are a shifting residue of history, and lags in adjustment are important (Stinchcombe, 1965; Hannan and Freeman, 1984; Astley, 1985). It is a problem familiar to every generation of political actors. Long before a new constellation of forces can transform the polity, that constellation is likely to have been supplanted by another, which will, in its turn, be equally short-lived; and the disparity between the rate of environmental change and the rate of adjustment is itself self-sustaining. By constraining political change, institutional stability contributes to regime instability.

The model is a more generalized version of the competency trap discussed in Chapter 4. As institutions develop competence at acting within a particular political system, those enhanced capabilities are accompanied by an even more significant increase in the disparity between the fit of the institutions to the existing system and their fit to changing demands. Attempts by the regime to impose small changes on the institutional structure either fail, in which case the regime suffers, or they succeed, in which case performance declines in the short run and the regime suffers also. The process is bounded, however. While institutions become increasingly efficient relative to near-neighborhood changes, they tend to become increasingly obsolescent (Hall, 1976). The narrow focusing of competences assures that incremental change will not succeed, but leaves institutions susceptible to radical change.

Thus, political discontent tends to lead simultaneously to increasing stability in institutions and instability in regimes. If a change can be introduced and imposed for the relatively brief time required to achieve modest competence on the new (better) technology, a new fundamental perspective is established, and the old institutional order falls apart rapidly

(Tushman and Romanelli, 1985). The ''stickiness'' of adaptation means both that improved rules or forms will not be adopted immediately and that there will be a relatively large number of quite different alternative radical steps that can be taken. Thus, history can take a number of different routes, and the particular route that is followed may be heavily influenced by the political institution itself.

Note that there is no assurance that the last part of the story will occur very soon, or even at all. Histories of organizational and institutional change are replete with stories of long stabilities of suboptimal strategies or technologies. A familiar example to anyone in the United States is the persistence of inches, feet, and miles as measures of distance. Similarly, just as pervasive clerical and production competences associated with the QWERTY keyboard have kept that technology as standard against the claims of demonstrably more efficient forms, pervasive experience in political institutions can stabilize institutional rules or forms against alternatives that one would think were demonstrably more effective from a political point of view (Arthur, 1984). A conspicuous political example is the stability of political parties and cleavages (Lipset and Rokkan, 1967).

The story calls attention to a general feature of adaptive systems. In most adaptive processes there is a trade-off between exploitation of known alternatives or knowledge and exploration of new alternatives or new areas of knowledge. The issue is discussed as a matter of deliberate choice in treatments of the so-called two-armed bandit problem and optimal research policy. In both cases, the objective is to define an optimal strategy for dividing resources between using technologies currently believed to be best and gathering additional information about alternatives. Where adaptation comes through learning from experience, increases in competence or knowledge tend to lead to the substitution of exploitation for exploration, and thereby tend to limit the discovery of, and experience with, new possibilities that are required for effective learning. That is, learning as a process tends to eliminate the prerequisites of learning as a form of intelligence.

Because of this, the literature on change exhibits considerable concern about the processes by which pressures for experimentation or exploration are sustained. In the political arena, politics has traditionally been viewed as producing pressures toward experimentation, and one of the prime concerns of political philosophy has been how to keep volatile political impulses compatible with a stable social and political order (Wolin, 1960:4). From the point of view of sensible adaptation, the problems, disagreements, cleavages, and conflicts that fill politics can be seen as providing the basis for exploring new alternatives. Thus, a political penchant for change counterbalances institutional stability and facilitates learning.

Experimentation is important, but the present analysis calls attention to some less obvious features of institutional adaptation and particularly the way in which stability and change are related. Consider, for example, incremental trial and error learning. Incrementalism involves learning from frequent, small, reversible steps. Studies of the requirements for effective learning in complicated learning environments indicate that taking frequent, small, reversible steps is likely to make learning difficult (Lounamaa and March, 1987). Frequent changes provide too little experience with any one strategy to assess its value reliably; small changes tend to be lost in the noise of ordinary historical experience; and reversibility encourages frequent changes. The political institutions we have described are, from such a point of view, surprisingly efficient instruments for learning. They allow incremental drift, but they constrain incrementalism in a way that tends to produce relatively long periods of considerable stability punctuated by rather substantial, rather abrupt changes.

Discussions of the efficiency of learning, however, can be misleading. Political institutions form a complicated ecology of interconnected rules. Within such a system, concepts of efficiency, optimality, or equilibrium are elusive (March and Sproull, 1989). Adjustments made in one part of the ecology may affect appropriate adjustments in another part (Krehbiel, 1987; Shepsle and Weingast, 1987b). Experiments run in one part benefit other parts. Institutions are "nested" in the sense that groups are contained within communities which are contained within larger polities. Actions that contribute to survival of a "higher level" of the system may endanger the survival of a "lower level," yet the existence of the latter may be vital to the former. These complications are not unique to political institutions. They are standard in theories of variation and selection or learning. They lead naturally to variations in the rate of adaptation of different political institutions. The focus of politics on changes in substantive policies buffers political institutions from change, which in turn buffer constitutions. These variations are reinforced by rules of behavior in democratic polities, rules that assume stability in constitutions and institutions while debating changes in substantive policies.

These features of the processes of change have implications both for understanding political institutions and for changing them. The transformation of institutions is neither dictated completely by exogenous conditions nor controllable precisely by intentional actions. For the most part, institutions evolve through a relatively mundane set of procedures sensitive to relatively diffuse mechanisms of control. Ideas about appropriate behavior ordinarily change gradually through the development of experience and the elaboration of worldviews. Such processes tend to result in significant lags in the adjustment of institutions to their environments. The lags, in turn, make institutional history somewhat jerky and sensitive to major shocks that lead not only to occasional periods of rapid change, but also to considerable indeterminacy in the direction of change.

ENDING

We began this book by observing that contemporary styles of theories of politics tended to describe political behavior as institution-free. We have tried to explain why we think that posture is a mistake, why an adequate theory of politics must include not only a conception of elementary processes such as those organized by political competition or temporal sorting, but also systematic attention to political institutions. We have tried to show how such attention deepens our understanding of political phenomena and enriches our efforts to bring political life closer to democratic ideals. In a broad sense, we have been urging that a perspective of politics as organized around the interactions of a collection of individual actors or events be supplemented with (or replaced by) a perspective that sees the polity as a community of rules, norms, and institutions.

Such a vision is an old one. It is also a part of several recent criticisms of individualism in contemporary life (Mansbridge, 1980; MacIntyre, 1988). It has become rather fashionable to speak of the need to reconstruct our lives and our political systems in a new image based on a sense of community and a commitment to tradition-dependent institutions. We are sympathetic to such a reconstruction, but our viewpoint is basically somewhat different. We object to contemporary descriptions of politics, not so much because they describe an unattractive political world but because they describe the real world badly. We believe that theories and philosophies of politics have obscured important realities of political life.

Our objective has been to suggest changes in the way we think about that life, to lay a basis for bringing theories of politics closer to our experience of it. We are convinced that norms of appropriateness, rules, routines, and the elaboration of meaning are central features of politics, that an understanding of stability and change in politics requires a theory of political institutions. Political institutions simplify the potential confusions of action by providing action alternatives; they simplify the potential confusions of meaning by creating a structure for interpreting history and anticipating the future; and they simplify the complications of heterogeneity by shaping the preferences of participants. All of those features are not utopian dreams but descriptions of politics as it occurs. As a result, it is hard to be sanguine about contemporary theories of politics, or contemporary efforts to reform politics, that ignore institutions, or relegate them to a secondary role.

Notes

CHAPTER 5: *INSTITUTIONAL REFORM AS AN AD HOC ACTIVITY*

1. We include such efforts as: (1) the Commission on Department Methods (the Keep Commission), 1905–1909, chaired by Charles H. Keep; (2) the Commission on Economy and Efficiency, 1910–1913, chaired by F. A. Cleveland; (3) the Joint Committee on the Reorganization of the Administrative Branch of the Government, 1920–1923, chaired by W. F. Brown; (4) the President's Committee on Administrative Management (Brownlow Committee), 1936–1937, chaired by Louis Brownlow; (5) the Senate Select Committee to Investigate the Executive Agencies of the Government, 1936, chaired by Senator H. F. Byrd; (6) the U.S. Commission on the Organization of the Executive Branch of Government (First Hoover Commission), 1947–1949, chaired by Herbert Hoover; (7) the Second Commission on Organization of the Executive Branch (Second Hoover Commission), 1953–1955, chaired by Herbert Hoover; (8) the President's Advisory Committee on Government Organization, 1953–1961, chaired by Nelson Rockefeller (1953–1958) and by Don Price (1958–1961); (9) the Price Task Force, 1964, chaired by Don Price; (10) the Heineman Task Force, 1966–1967, chaired by Ben Heineman, Sr.; (11) the President's Advisory Council on Executive Organization (Ash Council), 1969–1971, chaired by Roy Ash; (12) the President's Reorganization Project, 1977–1980, several task forces appointed by President Carter and led by Bert Lance; and (13) the Cabinet Council on Management and Administration, the President's Council on Integrity and Efficiency, the President's Council on Management Improvement, and a variety of projects under the "Reform '88" umbrella, and the President's Private Sector Survey on Cost Control (the Grace Commission), appointed by President Reagan, 1981–1988.

CHAPTER 6: *INSTITUTIONAL REFORM AS PUBLIC POLICY*

1. The number of documents relating to the reform programs in Denmark, Finland, Norway, and Sweden is rather large. Some of the more important ones are listed in Olsen (1988b).

2. In a similar spirit, in 1987, after the Norwegian social democratic government called its program "Den nye staten" (the new state), the conservative party called its own program "Den moderne staten" (the modern state).

3. It should be noted that these effects were not associated with commensurate effects on the total budget. Achievements in cutting total public spending fell well short of what was hoped by the Thatcher government (Metcalfe and Richards, 1987:177). Cutbacks in some policy fields were matched by unanticipated increases in others, driven by quasi-automatic mechanisms of growth built into most welfare states.

References

NOTE: Scandinavian authors with names using the three Scandinavian letters of Æ, Å, and Ø (Danish and Norwegian) or Ä, Å, and Ö (Swedish) are alphabetized as though the letters were English letters of AE, A, and O and not as separate letters.

AARRESTAD, J. 1984. *Oljen og norsk økonomi*. Oslo: NKS-forlaget.

ABELSON, R. P., ed. 1968. *Theories of Cognitive Consistency: A Sourcebook*. Chicago: Rand McNally.

ABRAHAMSON, L. Y., M. E. P. SELIGMAN, AND J. D. TEASDALE. 1978. Learned Helplessness in Humans: Critique and Reformulation. *Abnormal Psychology*, 87:49–74.

AIKIN, C., AND L. W. KOENIG. 1949. Introduction to Hoover Commission: A Symposium. *American Political Science Review*, 43:933–940.

AKERLOF, G. A. 1970. The Market for "Lemons": Qualitative Uncertainty and the Market Mechanism. *Quarterly Journal of Economics*, 84:488–500.

AKERLOF, G. A. 1980. The Economics of Social Customs, of Which Unemployment May Be One Consequence. *Quarterly Journal of Economics*, 95:749–775.

ALDRICH, H. E. 1979. *Organizations and Environments*. Englewood Cliffs, N.J.: Prentice-Hall.

ALLARDT, E., ed. 1981. *Nordic Democracy*. Copenhagen: Det Danske Selskab.

ALLISON, G. T. 1971. *Essence of Decision*. Boston: Little, Brown.

ANDENÆS, K. 1985. Domstolene—Statsmakt på nedtur. *Hefte for Kritisk Juss*, 3/4:48–51.

ANDERSEN, S. 1988. *Industrial Relations in British and Norwegian Offshore Industrial Relations*. London: Gower.

175

ANDERSON, C. W. 1979. The Place of Principles in Policy Analysis. *American Political Science Review,* 73:711–723.

ANDERSON, P. 1983. Decision Making by Objection and the Cuban Missile Crises. *Administrative Science Quarterly,* 28:201–222.

ANDERSON, P., AND G. W. FISCHER. 1986. A Monte Carlo Model of a Garbage Can Decision Process. In J. G. March and R. Weissinger-Baylon, eds., *Ambiguity and Command: Organizational Perspectives on Military Decision Making.* Marshfield, Mass.: Pitman.

ARENDT, H. 1958. *The Human Condition.* Chicago: University of Chicago Press.

ARGYRADES, D. C. 1965. Some Aspects of Civil Service Reorganization in Greece. *International Review of Administrative Sciences,* 31:297–307.

ARGYRIS, C. 1965. *Organization and Innovation.* Homewood, Ill.: Irwin-Dorsey.

ARGYRIS, C., AND D. SCHÖN. 1978. *Organizational Learning.* Reading, Mass.: Addison-Wesley.

ARNOLD, P. E. 1974. Reorganization and Politics: A Reflection on the Adequacy of Administration Theory. *Public Administration Review,* 34:205–211.

ARNOLD, P. E. 1976. The First Hoover Commission and the Managerial Presidency. *Journal of Politics,* 38:46–70.

ARNOLD, P. E. 1988. Reorganization and Regime in United States and Britain. *Public Administration Review,* 48:726–734.

ARNOLD, P. E., AND L. J. ROOS. 1974. Toward a Theory of Congressional-Executive Relations. *Review of Politics,* 26:410–429.

ARROW, K. 1974. *Limits of Organization.* New York: Norton.

ARTHUR, W. B. 1984. Competing Technologies and Economic Prediction. *IIASA Options,* 2:10–13.

ASHFORD, D. E., ed. 1978. *Comparing Public Policies: New Concepts and Methods.* Beverly Hills, Calif.: Sage Publications.

ASHFORD, D. E. 1986. *The Emergence of Welfare States.* Oxford: Basil Blackwell.

ASTLEY, W. G. 1985. The Two Ecologies: Population and Community Perspectives on Organizational Evolution. *Administrative Science Quarterly,* 30:224–241.

AXELROD, R. 1980. More Effective Choice in Prisoners' Dilemma. *Journal of Conflict Resolution,* 24:379–403.

AXELROD, R. 1984. *The Evolution of Cooperation.* New York: Basic Books.

AXELROD, R., AND W. D. HAMILTON. 1981. The Evolution of Cooperation. *Science,* 211:1390–96.

BACHRACH, P., AND M. BARATZ. 1962. The Two Faces of Power. *American Political Science Review,* 56:947–952.

BAIER, V. E., J. G. MARCH, AND H. SÆTREN. 1986. Implementation and Ambiguity. *Scandinavian Journal of Management Studies,* 2:197–212.

176

References

BALBUS, I. 1971. The Concept of Interest in Pluralist and Marxian Analysis. *Politics and Society,* 1:151–174.

BARDACH, E. 1977. *The Implementation Game.* Cambridge, Mass.: MIT Press.

BARKER, A., ed. 1982. *Quangos in Britain.* London: Macmillan.

BARLEY, S. R. 1987. The Social Construction of a Machine: Ritual, Superstition, Magical Thinking and Other Pragmatic Responses to Running a CT Scanner. In M. Lock and D. Gordon, eds., *Knowledge and Practice in Medicine: Social, Cultural and Historical Approaches.* Hingham, Mass.: Reidel Publishing.

BARNARD, C. I. 1938. *Functions of the Executive.* Cambridge, Mass.: Harvard University Press.

BARTUNEK, J. M., AND C. B. KEYS. 1979. Participation in School Decision Making. *Urban Education,* 14:52–75.

BEAM, D. R. 1978. Public Administration is Alive and Well and Living in the White House. *Public Administration Review,* 38:72–77.

BECKER, B. 1978. Ambiguity and Choice in Organizations (review). Die Verwaltung. *Zeitschrift für Verwaltungswissenschaft,* II:255–256.

BECKER, G. S., AND G. J. STIGLER. 1977. De Gustibus Non Est Disputandum. *American Economic Review,* 67:76–90.

BEM, D. J. 1970. *Beliefs, Attitudes and Human Affairs.* Belmont, Calif.: Brooks/ Cole.

BENDA, P. M., AND C. H. LEVINE. 1986. OMB and the Central Management Problem: Is Another Reorganization the Answer? *Public Administration Review,* 46:379–391.

BENDA, P. M., AND C. H. LEVINE. 1988. Reagan and the Bureaucracy: The Bequest, the Promise, and the Legacy. In C. O. Jones, ed., *The Reagan Legacy: Promise and Performance.* Chatham, N.J.: Chatham House.

BENSON, J. K. 1975. The Interorganizational Network as Political Economy. *Administrative Science Quarterly,* 20:229–249.

BENVENISTE, G. 1972. *The Politics of Expertise.* Berkeley and London: The Glendessary Press and Croom Helm.

BERG, C. C. 1986. Aspiration Level Adaptation of Members within Project Groups. In E. Witte and H.-J. Zimmermann, eds., *Empirical Research on Organizational Decision Making.* Amsterdam: Elsevier.

BERG, C. L. 1975. Lapse of Reorganization Authority. *Public Administration Review,* 35:195–199.

BERGER, R. A. 1987. Private-Sector Initiatives in the Reagan Era: New Actors Rework an Old Theme. In L. M. Salamon and M. S. Lund, eds., *The Reagan Presidency and the Governing of America.* Washington, D.C.: The Urban Institute Press.

BERGER, S., ed. 1981. *Organizing Interests in Europe: Pluralism, Corporatism,*

177

and the Transformation of Politics. Cambridge: Cambridge University Press.

BERGEVÄRN, L.-E., AND O. OLSON. 1987. *Kommunal redovisning då och nu - Om längtan efter likformighet, rättvisa och affärsmässighet.* Lund: Doxa.

BERKI, R. N. 1979. State and Society: An Antithesis of Modern Political Thought. In J. E. S. Hayward and R. N. Berki, eds., *State and Society in Contemporary Europe.* Oxford: Martin Robertson.

BEYME, K. VON. 1985. The Role of the State and the Growth of Government. *International Political Science Review,* 6:11–34.

BIRNBAUM, P., J. LIVELY, AND G. PARRY. 1978. *Democracy, Consensus and Social Contract.* London: Sage.

BLACK, D. 1958. *The Theory of Committees and Elections.* Cambridge: Cambridge University Press.

BLEIKLIE, I. 1983. The Selective Providers: Organization and Distribution Effects of Public Service Provision. *Tidsskrift för Rättssociologi,* 1:55–80.

BLICHNER, L. C., AND J. P. OLSEN. 1986. *Spørsmål i Stortinget. Sikkerhetsventil i petroleumspolitikken.* Bergen: Universitetsforlaget.

BORKENAU, F. 1937. State and Revolution in the Paris Commune, the Russian Revolution and the Spanish Civil War. *Sociological Review,* 29:41–75.

BOZEMAN, B. 1987. *All Organizations Are Public.* San Francisco: Jossey-Bass.

BRADEMAS, J. 1978. Federal Reorganization and Its Likely Impact on State and Local Government. *Publius,* 8:25–37.

BRADY, D. W. 1988. *Critical Elections and Congressional Policy Making.* Stanford: Stanford University Press.

BREHMER, B. 1980. In One Word: Not From Experience. *Acta Psychologica,* 45:223–241.

BRENNAN, G., AND J. M. BUCHANAN. 1985. *The Reason of Rules.* Cambridge: Cambridge University Press.

BREWER, G. D. 1973. *Politicians, Bureaucrats and the Consultant: A Critique of Urban Problem Solving.* New York: Basic Books.

BRIGGS, A. 1961. The Welfare State in Historical Perspective. *Archives Européennes de Sociologie,* 2:221–258.

BROWN, D. S. 1977. Reforming the Bureaucracy: Some Suggestions for the New President. *Public Administration Review,* 37:163–170.

BROWN, R. G. 1979. *Reorganizing the National Health Service: A Case Study in Administrative Change.* Oxford: Basil Blackwell/Martin Robertson.

BROWN, R. H. 1978. Bureaucracy as Praxis: Toward a Political Phenomenology of Formal Organizations. *Administrative Science Quarterly,* 23:365–382.

BROWNING, R. P. 1968. Innovation and Non-Innovation Decision Processes in Government Budgeting. In R. T. Golembiewski, ed., *Public Budgeting and Finance.* Itasca, Ill.: Peacock.

References

BROWNLOW COMMITTEE. *See* President's Committee on Administrative Management.

BRUNSSON, N. 1982. The Irrationality of Action and Action Rationality: Decisions, Ideologies, and Organizational Actions. *Journal of Management Studies,* 19:29–44.

BRUNSSON, N. 1985. *The Irrational Organization: Irrationality as a Basis for Organizational Action and Change.* Chichester: Wiley.

BRUNSSON, N. 1989. *The Organization of Hypocrisy.* Chichester: Wiley.

BUCK, A. E. 1938. *The Reorganization of State Governments in the United States.* New York: Columbia University Press.

BURCHELL, S., C. COLIN, AND A. G. HOPWOOD. 1985. Accounting in Its Social Context: Towards a History of Value Added in the United Kingdom. *Accounting, Organizations, and Society,* 10:381–413.

BURGELMAN, R. A. 1988. Strategy-Making as a Social Learning Process: The Case of Internal Corporate Venturing. *Interfaces,* 18:74–85.

BURNS, J. M. 1978. *Leadership.* New York: Harper and Row.

BURNS, T., AND G. M. STALKER. 1961. *The Management of Innovation.* London: Tavistock.

BURNS, T. R., AND H. FLAM. 1987. *The Shaping of Social Organization.* London: Sage.

BUTLER, S. 1927. *Erewhon and Erewhon Revisited.* New York: Random House.

CAIDEN, G. 1984. Reform and Revitalization in American Bureaucracy. In R. Miewald and M. Steineman, eds., *Problems in Administrative Reform.* Chicago: Nelson-Hall.

CALIFANO, J. A., JR. 1981. *Governing America: An Insider's Report from the White House and the Cabinet.* New York: Simon and Schuster.

CANOVAN, M. 1985. Politics as Culture: Hannah Arendt and the Public Realm. *History of Political Thought,* 6:617–642.

CARLEY, K. 1986. Measuring Efficiency in a Garbage Can Hierarchy. In J. G. March and R. Weissinger-Baylon, eds., *Ambiguity and Command: Organizational Perspectives on Military Decision Making.* Marshfield, Mass.: Pitman.

CARROLL, G. R. 1984. Organizational Ecology. *Annual Review of Sociology,* 10:71–93.

CARROLL, J. D., A. L. FRITSCHLER, AND B. L. R. SMITH. 1985. Supply-Side Management in the Reagan Administration. *Public Administration Review,* 45:805–814.

CHAPMAN, R. A., AND J. R. GREENWAY. 1980. *The Dynamics of Administrative Reform.* London: Croom Helm.

CHILD, J., AND A. KIESER. 1981. Development of Organizations Over Time. In P. C. Nystrom and W. H. Starbuck, eds., *Handbook of Organizational Design.* Oxford: Oxford University Press.

CHRISTENSEN, J. G. 1980. *Centraladministrationen, organisation og politisk placering*. Copenhagen: Samfunnsvitenskabelig Forlag.

CHRISTENSEN, J. G. 1987. Deregulation, Recent Danish Experience. Aarhus, Denmark: Unpublished manuscript.

CHRISTENSEN, S. 1976. Decision Making and Socialization. In J. G. March and J. P. Olsen, eds., *Ambiguity and Choice in Organizations*. Bergen: Universitetsforlaget.

CHRISTENSEN, T. 1985. Styrt endring og planlagte konsekvenser: en organisasjonsanalyse av omorganiseringen i den sentrale helseforvaltning, 1982–83. Troms: Unpublished manuscript.

COCH, L., AND J. R. P. FRENCH, JR. 1948. Overcoming Resistance to Change. *Human Relations,* 1:512–532.

COHEN, A. P. 1974. *Two-dimensional Man: An Essay on the Anthropology of Power and Symbolism in Complex Societies*. London: Routledge and Kegan Paul.

COHEN, M. 1977. Religious Revivalism and the Administrative Centralization Movement. *Administration and Society,* 9:219–232.

COHEN, M. D., AND R. AXELROD. 1984. Coping With Complexity: The Adaptive Value of Changing Utility. *American Economic Review,* 74:30–42.

COHEN, M. D., AND J. G. MARCH. 1986. *Leadership and Ambiguity,* 2nd ed. Boston: Harvard Business School Press.

COHEN, M. D., J. G. MARCH, AND J. P. OLSEN. 1972. A Garbage Can Model of Organizational Choice. *Administrative Science Quarterly,* 17:1–25.

COKER, F. W. 1922. Dogmas of Administrative Reform as Exemplified in the Recent Reorganization in Ohio. *American Political Science Review,* 16:399–411.

COLEMAN, J. S. 1986. *Individual Interests and Collective Action*. Cambridge: Cambridge University Press.

COOPER, D. J., D. HAYES, AND F. WOLF. 1981. Accounting in Organized Anarchies: Understanding and Designing Accounting Systems in Ambiguous Situations. *Accounting, Organizations, and Society,* 6:175–191.

CORONEL, G. 1983. *The Nationalization of the Venezuelan Oil Industry*. Lexington, Mass.: Lexington Books.

COUNCIL OF STATE GOVERNMENTS. 1950. *Reorganizing State Government*. Chicago: Council of State Governments.

COY, W. 1946. Basic Problems in Federal Executive Reorganization Re-examined: A Symposium. *American Political Science Review,* 40:1124–1137.

CRESPIGNY, A. DE, AND A. WERTHEIMER, eds. 1970. *Contemporary Political Theory*. London: Nelson.

CRICK, B. 1982. *In Defence of Politics*. Harmondsworth, Middlesex: Penguin.

CROZIER, M. 1964. *The Bureaucratic Phenomenon*. Chicago: University of Chicago Press.

References

CROZIER, M., S. P. HUNTINGTON, AND J. WATANUKI. 1975. *The Crises of Democracy: Report on the Governability of Democracies to the Trilateral Commission.* New York: New York University Press.

CYERT, R. M., W. DILL, AND J. G. MARCH. 1958. The Role of Expectations in Business Decision Making. *Administrative Science Quarterly,* 3:307–340.

CYERT, R. M., AND J. G. MARCH. 1963. *A Behavioral Theory of the Firm.* Englewood Cliffs, N.J.: Prentice-Hall.

CZARNIAWSKA, B. 1985. The Ugly Sister: On Relationships Between the Private and the Public Sectors in Sweden. *Scandinavian Journal of Management Studies,* 2:2, 83–103.

DAFT, R. L., AND S. W. BECKER. 1978. *The Innovative Organization.* New York: Elsevier.

DAFT, R. L., AND K. E. WEICK. 1984. Toward a Model of Organizations as Interpretation Systems. *Academy of Management Review,* 9:284–295.

DAHL, R. A. 1950. *Congress and Foreign Policy.* New York: Harcourt, Brace.

DAHL, R. A. 1956. *A Preface to Democratic Theory.* Chicago: University of Chicago Press.

DAHL, R. A. 1957. The Concept of Power. *Behavioral Science,* 2:201–215.

DAHL, R. A. 1971. *Polyarchy: Participation and Opposition.* New Haven: Yale University Press.

DAHL, R. A. 1977. On Removing Certain Impediments to Democracy in the United States. *Political Science Quarterly,* 92:1–20.

DAHL, R. A. 1978. Pluralism Revisited. *Comparative Politics,* 10:191–203.

DAHL, R. A. 1979. Procedural Democracy. In P. Laslett and J. Fishkin, eds., *Philosophy, Politics, and Society,* 5th series. Oxford: Basil Blackwell.

DAHL, R. A. 1980a. Introduction. In J. Jersey, *Aspects of the Presidency.* New York: Ticknor and Fields.

DAHL, R. A. 1980b. The Moscow Discourse: Fundamental Rights in a Democratic Order. *Government and Opposition,* 15:3–30.

DAHL, R. A. 1982. *Dilemmas of Pluralist Democracy: Autonomy vs. Control.* New Haven: Yale University Press.

DAHL, R. A. 1983. Federalism and the Democratic Process. *Nomos,* 25:95–108.

DAHL, R. A. 1984a. Polyarchy, Pluralism, and Scale. *Scandinavian Political Studies,* 7:225–241.

DAHL, R. A. 1984b. *Modern Political Analysis,* 4th ed. Englewood Cliffs, N.J.: Prentice-Hall.

DAHL, R. A. 1986. *Democracy, Liberty, and Equality.* Oslo: Norwegian University Press.

DAHL, R. A., AND C. E. LINDBLOM. 1953. *Politics, Economics, and Welfare.* New York: Harper and Row.

DAHL, R. A., AND E. R. TUFTE. 1973. *Size and Democracy*. Stanford: Stanford University Press.

DAHRENDORF, R. 1959. *Class and Class Conflict in Industrial Society*. Stanford: Stanford University Press.

DAHRENDORF, R. 1968. Homo Sociologicus. In R. Dahrendorf, *Essays in the Theory of Society*. Stanford: Stanford University Press.

DALBERG-LARSEN, J. 1984. *Retsstaten, velfærdsstaten og hvad så?* Copenhagen: Akademisk Forlag.

DALLMAYR, F. R., ed. 1978. *From Contract to Community*. New York/Basel: Marcel Dekker.

DAN-COHEN, M. 1986. *Rights, Persons, and Organizations: A Legal Theory for Bureaucratic Society*. Berkeley: University of California Press.

DAY, R. H., AND T. GROVES, eds. 1975. *Adaptive Economic Models*, New York: Academic Press.

DEMPSEY, J. R. 1979. Carter Reorganization: A Midterm Appraisal. *Public Administration Review*, 39:74–78.

DEMSKI, J. 1980. *Information Analysis*. Reading, Mass.: Addison-Wesley.

DEN MODERNE STATEN. 1987. *Innstilling fra et utvalg nedsatt av Høyres stortings-gruppe* [Norway]. Oslo: Høyre.

DEN NYE STATEN. 1987. *Program for fornyelse av statsforvaltningen* [Norway]. Oslo: Forbruker- og administrasjonsdepartementet.

DESTLER, A. M. 1981. Implementing Reorganization. In P. Szanton, ed. *Federal Reorganization: What Have We Learned?* Chatham, N.J.: Chatham House.

DEUTSCH, K. W. 1981. The Crisis of the State. *Government and Opposition*, 16:331–343.

DEUTSCH, M., AND H. GERARD. 1955. A Study of Normative and Informational Social Influences Upon Individual Judgment. *Journal of Abnormal and Social Psychology*, 51:629–636.

DIMAGGIO, P. 1985. Interest and Agency in Institutional Theory. New Haven, Yale University, Department of Sociology: Unpublished manuscript.

DIMAGGIO, P., AND W. W. POWELL. 1983. The Iron Cage Revisited: Institutional Isomorphism and Collective Rationality in Organizational Fields. *American Sociological Review*, 48:147–160.

DIMOCK, M. E. 1951. The Objectives of Governmental Reorganization. *Public Administration Review*, 11:233–241.

DOWNS, A. 1957. *An Economic Theory of Democracy*. New York: Harper and Row.

DOWNS, A. 1967. *Inside Bureaucracy*. Boston: Little, Brown.

DOWNS, G. W., AND P. D. LARKEY. 1986. *The Search for Government Efficiency: From Hubris to Helplessness*. Philadelphia: Temple University Press.

DURHAM, G. H. 1949. An Appraisal of the Hoover Commission Approach to

182

References

Administrative Reorganization in the National Government. *Western Political Science Quarterly,* 2:615–623.

DURKHEIM, E. [1893] 1933. *The Division of Labor in Society.* Translated by George Simpson. New York: Macmillan.

DYSON, K. 1980. *The State Tradition in Western Europe.* Oxford: Martin Robertson.

EASTON, D. 1968. Political Science. In D. L. Sills, ed., *International Encyclopedia of the Social Sciences,* Vol. 12. New York and London: Macmillan and Free Press.

ECKHOFF, T. 1976. The Relationship Between Judicial and Political Branches of Government. *Jahrbuch für Rechtssoziologie und Rechts Theorie,* 4:14–23.

ECKHOFF, T., AND K. D. JACOBSEN. 1960. *Rationality and Responsibility in Administrative and Judicial Decision-Making.* Copenhagen: Munksgaard.

ECKSTEIN, H. 1982. The Idea of Political Development: From Dignity to Efficiency. *World Politics,* 34:451–486.

EDELMAN, M. 1964. *The Symbolic Uses of Politics.* Urbana: University of Illinois Press.

EDLEFSON, C. J. 1978. Participatory Planning for Organizational Change: The Case of Project Redesign. Stanford University, School of Education: Ph.D. dissertation.

EGEBERG, M. 1981. *Stat og organisasjoner.* Bergen: Universitetsforlaget.

EGEBERG, M. 1984. *Organisasjonsutforming.* Oslo: Aschehoug/Tanum, Nordli.

EGEBERG, M. 1987. Designing Public Organizations. In J. Kooiman and K. A. Eliassen, eds., *Managing Public Organizations: Lessons From Contemporary European Experience.* London: Sage.

EGEBERG, M., AND I. STIGEN. 1985. The Management of Competing Norms and Decision Principles: The Organizational Context of Norwegian Directorates. Oslo: University of Oslo, Department of Political Science: Unpublished manuscript.

EINHORN, H. J., AND R. M. HOGARTH. 1981. Behavioral Decision Theory: Processes of Judgement and Choice. *Annual Review of Psychology,* 32:53–88.

EISENSTADT, S. N. 1958. Bureaucracy and Bureaucratization. *Current Sociology,* 7:99–164.

EISENSTADT, S. N. 1964. Institutionalization and Change. *American Sociological Review,* 29:235–247.

EISENSTADT, S. N. 1965. *Essays on Comparative Institutions.* New York: Wiley.

ELSTER, J. 1979. *Ulysses and the Sirens: Studies in Rationality and Irrationality.* Cambridge: Cambridge University Press.

ELSTER, J. 1983a. Offentlighet og deltakelse. In T. Bergh, ed., *Deltakerdemokratiet*. Oslo: Universitetsforlaget.

ELSTER, J. 1983b. *Sour Grapes: Studies in the Subversion of Rationality*. Cambridge: Cambridge University Press.

EMMERICH, H. 1971. *Federal Organization and Administrative Management*. University: University of Alabama Press.

ENDERUD, H. 1976. The Perception of Power. In J. G. March and J. P. Olsen, eds., *Ambiguity and Choice in Organizations*. Bergen: Universitetsforlaget.

ENGWALL, L. 1976. Response Time of Organizations. *Journal of Management Studies*, 13:1–15.

ERIKSEN, E. O. 1987. Symbols, Stratagems, and Legitimacy in Political Analysis. *Scandinavian Political Studies*, 10:259–278.

ETHEREDGE, L. S. 1976. *The Case of the Unreturned Cafeteria Trays*. Washington, D.C.: American Political Science Association.

EVAN, W. M. 1966. The Organization Set: Toward a Theory of Interorganizational Relations. In J. D. Thompson, ed., *Approaches to Organizational Design*. Pittsburgh: University of Pittsburgh Press.

EVANS, P., D. RUESCHEMEYER, AND T. SKOCPOL, eds. 1985. *Bringing the State Back In*. Cambridge: Cambridge University Press.

EXECUTIVE OFFICE OF THE PRESIDENT (NIXON). Office of the Management and Budget. Revised February 1972. *Papers Relating to the President's Departmental Reorganization Program: A Reference Compilation*. Washington, D.C.: U.S. Government Printing Office.

FAIN, T. G., ed. 1977. *Federal Reorganization: The Executive Branch*. New York: Bowker.

FAMA, E. F. 1980. Agency Problems and the Theory of the Firm. *Journal of Political Economy*, 88:288–307.

FELDMAN, M. S. 1989. *Information Production and Policy Making*. Stanford: Stanford University Press.

FELDMAN, M. S., AND J. G. MARCH. 1981. Information as Signal and Symbol. *Administrative Science Quarterly*, 26:171 186.

FEREJOHN, J. 1987. Notes on the New Institutionalism. Stanford University, Department of Political Science: Unpublished manuscript.

FESLER, J. R. 1975. Public Administration and the Social Sciences: 1946 to 1960. In F. C. Mosher, ed. *American Public Administration: Past, Present, Future*. University: University of Alabama Press.

FESLER, J. W. 1957. Administrative Literature and the Second Hoover Commission Reports. *American Political Science Review*, 51:135–157.

FESTINGER, L., H. W. RIECKEN, AND S. SCHACHTER. 1956. *When Prophecy Fails*. Minneapolis: University of Minnesota Press.

FINER, H. 1941. Administrative Responsibility in Democratic Government. *Public Administration Review*, 1:335–350.

References

FINER, H. 1949. The Hoover Commission Reports. *Political Science Quarterly,* 64, Part I: 405–419.

FINANSMINISTERIET (Denmark). 1983. *Redegørelse til Folketinget om regeringens program for modernisering af den offentlige sektor.* Copenhagen: Danish Government.

FINANSMINISTERIET (Denmark). 1987. *Redegørelse til Folketinget om moderniseringsarbejdet i den offentlige sektor.* Copenhagen: Danish Government.

FIRST HOOVER COMMISSION. *See* U.S. Commission on the Organization of the Executive Branch of the Government.

FISCHHOFF, B., AND R. BEYTH. 1975. "I Knew It Would Happen"—Remembered Probabilities of Once-Future Things. *Organizational Behavior and Human Performance,* 13:1–16.

FISCHHOFF, B., P. SLOVIC, AND S. LICHTENSTEIN. 1980. Knowing What You Want: Measuring Labile Values. In T. S. Wallsten, ed., *Cognitive Processes in Choice and Decision Behavior.* Hillsdale, N.J.: Erlbaum.

FISCHHOFF, F. 1975. Hindsight / Foresight: The Effect of Outcome Knowledge on Judgment Uncertainty. In J. H. Harvey, W. J. Ickes, and R. F. Kidd, eds., *New Directions in Attribution Research.* Hillsdale, N.J.: Erlbaum.

FOLLETT, M. P. 1918. *The New State.* Gloucester, Mass.: Peter Smith.

FOX, D. M., ed. 1974. President Nixon's Proposals for Executive Reorganization. *Public Administration Review,* 34:487–495.

FREY, B. S. 1983. *Democratic Economic Policy: A Theoretical Introduction.* Oxford: Martin Robertson.

FRIED, C. 1978. *Right and Wrong.* Cambridge, Mass.: Harvard University Press.

FRIEDMAN, M. 1953. *Essays in Positive Economics.* Chicago: University of Chicago Press.

FRIEDRICH, C. J. 1937. *Constitutional Government and Politics.* New York: Harper and Row.

FRIEDRICH, C. J. 1940. Public Policy and the Nature of Administrative Responsibility. In C. J. Friedrich and E. S. Mason, eds., *Public Policy.* Cambridge, Mass.: Harvard University Press.

FRY, G. K. 1988. The Thatcher Government: The Financial Management Initiative and the "New Civil Service." *Public Administration,* 66:1–20.

FURUBOTN, E. G., AND R. RICHTER, eds. 1984. The New Institutional Economics: A Symposium. *Journal of Institutional and Theoretical Economics,* 150:1–232.

GALBRAITH, J. K. 1967. *The New Industrial State.* London: Hamish Hamilton.

GAMSON, W. A. 1968. *Power and Discontent.* Homewood, Ill.: Dorsey.

GARNETT, J. L. 1980. *Reorganizing State Government: The Executive Branch.* Boulder, Colo.: Westview Press.

GARNETT, J. L., AND C. H. LEVINE. 1980. State Executive Branch Reorganization: Patterns and Perspectives. *Administration and Society,* 12:227–276.

185

GECAS, V. 1982. The Self-Concept. *Annual Review of Sociology,* 8:1–33.

GEERTZ, C. 1980. *Negara: The Theater State in Nineteenth-Century Bali.* Princeton: Princeton University Press.

GEORGE, A. L. 1980. *Presidential Decisionmaking in Foreign Policy: The Effective Use of Information and Advice.* Boulder, Colo.: Westview Press.

GIBBONS, M., AND B. WITTROCK, eds. 1984. *Science as a Commodity: Threats to the Open Community of Scholars.* London: Longman.

GIPLIN, R., AND C. WRIGHT, eds. 1964. *Scientists and National Policy Making.* New York: Columbia University Press.

GJERDE, I. 1983. Planleggingssekretariatet-En studie av etablering og virkemåte. Bergen: Institutt for offentlig administrasjon og organisasjonskunnskap: Hovedfags Dissertation.

GLASSMAN, R. B. 1973. Persistence and Loose Coupling in Living Systems. *Behavioral Science,* 18:83–98.

GOLDBERG, E. N. 1987. The Permanent Government in an Era of Retrenchment and Redirection. In L. M. Salamon and M. S. Lund, eds., *The Reagan Presidency and the Governing of America.* Washington, D.C.: The Urban Institute Press.

GOODIN, R. E. 1982. Freedom and the Welfare State: Theoretical Foundations. *Journal of Social Policy,* 2:149–176.

GOODIN, R. E. 1986. Laundering Preferences. In J. Elster and A. Hylland, eds., *Foundations of Social Choice Theory.* Oslo: Universitetsforlaget.

GOODMAN, P. S., AND L. B. KURKE. 1982. Studies of Change in Organizations: A Status Report. In Paul Goodman, ed., *Change in Organizations.* San Francisco: Jossey-Bass.

GOODSELL, C. 1984. The Grace Commission: Seeking Efficiency for the Whole People? *Public Administration Review,* 44:196–204.

GORVINE, A. 1966. *Administrative Reform: Function of Political and Economic Change.* In G. S. Birkhead, ed., Administrative Problems in Pakistan. Syracuse, N.Y.: Syracuse University Press.

GRACE, J. P. 1984. *Burning Money: The Waste of Your Tax Dollars.* New York: Macmillan.

GRAFTON, C. 1979. The Reorganization of Federal Agencies. *Administration and Society,* 10:437–464.

GRAHAM, G. A. 1938. Reorganization—A Question of Executive Institutions. *American Political Science Review,* 32:708–718.

GRAVES, W. B. 1949. *Reorganization of the Executive Branch of the Government of the United States: A Compilation of Basic Information and Significant Documents, 1912–1948.* Public Affairs Bulletin No. 66. Washington, D.C.: Library of Congress Legislative Reference Service.

GRAY, A., AND W. I. JENKINS. 1985. *Administrative Politics in British Government.* London: Harvester.

186

References

GRØNLIE, T. 1977. Norsk industripolitikk. In T. Bergh and H. Ø. Pharo, eds., *Vekst og Velstand*. Oslo: Universitetsforlaget.

GRØNLIE, T. 1989. *Statsdrift*. Oslo: Tano.

GROVES, R. T. 1967. Administrative Reform and the Politics of Reform: The Case of Venezuela. *Public Administration Review*, 27:436–445.

GULICK, L. 1937. Values and Public Administration. In L. Gulick and L. Urwick, eds., *Papers on the Science of Administration*. New York: Institute of Public Administration.

HABERMAS, J. 1975. *Legitimation Crisis*. Boston: Beacon.

HAGUE, D. C., W. J. M. MACKENZIE, AND A. BARKER. 1975. *Public Policy and Private Interests, the Institutions of Compromise*. London: Macmillan.

HAIDER, D. 1979. Presidential Management Initiatives: A Ford Legacy to Executive Management Improvement. *Public Administration Review*, 39:248–259.

HALL, R. H. 1968. Professionalization and Bureaucratization. *American Sociological Review*, 33:92–104.

HALL, R. I. 1976. A System Pathology of an Organization: the Rise and Fall of the Old Saturday Evening Post. *Administrative Science Quarterly*, 21:185–211.

HAMILTON, A., J. JAY, AND J. MADISON. [1787] 1964. *The Federalist Papers*. New York: Pocket Books.

HANF, K., AND F. SCHARPF, eds. 1978. *Interorganizational Policy Making: Limits to Coordination and Central Control*. London: Sage.

HANNAN, M. T., AND J. FREEMAN. 1977. The Population Ecology of Organizations. *American Journal of Sociology*, 82:929–964.

HANNAN, M. T., AND J. FREEMAN. 1984. Structural Inertia and Organizational Change. *American Sociological Review*, 49:149–164.

HANSEN, M. G. 1985. Management Improvement Initiatives in the Reagan Administration: Round Two. *Public Administration Review*, 45:441–446.

HANSOT, E. 1974. *Perfection and Progress: Two Modes of Utopian Thought*. Cambridge, Mass.: MIT Press.

HARBO, H. 1985. Organisasjon og symbol. En analyse av beslutningsprosessen i forbindelse med emblemendringer i Televerket. Oslo: University of Oslo, Department of Political Science: Hovedfags Dissertation.

HARDING, W. G. 1921. Business in Government and the Problem of Governmental Reorganization for Greater Efficiency. *Academy of Political Science Proceedings*, 9:430–431.

HARRIS, J. P. 1937. The Progress of Administrative Reorganization in the Seventy-fifth Congress. *American Political Science Review*, 31:862–870.

HARRIS, J. P. 1946. Wartime Currents and Peacetime Trends. *American Political Science Review*, 40:1137–1154.

HARRISON, A., AND J. GRATTON, eds. 1987. *Reshaping Central Government*. New Brunswick, N.J., and Oxford: Transaction Books.

HARRISON, J. R., AND J. G. MARCH. 1984. Decision Making and Post-Decision Surprises. *Administrative Science Quarterly,* 29:26–42.

HARSANYI, J. 1977. *Rational Behaviour and Bargaining Equilibrium in Games and Social Situations.* Cambridge: Cambridge University Press.

HART, J. 1948. *The American Presidency in Action.* New York: Macmillan.

HAUSCHILDT, J. 1986. Goals and Problem-Solving in Innovative Decisions. In E. Witte and H.-J. Zimmermann, eds., *Empirical Research on Organizational Decision Making.* Amsterdam: Elsevier.

HAWKINS, R. B., JR. 1978. Government Reorganization: A Federal Interest. *Publius,* 8:3–12.

HAYES, D. A., AND J. G. MARCH. 1970. The Normative Problem of University Governance. Assembly on University Goals and Governance, University of Pennsylvania: Unpublished essay.

HAYWARD, J. E. S., AND R. N. BERKI, eds. 1979. *State and Society in Contemporary Europe.* Oxford: Martin Robertson.

HEADY, F. 1947. A New Approach to Federal Executive Reorganization. *American Political Science Review,* 41:1118–1126.

HEADY, F. 1949a. The Reports of the Hoover Commission. *Review of Politics,* 11:355–378.

HEADY, F. 1949b. The Reorganization Act of 1949. *Public Administration Review,* 9:165–174.

HEADY, F. 1949c. The Operation of a Mixed Commission. *American Political Science Review,* 43:940–952.

HECLO, H. 1974. *Modern Social Policies in Britain and Sweden.* New Haven: Yale University Press.

HECLO, H. 1978. Issue Networks and the Executive Establishment. In A. King, ed., *The New American Political System.* Washington, D.C.: American Enterprise Institute.

HEDBERG, B. L. T., P. C. NYSTROM, AND W. H. STARBUCK. 1976. Camping on Seesaws: Prescriptions for a Self-Designing Organization. *Administrative Science Quarterly,* 21:41–65.

HEDBORG, A., AND R. MEIDNER. 1984. *Folkhemms modellen.* Borås: Rabén og Sjögren.

HEIDER, F. 1958. *The Psychology of Interpersonal Relations.* New York: Wiley.

HEINEMAN, B. W., JR., AND C. A. HESSLER, 1980. *Memorandum for the President.* New York: Random House.

HEISLER, M. O., AND R. B. KVAVIK. 1974. Patterns in European Politics: The "European Polity" Model. In M. O. Heisler, ed., *Politics in Europe.* New York: David McKay.

HELD, D. 1987. *Models of Democracy.* Cambridge: Polity Press.

HELLER, H. [1933] 1957. Political Science. In E. R. A. Seligman and A. Johnson, eds., *Encyclopedia of the Social Sciences.* New York: Macmillan.

References

HERNES, G. 1978. *Forhandlingsøkonomi og blandingsadministrasjon*. Bergen: Universitetsforlaget.

HERRING, E. P. 1934. Social Forces and the Reorganization of the Federal Bureaucracy. *Southwestern Social Science Quarterly*, 15:185–200.

HERRIOTT, S. R., D. LEVINTHAL, AND J. G. MARCH. 1985. Learning From Experience in Organizations. *American Economic Review*, 75:298–302.

HESS, S. 1976. *Organizing the Presidency*. Washington, D.C.: Brookings.

HIRSCHLEIFER, J., AND J. G. RILEY. 1979. The Analytics of Uncertainty and Information—An Expository Survey. *Journal of Economic Literature*, 17:1375–1421.

HIRSCHMAN, A. O. 1970. *Exit, Voice and Loyalty*. Cambridge, Mass.: Harvard University Press.

HOBBS, E. H. 1953. *Executive Reorganization in the National Government*. Oxford, Miss.: University of Mississippi Press.

HØGETVEIT, A. 1985. Organisasjon og symbol. En analyse an beslutningsprosessen i forbindelse med emblemendringen i Norges Statsbaner. Oslo: University of Oslo, Department of Political Science: Hovedfags Dissertation.

HOLCOMBE, A. N. 1921. Administrative Reorganization in the Federal Government. *Annals of the American Academy of Political and Social Science*, 95:242–251.

HOLMBERG, D. 1989. *Order in Paradox: Exchange, Ritual and Myth among Nepal's Tamang*. Ithaca, N.Y.: Cornell University Press.

HOOD, C. 1986. The Hidden Public Sector: The Quangocratization of the World. In F. X. Kaufman, V. Ostrom, and G. Majone, eds., *Guidance, Control and Performance Evaluation in the Public Sector*. Berlin: de Gruyter.

HOOD, C., AND G. F. SCHUPPERT, eds. 1988. *Delivering Public Services in Western Europe*. London: Sage.

HURT, P. 1932. Who Should Reorganize the National Administration? *American Political Science Review*, 26:1082–1098.

HYMAN, H. H., ed. 1973. *The Politics of Health Care: Nine Case Studies of Innovative Planning in New York City*. New York: Praeger.

HYNEMAN, C. S. 1939. Administrative Reorganization. *Journal of Politics*, 1:62–75.

HYNEMAN, C. S. 1950. *Bureaucracy in a Democracy*. New York: Harper and Row.

JACOBSEN, K. D. 1960. Lojalitet, nøytralitet og faglig uavhengighet. *Tidsskrift for Samfunnsforskning*, 1:231–248.

JACOBSEN, K. D. 1964. *Teknisk hjelp og politisk struktur*. Oslo: Universitetsforlaget.

JACOBSEN, K. D. 1966. Public Administration Under Pressure: The Role of the Expert in the Modernization of Traditional Agriculture. *Scandinavian Political Studies*, 1:159–193.

189

JACOBSSON, B. 1984. *Hur styrs förvalningen—myt och verklighet kring departementenes styrning av ämbetsverken.* Stockholm: EFI—Studentlitteratur.

JANIS, I. L., AND L. MANN. 1977. *Decision Making: A Psychological Analysis of Conflict, Choice and Commitment.* New York: Free Press.

JENKINS, B. 1986. Reexamining the "Obsolescing Bargain": A Study of Canada's Decision Making. *International Organization,* 40:139–165.

JESSOP, B. 1977. Recent Theories of the Capitalist State. *Cambridge Journal of Economics,* 1:353–373.

JOHNSON, N. 1976. Recent Administrative Reform in Britain. In A. F. Leemans, ed., *The Management of Change in Government.* The Hague: Martinus Nijhoff.

JOINT COMMITTEE, U.S. CONGRESS. 1924. House. Joint Committee on Reorganization of the Administrative Branch of the Government. *Report of the Joint Committee on Reorganization.* 68th Congress, 1st Session: Doc. No. 356. Washington, D.C.: U.S. Government Printing Office.

JONES, C. O., ed. 1988. *The Reagan Legacy: Promise and Performance.* Chatham, N.J.: Chatham House.

JORDAN, A. G. 1981. Iron Triangles, Wolly Corporatism and Elastic Nets: Images of the Policy Process. *Journal of Public Policy,* 1:95–123.

JOUVENAL, B. DE. 1949. *On Power.* New York: Viking Press.

KAHNEMAN, D. 1982. Bureaucracies, Minds and the Human Engineering of Decisions. In G. R. Ungson and D. N. Braunstein, eds., *Decision Making: An Interdisciplinary Inquiry.* Boston: Kent.

KAHNEMAN, D., P. SLOVIC, AND A. TVERSKY, eds. 1982. *Judgment Under Uncertainty: Heuristics and Biases.* Cambridge: Cambridge University Press.

KALBERG, S. 1980. Max Weber's Types of Rationality: Cornerstones for the Analysis of Rationalization Processes in History. *American Journal of Sociology,* 85:1145–1178.

KAMIEN, M. I., AND N. SCHWARTZ. 1975. Market Structure and Innovation: A Survey. *Journal of Economic Literature,* 13:1–37.

KARL, B. D. 1963. *Executive Reorganization and Reform in the New Deal: The Genesis of Administrative Management, 1900–1939.* Cambridge, Mass.: Harvard University Press.

KARL, T. 1986. Oil Booms and Petro States. Stanford: Stanford University, Department of Political Science: Unpublished manuscript.

KATZ, D. B. 1975. *Bureaucratic Encounters: A Pilot Study in the Evaluation of Government Services.* Ann Arbor: University of Michigan Institute for Social Research.

KATZENSTEIN, P. J., ed. 1978. *Between Power and Plenty: Foreign Economic Policies of Advanced Industrial States.* Madison: University of Wisconsin Press.

KATZENSTEIN, P. J. 1985. *Small States in World Markets.* Ithaca, N.Y.: Cornell University Press.

190

References

KAUFMAN, H. 1956. Emerging Conflicts in the Doctrine of American Public Administration. *American Political Science Review,* 50:1057–1073.

KAUFMAN, H. 1963. *Politics and Policies in State and Local Governments.* Englewood Cliffs, N.J.: Prentice-Hall.

KAUFMAN, H. 1971. *The Limits of Organizational Change.* University: University of Alabama Press.

KAUFMAN, H. 1976. *Are Government Organizations Immortal?* Washington, D.C.: Brookings.

KAUFMAN, H. 1977. Reflections on Administrative Reorganization. In J. A. Pechman, ed., *Setting National Priorities: The 1978 Budget.* Washington, D.C.: Brookings.

KAY, J. A., AND D. J. THOMPSON. 1986. Privatisation: A Policy in Search of a Rationale. *The Economic Journal,* 90:18–32.

KAY, N. M. 1979. *The Innovating Firm: A Behavioral Theory of Corporate R&D.* New York: St. Martin's Press.

KELLEY, H. H. 1967. Attribution Theory in Social Psychology. In D. Levine, ed., *Nebraska Symposium on Motivation.* Lincoln: University of Nebraska Press.

KELMAN, S. 1985. The Grace Commission: How Much Waste in Government? *Public Interest,* 78:62–82.

KENNEDY, W. R., JR., AND R. W. LEE. 1984. *A Taxpayer Survey of the Grace Commission Report.* Ottawa, Ill.: Jameson Books.

KIESLER, S., AND L. S. SPROULL. 1982. Managerial Response to Changing Environments: Perspectives on Problem Sensing from Social Cognition. *Administrative Science Quarterly,* 27:548–570.

KINGDON, J. W. 1984. *Agendas, Alternatives, and Public Policies.* Boston: Little, Brown.

KINGSLEY, D. 1944. *Representative Bureaucracy.* Yellow Springs, Ohio: Antioch Press.

KISER, L. L., AND E. OSTROM. 1982. The Three Worlds of Action: A Metatheoretical Synthesis of Institutional Approaches. In E. Ostrom, ed., *Strategies of Political Inquiry.* Beverly Hills, Calif.: Sage Publications.

KISTIAKOWSKY, G. B. 1976. *A Scientist in the White House.* Cambridge, Mass.: Harvard University Press.

KJELLBERG, F. 1975. *Political Institutionalization.* London: Wiley.

KLAPP, M. G. 1987. *The Sovereign Entrepreneur: Oil Policies in Advanced and Less Developed Countries.* Ithaca, N.Y.: Cornell University Press.

KLOSTER, K. 1984. U-hjelpsforvaltningen: En analyse av (re) organiseringsprosessen, og en drofting av mulige konsekvenser av reorganiseringen for politikkens innhold. Oslo: Institutt for Statsvitenskap: Hovedfags dissertation.

KOHN, M. G., AND S. SHAVELL. 1974. Optimal Adaptive Search. *Journal of Economic Theory,* 9:93–124.

KRAINES, O. 1958. *Congress and the Challenge of Big Government*. New York: Bookman.

KRAINES, O. 1970. The President Versus Congress: the Keep Commission, 1905–1909, First Comprehensive Presidential Inquiry Into Administration. *Western Political Science Quarterly*, 23:5–54.

KRASNER, S. D. 1978. *Defending the National Interest: Raw Materials, Investments and the U.S. Foreign Policy*. Princeton: Princeton University Press.

KRASNER, S. D. 1984. Approaches to the State: Alternative Conceptions and Historical Dynamics. *Comparative Politics*, 1:223–246.

KRASNER, S. D. 1988. Sovereignty: An Institutional Perspective. *Comparative Political Studies*, 21:66–94.

KREHBIEL, K. 1987. Why are Congressional Committees Powerful? *American Political Science Review*, 81:929–935.

KREINER, K. 1976. Ideology and Management in a Garbage Can Situation. In J. G. March and J. P. Olsen, eds., *Ambiguity and Choice in Organizations*. Bergen: Universitetsforlaget.

KREPS, D., AND R. WILSON. 1982. Reputation and Imperfect Information. *Journal of Economic Theory*, 27:253–279.

KRIEGER, S. 1979. *Hip Capitalism*. Beverly Hills, Calif.: Sage Publications.

KRISLOV, S. 1974. *Representative Bureaucracy*. Englewood Cliffs, N.J.: Prentice-Hall.

KRISLOV, S., AND D. H. ROSENBLOOM. 1981. *Representative Bureaucracy and the American Political System*. New York: Praeger.

KRISTENSEN, O. P. 1984. Privatisering: modernisering af den offentlige sektor eller ideologisk korstog. *Nordisk Administrativt Tidsskrift*, 65:96–117.

KRISTENSEN, O. P. 1987a. Alliancer og konflikter i forbindelse med privatisering. Paper presented at the FAFO Seminar on Privatization, Oslo.

KRISTENSEN, O. P. 1987b. *Væksten i den offentlige sektor: Institutioner og politik*. Copenhagen:Jurist-og Økonomiforbundets forlag.

KRISTENSEN, O. P. 1987c. Privatization. In J. Kooiman and K. A. Eliassen, eds., *Managing Public Organizations: Lessons From Contemporary European Experience*. London: Sage.

KROGH, F. E. 1987. *Reoganiseringen av Statoil*. Bergen:University of Bergen, Department of Administration: Hovedfags dissertation.

KURZ, M. 1978. Altruism as an Outcome of Social Interaction. *American Economic Review*, 68:216–222.

LA FOLLETTE, R. M., JR. 1947. Systematizing Congressional Control. In Federal Executive Reorganization Reexamined: A Symposium, II. *American Political Science Review*, 41:58–68.

LADD, E. C. 1987. The Reagan Phenomenon and Public Attitudes Toward Government. In L. M. Salamon and M. S. Lund, eds., *The Reagan Presidency and the Governing of America*. Washington, D.C.: The Urban Institute Press.

References

LÆGREID, P. 1983. Medbestemmingsretten i den offentlige sektor og det politiske demokrati. In T. Bergh, ed., *Deltakerdemokratiet*. Oslo: Universitetsforlaget.

LÆGREID, P., AND J. P. OLSEN. 1978. *Byråkrati og beslutninger*. Bergen: Universitetsforlaget.

LÆGREID, P., AND J. P. OLSEN. 1984. Top Civil Servants in Norway: Key Players—On Different Teams. In E. N. Suleiman, ed., *Bureaucrats and Policy Making*. New York: Holmes and Meier.

LAFFERTY, W. M. 1981. *Participation and Democracy in Norway*. Oslo: Universitetsforlaget.

LAKOFF, S. A. 1966. *Knowledge and Power: Essays on Science and Government*. New York: Free Press.

LANCE, B. 1977. Foreword. In T. G. Fain, ed., *Federal Reorganization: The Executive Branch*. New York: Bowker.

LANGER, E. J. 1975. The Illusion of Control. *Journal of Personality and Social Psychology*, 32:311–328.

LAVE, C. A., AND J. G. MARCH. 1975. *An Introduction to Models in the Social Sciences*. New York: Harper and Row.

LEE, W. 1971. *Decision Theory and Human Behavior*. New York: Wiley.

LEEMANS, A. F., ed. 1976. *The Management of Change in Government*. The Hague: Martinus Nijhoff.

LEGRAND, J., AND R. ROBINSON. 1984. *Privatisation and the Welfare State*. London: Allen and Unwin.

LEHMBRUCH, G. 1984. Concertation and the Structure of Corporatist Networks. In J. H. Goldthorpe, ed., *Order and Conflict in Contemporary Capitalism*. Oxford: Clarendon.

LEHMBRUCH, G. 1985. Neo Corporatism in Western Europe: A Reassessment of the Concept in Cross-National Perspective. Constance: University of Constance, Department of Political Science: Unpublished manuscript.

LEIBFRIED, S. 1979. *The Bureaucracy of the "Statist Reserve": The Case of the U.S.A.* Ithaca, N.Y.: Cornell University, Western Societies Program: Occasional Papers No. 12.

LEISERSON, A. 1947. Political Limitations on Executive Reorganization. In Federal Executive Reorganization Reexamined: A Symposium, II. *American Political Science Review*, 41:68–84.

LEVI, E. H. 1949. *An Introduction to Legal Reasoning*. Chicago: University of Chicago Press.

LEVI, M. 1981. The Predatory Theory of Rule. *Politics and Society*, 10:431–465.

LEVINE, C. H. 1986. The Federal Government in the Year 2000: Administrative Legacies in the Reagan Years. *Public Administration Review*, 46:195–206.

LEVINE, C. H., AND M. G. HANSEN. 1985. The Centralization-Decentralization Tug-of-War in the New Executive Branch. Paris: Unpublished manuscript.

193

LEVINTHAL, D. 1988. A Survey of Agency Models of Organizations. *Journal of Economic Behavior and Organization*, 9:153–185.

LEVINTHAL, D., AND J. G. MARCH. 1981. A Model of Adaptive Organizational Search. *Journal of Economic Behavior and Organization*, 2:307–333.

LEVITT, B. 1988. Institutional Constraints on Decision-making in the Textbook Industry. Stanford University, Department of Sociology: Ph.D. dissertation.

LEVITT, B., AND J. G. MARCH. 1988. Organizational Learning. *Annual Review of Sociology*, 14:319–340.

LINDBLOM, C. E. 1959. The "Science" of Muddling Through. *Public Administration Review*, 19:79–88.

LINDBLOM, C. E. 1977. *Politics and Markets*. New York: Basic Books.

LINDLEY, D. V. 1973. *Making Decisions*. New York: Wiley.

LIPSET, S. M. 1986. Historical Traditions and National Characteristics: A Comparative Analysis of Canada and the United States. *Canadian Journal of Sociology*, 11:113–155.

LIPSET, S. M., AND S. ROKKAN. 1967. Cleavage Structures, Party Systems, and Voter Alignments: An Introduction. In S. M. Lipset and S. Rokkan, eds., *Party Systems and Voter Alignments*. New York: Free Press.

LIPSET, S. M., AND W. SCHNEIDER. 1987. *The Confidence Gap*, revised ed. Baltimore: The Johns Hopkins University Press.

LIPSON, L. 1964. *The Democratic Civilization*. New York: Oxford University Press.

LO [Sweden]. 1986. *Fackföreningsrörelsen och välfärdsstaten. Rapport till 1986 års LO-kongress från LOs utredning om den offentliga sektorn*. Stockholm: Swedish Federation of Trade Unions (LO).

LONG, N. 1958. The Local Community as an Ecology of Games. *American Journal of Sociology*, 44:251–261.

LOPES, L. L. 1987. Between Hope and Fear: The Psychology of Risk. *Advances in Social Psychology*, 20:255–295.

LOTTO, L. S. 1982. Revisiting the Role of Organizational Effectiveness in Educational Evaluation. Presented at meetings of the American Educational Research Association, New York.

LOTTO, L. S. 1983. More on Loose Coupling. *Administrative Science Quarterly*, 28:294–296.

LOUNAMAA, P., AND J. G. MARCH. 1987. Adaptive Coordination of a Learning Team. *Management Science*, 33:107–123.

LOWI, T. J. 1969. *The End of Liberalism*. New York: Norton.

LUCE, R. D., AND H. RAIFFA. 1957. *Games and Decisions*. New York: Wiley.

LUNDQUIST, L. 1988. Byråkratisk etik. Lund: University of Lund, Department of Political Science: Unpublished manuscript.

LUNDQUIST, L., AND K. STÅHLBERG. 1982. *Byråkrater i Norden*. Åbo: Åbo Akademi, Meddelande No. 83.

194

References

MACHIAVELLI, N. [1513] 1940. *The Prince and the Discourses*. New York: Modern Library.

MACINTYRE, A. 1988. *Whose Justice? Which Rationality?* Notre Dame, Ind.: University of Notre Dame Press.

MACNEIL, N., AND H. W. METZ. 1956. *The Hoover Report 1953–55: What It Means to You as a Citizen and Taxpayer*. New York: Macmillan.

MANNS, C., AND J. G. MARCH. 1978. Financial Adversity, Internal Competition, and Curriculum Change in a University. *Administrative Science Quarterly*, 23:541–552.

MANSBRIDGE, J. 1980. *Beyond Adversary Democracy*. New York: Basic Books.

MANSFIELD, H. C. 1969. Federal Executive Reorganization: Thirty Years of Experience. *Public Administration Review*, 29:332–345.

MANSFIELD, H. C. 1970. Reorganizing the Federal Executive Branch: Limits of Institutionalization. *Law and Contemporary Problems*, 35:461–495.

MARCH, J. C., AND J. G. MARCH. 1977. Almost Random Careers: The Wisconsin School Superintendency, 1940–1972. *Administrative Science Quarterly*, 22:377–409.

MARCH, J. C., AND J. G. MARCH. 1978. Performance Sampling in Social Matches. *Administrative Science Quarterly*, 23:434–453.

MARCH, J. G. 1962. The Business Firm as a Political Coalition. *Journal of Politics*, 24:662–678.

MARCH, J. G. 1966. The Power of Power. In D. Easton, ed., *Varieties of Political Theory*. Englewood Cliffs, N.J.: Prentice-Hall.

MARCH, J. G. 1970. Politics and the City. In K. Arrow, J. S. Coleman, A. Downs, and J. G. March, eds., *Urban Processes as Viewed by the Social Sciences*. Washington, D.C.: The Urban Institute Press.

MARCH, J. G. 1971. The Technology of Foolishness. *Civiløkonomen*, 18:4–12.

MARCH, J. G. 1973. Model Bias in Social Action. *Review of Educational Research*, 42:413–429.

MARCH, J. G. 1978. Bounded Rationality, Ambiguity, and the Engineering of Choice. *Bell Journal of Economics*, 9:587–608.

MARCH, J. G. 1980. Science, Politics, and Mrs. Gruenberg. In *National Research Council in 1979*. Washington, D.C.: National Academy of Sciences.

MARCH, J. G. 1981a. Decisions in Organizations and Theories of Choice. In A. Van de Ven and W. Joyce, eds., *Perspectives on Organizational Design and Performance*. New York: Wiley.

MARCH, J. G. 1981b. Footnotes to Organizational Change. *Administrative Science Quarterly*, 26:563–577.

MARCH, J. G. 1982. Theories of Choice and Making Decisions. *Transaction/SOCIETY*, 20:29–39.

MARCH, J. G. 1984. How We Talk and How We Act: Administrative Theory and Administrative Life. In T. J. Sergiovanni and John E. Corbally, eds., *Leadership and Organizational Cultures*. Urbana: University of Illinois Press.

MARCH, J. G. 1987. Ambiguity and Accounting: The Elusive Link Between Information and Decision Making. *Accounting, Organizations, and Society*, 12:153–168.

MARCH, J. G. 1988a. *Decisions and Organizations*. Oxford: Basil Blackwell.

MARCH, J. G. 1988b. Variable Risk Preferences and Adaptive Aspirations. *Journal of Economic Behavior and Organization*, 9:5–24.

MARCH, J. G. 1988c. Preferences, Power, and Democracy. In I. Shapiro and G. Reeher, eds., *Power, Inequality and Democratic Politics*. Boulder, Colo.: Westview Press.

MARCH, J. G., AND J. P. OLSEN. 1975. The Uncertainty of the Past: Organizational Learning Under Ambiguity. *European Journal of Political Research*, 3:147–171.

MARCH, J. G., AND J. P. OLSEN. 1976. *Ambiguity and Choice in Organizations*. Bergen: Universitetsforlaget.

MARCH, J. G., AND J. P. OLSEN. 1983. Organizing Political Life: What Administrative Reorganization Tells Us About Government. *American Political Science Review*, 77:281–297.

MARCH, J. G., AND J. P. OLSEN. 1984. The New Institutionalism: Organizational Factors in Political Life. *American Political Science Review*, 78:734–749.

MARCH, J. G., AND J. P. OLSEN. 1986a. Garbage Can Models of Decision Making in Organizations. In J. G. March and R. Weissinger-Baylon, eds., *Ambiguity and Command: Organizational Perspectives on Military Decision Making*. Cambridge, Mass.: Ballinger.

MARCH, J. G., AND J. P. OLSEN. 1986b. Popular Sovereignty and the Search for Appropriate Institutions. *Journal of Public Policy* (Cambridge University Press), 6:341–370.

MARCH, J. G., AND P. ROMELAER. 1976. Position and Presence in the Drift of Decisions. In J. G. March and J. P. Olsen, eds., *Ambiguity and Choice in Organizations*. Bergen: Universitetsforlaget.

MARCH, J. G., AND G. SEVÓN. 1984. Gossip, Information and Decision Making. In L. S. Sproull and P. D. Larkey, eds. *Advances in Information Processing in Organizations*, Vol. 1. Greenwich, Conn.: JAI Press.

MARCH, J. G., AND Z. SHAPIRA. 1982. Behavioral Decision Theory and Organizational Decision Theory. In G. R. Ungson and D. N. Braunstein, eds. *Decision Making: An Interdisciplinary Inquiry*. Boston: Kent.

MARCH, J. G., AND Z. SHAPIRA. 1987. Managerial Perspectives on Risk and Risk Taking. *Management Science*, 33:1404–1418.

MARCH, J. G., AND H. A. SIMON. 1958. *Organizations*. New York: Wiley.

MARCH, J. G., AND L. S. SPROULL. 1989. Technology, Management, and Competitive Advantage. In P. S. Goodman and L. S. Sproull, eds., *Technology and Organizations*. San Francisco: Jossey-Bass.

References

MARSHALL, T. H. 1950. *Citizenship and Social Class and Other Essays.* Cambridge: Cambridge University Press.

MARTINUSSEN, W. 1988. *Solidaritetens grenser.* Oslo: Universitetsforlaget.

MARX, K. [1838] 1961. *Capital: A Critical Analysis of Capitalist Production.* Translated by S. Moore and E. Aveling. Moscow: Foreign Language Publishing House.

MASHAW, J. L. 1985. Prodelegation: Why Administrators Should Make Political Decisions. *Journal of Law, Economics, and Organization,* 1:81–100.

MASTERS, R. D. 1983. The Biological Nature of the State. *World Politics,* 35:161–193.

MAYNARD SMITH, J. 1978. Optimization Theory in Evolution. *Annual Review of Ecological Systems,* 9:31–56.

MAYNTZ, R. 1979. Public Bureaucracies and Policy Implementation. *International Social Science Journal,* 31:632–645.

MAYNTZ, R. 1983. The Conditions of Effective Public Policy: A New Challenge for Policy Analysis. *Policy and Politics,* 11:123–143.

MAYNTZ, R., AND F. SCHARPF. 1975. *Policy-Making in the German Federal Bureaucracy.* Amsterdam: Elsevier.

MAYR, E. 1963. *Population, Species, and Evolution.* Cambridge, Mass.: Harvard University Press.

McNEIL, K., AND J. THOMPSON, 1971. The Regeneration of Social Organizations. *American Sociological Review,* 36:624–637.

MEIER, K. J. 1980. Executive Reorganization of Government: Impact on Employment and Expenditures. *American Journal of Political Science,* 24:396–412.

MELLBOURN, A. 1986. *Bortom det starka samhället.* Stockholm: Carlssons.

MERIAM, L., AND L. F. SCHMECKEBIER. 1939. *Reorganization of the National Government: What Does It Involve?* Washington, D.C.: Brookings.

MERTON, R. K. 1957. *Social Theory and Social Structure.* New York: Free Press.

MESSINGER, S. L. 1955. Organizational Transformation: A Case Study of a Declining Social Movement. *American Sociological Review,* 20:3–10.

METCALFE, L., AND S. RICHARDS. 1987. *Improving Public Management.* London: Sage.

MEYER, J. W., AND B. ROWAN. 1977. Institutionalized Organizations: Formal Structure as Myth and Ceremony. *American Journal of Sociology,* 83:340–363.

MEYER, J. W., AND S. R. SCOTT. 1983. *Organizational Environments: Ritual and Rationality.* Beverly Hills, Calif.: Sage Publications.

197

MILES, R. E., JR. 1977. Considerations for a President Bent on Reorganization. *Public Administration Review,* 37:155–162.

MILL, J. S. [1861] 1962. *Considerations on Representative Government.* South Bend, Ind.: Gateway Editions.

MILL, J. S. [1862] 1950. Bentham. In *Mill on Bentham and Coleridge.* London: Chatto and Windus.

MILLER, D. 1982. Evolution and Revolution: A Quantum View of Structural Change in Organizations. *Journal of Management Studies,* 19:131–151.

MILLER, N. 1983. Pluralism and Social Choice. *American Political Science Review,* 77:734–747.

MILLETT, J. D. 1949. Departmental Management. *American Political Science Review,* 43:959–966.

MILLETT, J. D., AND L. ROGERS. 1941. The Legislative Veto and the Reorganization Act of 1939. *Public Administration Review,* 1:176–189.

MOE, R. C. 1978. *Executive Branch Reorganization: An Overview.* Washington, D.C.: Senate Committee on Governmental Affairs, Committee Print.

MOE, T. M. 1984. The New Economics of Organization. *American Journal of Political Science,* 28:739–777.

MOORE, W. E. 1970. *The Professions: Roles and Rules.* New York: Russell Sage Foundation.

MORGAN, D. R., AND J. P. PELISSERO. 1980. Urban Policy: Does Political Structure Matter? *American Political Science Review,* 74:999–1006.

MOSHER, F. C. 1965. Some Notes on Reorganizations in Public Agencies. In R. C. Martin, ed., *Public Administration and Democracy.* Syracuse, N.Y.: Syracuse University Press.

MOSHER, F. C., ed. 1967. *Government Reorganization: Cases and Commentary.* Indianapolis: Bobbs-Merrill.

MOSHER, F. C., ed. 1974. *Watergate: Implications for Responsible Government.* New York: Basic Books.

MOSHER, F. C., ed. 1975. *American Public Administration: Past, Present, Future.* University: University of Alabama Press.

MUSICUS, M. 1964. Reappraising Reorganization. *Public Administration Review,* 24:107–112.

NAGEL, J. H. 1975. *The Descriptive Analysis of Power.* New Haven: Yale University Press.

NAS, T. F., A. C. PRICE, AND C. T. WEBER. 1986. A Policy-Oriented Theory of Corruption. *American Political Science Review,* 80:107–119.

NATHAN, R. P. 1975. *The Plot that Failed: Nixon and the Administrative Presidency.* New York: Wiley.

NATHAN, R. P. 1976. The Administrative Presidency. *Public Interest,* 44:40–54.

NATHAN, R. P. 1986. Institutional Change Under Reagan. In J. L. Palmer, ed., *Perspectives on the Reagan Years*. Washington, D.C.: The Urban Institute Press.

NELSON, R. R., AND S. G. WINTER. 1982. *An Evolutionary Theory of Economic Change*. Cambridge, Mass.: Harvard University Press.

NELSON, R. R., AND D. YATES. 1978. *Innovation and Implementation in Public Organizations*. Lexington, Mass.: Lexington Books.

NEUMANN, S. 1957. Comparative Politics: A Half Century Appraisal. *Journal of Politics,* 19:369–390.

NEWLAND, C. A. 1984. Executive Office Policy Approaches: Enforcing the Reagan Agenda. In L. M. Salamon and M. S. Lund, eds., *The Reagan Presidency and the Governing of America*. Washington, D.C.: The Urban Institute Press.

NEWSLETTER. 1986. SSRC Study Group on the Structure and Organization of Government, Vol. 1, No. 1. New York: Social Science Research Council.

NISBET, R., AND L. ROSS. 1980. *Human Inference: Strategies and Shortcomings of Social Judgement*. Englewood Cliffs, N.J.: Prentice-Hall.

NISKANEN, W. A. 1971. *Bureaucracy and Representative Government*. Chicago: Rand McNally.

NIXON PAPERS. *See* Executive Office of the President (Nixon).

NOLL, R. G. 1971. *Reforming Regulation: An Evaluation of the Ash Council Proposals, A Staff Paper*. Washington, D.C.: Brookings.

NONET, P., AND P. SELZNICK. 1978. *Law and Society in Transition: Towards Responsive Law*. New York: Harper and Row.

NORDLINGER, E. 1981. *On the Autonomy of the Democratic State*. Cambridge, Mass.: Harvard University Press.

NORTH, D. C. 1981. *Structure and Change in Economic History*. New York: Norton.

NORTH, D. C. 1986. The New Institutional Economics. *Journal of Institutional and Theoretical Economics,* 142:230–237.

NYSTROM, P. C., AND W. H. STARBUCK, eds. 1981. *Handbook of Organizational Design*. Oxford: Oxford University Press.

OECD. 1980. *Strategies for Change and Reform in Public Management*. Paris: OECD.

OECD. 1983. *Positive Adjustment Policies: Managing Structural Change*. Paris: OECD.

OECD. 1987. *Administration as Service: The Public as Client*. Paris: OECD.

OFFE, C. 1984. *Contradictions of the Welfare State*. London: Hutchinson.

OFFERDAL, A. 1986. Om det rasjonelle og det rimelige. *Norsk Statsvitenskapelig Tidsskrift,* 1:3–19.

OLSEN, J. P. 1970. Local Budgeting: Decision Making or a Ritual Act? *Scandinavian Political Studies,* 5:85–118.

OLSEN, J. P. 1972. 'Voting,' 'Sounding Out,' and the Governance of Modern Organizations. *Acta Sociologica*, 15:267–283.

OLSEN, J. P. 1976a. Reorganization as a Garbage Can. In J. G. March and J. P. Olsen, eds., *Ambiguity and Choice in Organizations*. Bergen: Universitetsforlaget.

OLSEN, J. P. 1976b. The Process of Interpreting Organizational History. In J. G. March and J. P. Olsen, eds., *Ambiguity and Choice in Organizations*. Bergen: Universitetsforlaget.

OLSEN, J. P. 1976c. University Governance: Non-Participation as Exclusion or Choice. In J. G. March and J. P. Olsen, eds., *Ambiguity and Choice in Organizations*. Bergen: Universitetsforlaget.

OLSEN, J. P. 1976d. Choice in an Organized Anarchy. In J. G. March and J. P. Olsen, eds., *Ambiguity and Choice in Organizations*. Bergen: Universitetsforlaget.

OLSEN, J. P. 1981. Integrated Organizational Participation in Government. In P. C. Nystrom and W. H. Starbuck, eds., *Handbook of Organizational Design*, Vol. 2. New York: Oxford University Press.

OLSEN, J. P. 1983. *Organized Democracy*. Bergen: Universitetsforlaget.

OLSEN, J. P. 1985. Nyinstitusjonalismen og statsvitenskapen. *Statsvetenskaplig Tidsskrift* [Sweden], 88:1–14.

OLSEN, J. P. 1986a. Foran en ny offentlig revolusjon. *Nytt Norsk Tidsskrift*, 3:3–15.

OLSEN, J. P. 1986b. Privatisering og forvaltningspolitikk. *Norsk Statsvitenskapelig Tidsskrift*, 1:51–57.

OLSEN, J. P. 1988a. The Modernization of Public Administration in the Nordic Countries: Some Research Questions. *Hallinnon Tutkimus* [Administrative Studies, Finland], 7:2–17.

OLSEN, J. P. 1988b. Administrative Reform and Theories of Organization. In C. Campbell and B. G. Peters, eds., *Organizing Governance. Governing Organizations*. Pittsburgh: University of Pittsburgh Press.

OLSEN, J. P. 1988c. Political Science and Organization Theory: Parallel Agendas But Mutual Disregard. In *Festschrift to Gerhard Lehmbruch*. Constance, Forthcoming.

OLSEN, J. P. 1989. *Petroleum og politikk*. Oslo: Tano.

OLSEN, J. P., P. RONESS, AND H. SÆTREN. 1982. Still Peaceful Co-Existence and Revolution in Slow Motion? In J. J. Richardson, ed., *Policy Styles in Western Europe*. London: Allen and Unwin.

OLSEN, J. P., AND H. SÆTREN. 1980. *Aksjoner og demokrati*. Bergen: Universitetsforlaget.

OLSON, M. 1965. *The Logic of Collective Action*. Cambridge, Mass.: Harvard University Press.

References

OLSON, M. 1982. *The Rise and Decline of Nations*. New Haven: Yale University Press.

OLSON, O., ed. 1987. *Kommunal årsrapportering—om utviklingen til nå og et alternativ*. Oslo: Bedriftsøkonomens Forlag.

ORDESHOOK, P. C. 1986. *Game Theory and Political Theory: An Introduction*. Cambridge: Cambridge University Press.

OSTROM, V. 1973. *The Intellectual Crisis in American Public Administration*. University: University of Alabama Press.

ØVRELID, R. 1984. *Rettssikkerhet eller demokrati*. Oslo: Universitetsforlaget.

ØYSTESE, O. 1980. *Staten i en skjebnetime*. Oslo: Lunde.

PADGETT, J. F. 1981. Hierarchy and Ecological Control in Federal Budgetary Decision Making. *American Journal of Sociology*, 87:75–129.

PARENTI, M. 1978. *Power and the Powerless*. New York: St. Martin's Press.

PATEMAN, C. 1970. *Participation and Democratic Theory*. Cambridge: Cambridge University Press.

PATEMAN, C. 1985. *The Problem of Political Obligation*. Berkeley: University of California Press.

PATTANAIK, P. K. 1971. *Voting and Collective Choice*. Cambridge: Cambridge University Press.

PEMBERTON, W. E. 1979. *Bureaucratic Politics: Executive Reorganization During the Truman Administration*. Columbia: University of Missouri Press.

PETERS, B. G. 1984. *The Politics of Bureaucracy*, 2nd ed. New York: Longmans.

PETERS, T. J. 1978. Symbols, Patterns and Settings: An Optimistic Case for Getting Things Done. *Organizational Dynamics*, 7:3–23.

PETERSSON, O., AND J. FREDEN. 1987. *Statens symboler*. Uppsala: Maktutredningen.

PFEFFER, J. 1981a. Management as Symbolic Action: The Creation and Maintenance of Organizational Paradigms. In L. Cummings and B. M. Staw, eds., *Research in Organizational Behavior*. Vol. 3. Greenwich, Conn.: JAI Press.

PFEFFER, J. 1981b. Some Consequences of Organizational Demography: Potential Impacts of an Aging Work Force on Formal Organizations. In S. Kiesler, J. N. Morgan, and V. K. Oppenheimer, eds., *Aging: Social Change*. New York: Academic Press.

PFEFFER, J. 1981c. *Power in Organizations*. Marshfield, Mass.: Pitman.

PFEFFER, J. 1982. *Organizations and Organization Theory*. Marshfield, Mass.: Pitman.

PFEFFER, J., AND G. SALANCIK. 1978. *The External Control of Organizations: A Resource Dependence Perspective*. New York: Harper and Row.

PINKETT, H. T. 1965. The Keep Commission, 1905–1909: A Rooseveltian Effort for Administrative Reform. *Journal of American History*, 52:297–312.

PITKIN, H. 1967. *The Concept of Representation*. Berkeley: University of California Press.

PITKIN, H. 1981. Justice: On Relating Private and Public Political Theory. *Political Theory*, 9:327–352.

PITZ, G. F., AND N. J. SACHS. 1984. Judgment and Decision: Theory and Application. *Annual Review of Psychology*, 35:139–163.

POGGI, G. 1978. *The Development of the Modern State*. Stanford: Stanford University Press.

POLENBERG, R. 1966. *Reorganizing Roosevelt's Government: The Controversy Over Executive Reorganization 1936–39*. Cambridge, Mass.: Harvard University Press.

POLLITT, C. 1984. *Manipulating the Machine*. London: Allen and Unwin.

POLSBY, N. W. 1980. *Community Power and Political Theory*, 2nd ed. New Haven: Yale University Press.

PONDY, L. R. 1978. Leadership as a Language Game. In M. W. McCall, Jr., and M. M. Lombardo, eds., *Leadership*. Durham: Duke University Press.

POSNER, R. A. 1973. *Economic Analysis of Law*. Boston: Little, Brown.

POSNER, R. A. 1981. *Economic Analysis of Justice*. Cambridge, Mass.: Harvard University Press.

POTTER, A. L. 1979. Political Institutions, Political Decay and the Argentine Crises of 1930. Stanford University, Department of Political Science: Ph.D. dissertation.

POWELL, W. W. 1978. Publishers' Decision-Making: What Criteria Do they Use in Deciding Which Books to Publish? *Social Research*, 45:227–252.

PRESIDENT'S ADVISORY COMMITTEE ON MANAGEMENT. 1952. Improvement of Management in the Federal Government. Reprinted in *Public Administration Review*, 1953, 13:38–49.

PRESIDENT'S COMMITTEE ON ADMINISTRATIVE MANAGEMENT (BROWNLOW COMMITTEE). 1937. *Report of the President's Committee: Administrative Management in the Government of the United States*. Washington, D.C.: U.S. Government Printing Office.

PRESSMAN, J. L., AND A. B. WILDAVSKY. 1973. *Implementation*. Berkeley: University of California Press.

PRICE, D. K. 1975. 1984 and Beyond: Social Engineering or Political Values? In F. C. Mosher, ed., *American Public Administration: Past, Present, Future*. University: University of Alabama Press.

PRIMACK, J., AND F. VON HIPPEL. 1976. *Advice and Dissent: Scientists in the Political Arena*. New York: Basic Books.

PRZEWORSKI, A. 1986. Popular Sovereignty, State Autonomy, and Private Property. *Archives Européennes de Sociologie*, 27:215–259.

References

PYE, L., AND S. VERBA, EDS. 1965. *Political Culture and Political Development.* Princeton: Princeton University Press.

RAWLS, J. 1971. *A Theory of Justice.* Cambridge, Mass.: Harvard University Press.

REDFORD, E. S. 1950. The Value of the Hoover Commission Reports to the Educator. *American Political Science Review,* 44:283–298.

REDFORD, E. S., AND M. BLISSETT. 1981. *Organizing the Executive Branch.* Chicago: University of Chicago Press.

REES, J. 1985. *Natural Resources.* London: Methuen.

REGERINGENS SKRIVELSE. (#202) 1984/85. Den offentliga sektorns förnyelse. Stockholm: Swedish government.

RIKER, W. H. 1962. *The Theory of Political Coalitions.* New Haven: Yale University Press.

RIKER, W. H. 1982. *Liberalism Against Populism: A Confrontation Between the Theory of Democracy and Theory of Social Choice.* San Francisco: Freeman.

ROBERTS, C., ed. 1973. *Has the President Too Much Power?* New York: Harper's Magazine Press.

ROBINS, R. S. 1976. *Political Institutionalization and the Integration of Elites.* Beverly Hills, Calif.: Sage Publications.

ROGERS, E. M. 1962. *Diffusion of Innovations.* New York: Free Press.

ROGERS, E. M., AND F. F. SHOEMAKER. 1971. *Communication of Innovations.* New York: Free Press.

ROGERS, L. 1938. Reorganization: Post Mortem Notes. *Political Science Quarterly,* 53:161–172.

ROKKAN, S. 1966. Norway: Numerical Democracy and Corporate Pluralism. In R. A. Dahl, ed., *Political Oppositions in Western Democracies.* New Haven: Yale University Press.

ROMMETVEIT, K. 1976. Decision Making Under Changing Norms. In J. G. March and J. P. Olsen, eds., *Ambiguity and Choice in Organizations.* Bergen: Universitetsforlaget.

RONESS, P. 1979. *Reorganisering av departementa. Eit politisk styringsmiddel?* Bergen: Universitetsforlaget.

ROOS, L. L., JR., AND R. HALL. 1980. Influence Diagrams and Organizational Power. *Administrative Science Quarterly,* 25:57–71.

ROSE, R. 1984. *Understanding Big Government.* London: Sage.

ROSS, L. 1977. The Intuitive Psychologist and His Shortcomings: Distortion in the Attribution Process. In L. Berkowitz, ed., *Advances in Experimental Social Psychology.* New York: Academic Press.

ROSS, M., AND F. SICOLY. 1979. Egocentric Biases in Availability and Attribution. *Journal of Personality and Social Psychology,* 37:322–336.

203

Ross, S. A. 1973. The Economic Theory of Agency: The Principal's Problem. *American Economic Review,* 63:134–139.

Rourke, F. E. 1957. The Politics of Administrative Organization: A Case History. *Journal of Politics,* 19:461–478.

Rueschemeyer, D., and P. B. Evans. 1985. The State and Economic Transformation: Toward an Analysis of the Conditions Underlying Effective Intervention. In P. B. Evans, D. Rueschemeyer, and T. Skocpol, eds., *Bringing the State Back In.* Cambridge: Cambridge University Press.

Ruin, O. 1982. Sweden in the 1970's: Policy-Making Becomes More Difficult. In J. J. Richardson, ed., *Policy Styles in Western Europe.* London: Allen and Unwin.

Sætren, H. 1983. *Iverksetting av offentlig politikk.* Bergen: Universitetsforlaget.

Sait, E. M. 1938. *Political Institutions—A Preface.* New York: Appleton-Century Crofts.

Salamon, L. M. 1981a. The Goals of Reorganization. *Administration and Society,* 12:471–500.

Salamon, L. M. 1981b. The Question of Goals. In P. Szanton, ed., *Federal Reorganization: What Have We Learned?* Chatham, N.J.: Chatham House.

Salamon, L. M., and A. J. Abramson. 1984. Governance: The Politics of Retrenchment. In J. L. Palmer and I. V. Sawhill, eds., *The Reagan Record.* Cambridge, Mass.: Ballinger.

Salamon, L. M., and M. S. Lund, eds. 1987. *The Reagan Presidency and the Governing of America.* Washington, D.C.: The Urban Institute Press.

Sangolt, L. 1984. Institusjonell endring—Sjøfartsdirektoratets tilpasning til petroleumsvirksomheten, 1966–1984. Bergen: University of Bergen, Department of Administration: Hovedfags dissertation.

Sarason, S. B. 1986. And What is the Public Interest? *American Psychologist,* 41:899–905.

Savage, L. J. 1954. *Foundations of Statistics.* New York: Wiley.

Savas, E. S. 1982. *Privatizing the Public Sector: How to Shrink Government.* Chatham, N.J.: Chatham House.

Schaffer, B. B. 1980. Insiders and Outsiders: Insideness, Incorporation and Bureaucratic Politics. *Development and Change,* 1:187–210.

Scharpf, F. W. 1977a. Public Organization and the Waning of the Welfare State: A Research Perspective. *European Journal of Political Research,* 5:339–362.

Scharpf, F. W. 1977b. Does Organization Matter? Task Structure and Interaction in the Ministerial Bureaucracy. In E. H. Burack and A. R. Negandhi, eds., *Organization Design: Theoretical Perspectives and Empirical Findings.* Kent, Ohio: Kent State University Press.

Scharpf, F. W. 1986. Policy Failure and Institutional Reform: Why Should

Form Follow Function? *International Social Science Journal,* 37:179–189.

SCHATTSCHNEIDER, E. E. 1960. *The Semi-Sovereign People.* New York: Holt, Rinehard & Winston.

SCHELLING, T. C. 1960. *The Strategy of Conflict.* Cambridge, Mass.: Harvard University Press.

SCHELLING, T. C. 1978. *Micromotives and Macrobehavior.* New York: Norton.

SCHER, S. 1962. The Politics of Agency Organization. *Western Political Quarterly,* 15:328–344.

SCHICK, A. 1975. The Trauma of Politics: Public Administration in the Sixties. In F. C. Mosher, ed., *American Public Administration: Past, Present, and Future.* University: University of Alabama Press.

SCHMITTER, P., AND G. LEHMBRUCH, eds. 1979. *Trends Toward Corporatist Intermediation.* Beverly Hills, Calif.: Sage Publications.

SCHOEMAKER, P. J. H. 1982. The Expected Utility Model: Its Variants, Purposes, Evidence and Limitations. *Journal of Economic Literature.* 20:529–63.

SCHOFIELD, N. 1982. Bargaining Set Theory and Stability in Coalition Governments. *Mathematical Social Science,* 3:9–31.

SCOTT, W. R. 1987a. *Organizations: Rational, Natural, and Open Systems,* 2nd ed. Englewood Cliffs, N.J.: Prentice-Hall.

SCOTT, W. R. 1987b. The Adolescence of Institutional Theory. *Administrative Science Quarterly,* 32:493–511.

SEIDMAN, H. 1974. Remarks. In D. M. Fox, ed., President Nixon's Proposals for Executive Reorganization. *Public Administration Review,* 34:487–495.

SEIDMAN, H. 1980. *Politics, Position and Power: The Dynamics of Federal Organization,* 3rd ed. New York: Oxford University Press.

SEIP, J. 1958. *Teorien om Det Opinionsstyrte Eneveldet.* Oslo: Universitetsforlaget.

SEJERSTED, F. 1984. *Demokrati og rettsstat.* Oslo: Universitetsforlaget.

SELZNICK, P. 1949. *TVA and the Grass Roots.* Berkeley: University of California Press.

SELZNICK, P. 1957. *Leadership in Administration.* New York: Harper and Row.

SELZNICK, P. 1968. Law: The Sociology of Law. In D. Sills, ed., *International Encyclopedia of the Social Sciences.* New York: Macmillan and Free Press.

SEN, A. K. 1970. *Collective Choice and Social Welfare.* Edinburgh: Oliver and Boyd.

SEN, A. K. 1982. *Choice, Welfare, and Measurement.* Oxford: Basil Blackwell.

SEN, A. K. 1985. Goals, Commitment, and Identity. *Journal of Law, Economics, and Organization,* 1:341–355.

SHARKANSKY, I. 1979. *Whither the State?* Chatham, N.J.: Chatham House.

SHARPE, W. F. 1970. *Portfolio Theory and Capital Markets*. New York: McGraw-Hill.

SHEPSLE, K., AND B. WEINGAST. 1983. Institutionalizing Majority Rule: A Social Choice Theory With Policy Implications. *American Economic Review*, 73:357–372.

SHEPSLE, K., AND B. WEINGAST. 1987a. The Institutional Foundations of Committee Power. *American Political Science Review*, 81:85–104.

SHEPSLE, K., AND B. WEINGAST. 1987b. Why Are Congressional Committees Powerful? *American Political Science Review*, 81:935–945.

SHORT, L. M. 1923. *The Development of National Administrative Organization in the United States*. Baltimore: The Johns Hopkins University Press.

SHORT, L. M. 1947. Adjusting the Departmental System. In Federal Executive Reorganization Re-examined: A Symposium, II. *American Political Science Review*, 41:48–58.

SIEGEL, G. B., AND N. KLEBER. 1965. Formalism in Brazilian Administrative Reform. *International Review of Administrative Sciences*, 31:175–184.

SILLS, D. L. 1957. *The Volunteers*. New York: Free Press.

SIMON, H. A. 1957a. *Administrative Behavior*, 2nd ed. New York: Macmillan.

SIMON, H. A. 1957b. *Models of Man*. New York: Wiley.

SIMON, H. A., D. W. SMITHBURG, AND V. A. THOMPSON. 1950. *Public Administration*. New York: Knopf.

SINGH, J. V. 1986. Performance, Slack, and Risk Taking in Organizational Decision Making. *Academy of Management Journal*, 29:562–585.

SJÖBLOM, S., AND K. STÅHLBERG. 1987. *Att uveckla förvaltningen, En beskrivning av förvaltningsreformkomiteer i Finland årene 1975–1987*. Åbo: Åbo Akademi.

SKOCPOL, T. 1979. *States and Social Revolutions: A Comparative Analysis of France, Russia, and China*. Cambridge: Cambridge University Press.

SKOCPOL, T. 1980. Political Response to Capitalist Crises: Neo-Marxist Theories of the State and the Case of the New Deal. *Politics and Society*, 10:155–201.

SKOCPOL, T., AND K. FINEGOLD. 1982. State Capacity and Economic Intervention in the Early New Deal. *Political Science Quarterly*, 97:255–278.

SKOWRONEK, S. 1982. *Building a New American State*. Cambridge: Cambridge University Press.

SLAGSTAD, R. 1987. *Rett og politikk*. Oslo: Universitetsforlaget.

SLOVIC, P. 1966. Value as a Determiner of Subjective Probability. *IEEE Transactions on Human Factors in Electronics*, 7(1).

SMITH, R. M. 1988. Political Jurisprudence, the ''New Institutionalism,'' and the Future of Public Law. *American Political Science Review*, 82:89–108.

SNOW, C. P. 1961. *Science and Government*. Cambridge, Mass.: Harvard University Press.

SÖDERLIND, D., AND O. PETERSSON. 1986. *Svensk Förvaltningspolitik*. Uppsala: Diskurs.

SOU (#40). 1985. Regeringen, myndigheterna, och myndigheternas ledning. Stockholm: Swedish government.

SPROULL, L., S. WEINER, AND D. WOLF. 1978. *Organizing an Anarchy*. Chicago: University of Chicago Press.

STARBUCK, W. H. 1976. Organizations and Their Environments. In M. D. Dunnette, ed., *Handbook of Industrial and Organizational Psychology*. Chicago: Rand McNally.

STAVA, P. 1976. Constraints on Politics of Public Choice. In J. G. March and J. P. Olsen, eds., *Ambiguity and Choice in Organizations*. Bergen: Universitetsforlaget.

STAW, B. 1976. Knee-Deep in the Big Muddy: A Study of Escalating Commitment to a Chosen Course of Action. *Organizational Behavior and Human Performance*, 16:27–44.

STAW, B. 1981. The Escalation of Commitment to a Course of Action. *Academy of Management Review*, 6:577–587.

STAW, B., AND E. SZWAJKOWSKI. 1975. The Scarcity-Munificence Component of Organizational Environments and the Commission of Illegal Acts. *Administrative Science Quarterly*, 20:345–354.

STEPHAN, A. C. 1978. *The State and Society: Peru in Comparative Perspective*. Princeton: Princeton University Press.

STIGLER, G. J. 1952. *The Theory of Price*, rev. ed. New York: Macmillan.

STINCHCOMBE, A. 1965. Social Structure and Organizations. In J. G. March, ed., *Handbook of Organizations*. Chicago: Rand McNally.

STINCHCOMBE, A. 1974. *Creating Efficient Industrial Administration*. New York: Academic Press.

STINCHCOMBE, A. 1986a. *Stratification and Organization*. Cambridge: Cambridge University Press.

STINCHCOMBE, A. 1986b. Reason and Rationality. *Sociological Theory*, 4:151–166.

STONE, J. 1950. *The Province and Function of Law*. Cambridge, Mass.: Harvard University Press.

STREECK, W., AND P. C. SCHMITTER. 1985. Community, Market, State—and Associations? The Prospective Contribution of Interest Government to Social Order. In W. Streeck and P. C. Schmitter, eds., *Private Interest Government: Beyond Market and State*. London: Sage.

STUDY OF POWER AND DEMOCRACY IN SWEDEN (#36). 1985. *Committee Instructions*. Stockholm: Study of Power and Democracy in Sweden.

SULEIMAN, E. N. 1987. State Structures and Clientelism: The French State Versus the "Notaires." *British Journal of Political Science*, 17:257–79.

SUNSTEIN, C. R. 1988. Constitutions and Democracies: An Epilogue. In

J. Elster and R. Slagstad, eds., *Constitutionalism and Democracy*. Cambridge: Cambridge University Press.

SWIERINGA, R. J., AND J. H. WATERHOUSE. 1982. Organizational Views of Transfer Pricing. *Accounting, Organizations, and Society,* 7:149–155.

SZANTON, P., ed. 1981. *Federal Reorganization: What Have We Learned?* Chatham, N.J.: Chatham House.

TARSCHYS, D. 1978. *Den offentliga revolutionen.* Stockholm: Liber.

TARSCHYS, D., AND M. EDUARDS. 1975. *Petita: Hur svenska myndigheter argumenterar för högre anslag.* Stockholm: Liber.

TAYLOR, M. 1975. The Theory of Collective Choice. In F. I. Greenstein and N. W. Polsby, eds., *Handbook of Political Science,* Vol. 3. Reading, Mass.: Addison-Wesley.

TAYLOR, S. 1984. *Making Bureaucracies Think.* Stanford: Stanford University Press.

TEUBNER, G. 1983. Substantive and Reflexive Elements in Modern Law. *Law and Society,* 17:239–285.

TEUBNER, G. 1984. After Legal Instrumentalism? Strategic Models of Post-regulatory Law. *International Journal of the Sociology of Law,* 12:375–400.

THERBORN, G. 1980. *What Does the Ruling Class Do When It Rules?* London: Verso.

THOMAS, G. M., ed. 1987. *Institutional Structure: Constituting State, Society, and the Individual.* Beverly Hills, Calif.: Sage Publications.

THOMPSON, D. F. 1980. Moral Responsibility of Public Officials: The Problem of Many Hands. *American Political Science Review,* 74:905–916.

THOMPSON, J. D., AND W. J. MCEWEN. 1958. Organizational Goals and Environment. *American Sociological Review,* 23:23–31.

TILLY, C., ed. 1978. *From Mobilization to Revolution.* Reading, Mass.: Addison-Wesley.

TOLBERT, P. S., AND L. G. ZUCKER. 1983. Institutional Sources of Change in the Formal Structure of Organizations: The Diffusion of Civil Service Reform, 1880–1935. *Administrative Science Quarterly,* 28:22–39.

TRIBE, L. H. 1985. *Constitutional Choices.* Cambridge, Mass.: Harvard University Press.

TRIMBERGER, E. K. 1978. *Revolution From Above: Military Bureaucrats and Development in Japan, Turkey, Egypt, and Peru.* New Brunswick, N.J.: Transaction Books.

TRIVERS, R. 1971. The Evolution of Reciprocal Altruism. *Quarterly Review of Biology,* 46:35–37.

TUGWELL, F. 1975. *The Politics of Oil in Venezuela.* Stanford: Stanford University Press.

TULLOCK, G. 1967. *Toward a Mathematics of Politics.* Ann Arbor: University of Michigan Press.

References

Tushman, M. L., and E. Romanelli. 1985. Organizational Evolution: A Meta-morphosis Model of Convergence and Reorientation. In B. Staw and L. L. Cummings, eds., *Research in Organizational Behavior.* Greenwich, Conn.: JAI Press.

Tyack, D. B. 1976. Pilgrim's Progress: Toward a Social History of the School Superintendency, 1860–1960, *History of Education Quarterly,* 16:259–300.

U.S. Commission on the Organization of the Executive Branch of the Government (First Hoover Commission). 1971 (repint of 1949 edition). *Hoover Commission Report on the Organization of the Executive Branch of the Government.* Westport, Conn.: Greenwood.

Valen, H. 1981. *Valg og politikk.* Oslo: NKS-forlaget.

Van Maanen, J. 1973. Observations on the Making of Policemen. *Human Organization,* 32:407–418.

Vaughan, W., Jr., and R. J. Herrnstein. 1987. Stability, Melioration, and Natural Selection. In L. Green and J. H. Kagel, eds., *Advances in Behavioral Economics,* Vol. 1. Norwood, N.J.: Ablex.

Vickers, G. 1965. *The Art of Judgment.* New York: Basic Books.

Waldo, D. 1961. Organization Theory: An Elephantine Problem. *Public Administration Review,* 21:210–225.

Walker, J. L. 1969. The Diffusion of Innovations Among the American States. *American Political Science Review,* 63:800–899.

Walzer, M. 1983. *Spheres of Justice.* New York: Basic Books.

Wass, D. 1985. The Civil Service at the Crossroads. *Political Quarterly,* 50:227–241.

Waterstone, G. C. 1966. *Order and Counterorder: Dualism in Western Culture.* New York: Philosophical Library.

Weary, F. 1979. Self-Serving Attributional Biases: Perceptional or Response Distortions. *Journal of Personality and Social Psychology,* 37:1418–1420.

Weber, G. A. 1919. *Organized Efforts for the Improvement of Methods of Administration in the United States.* New York: Appleton.

Weber, M. [1924] 1978. *Economy and Society.* Edited by Guenther Roth and Claus Wittich, and translated by Ephraim Fischoff et al. from *Wirtschaft und Gesellschaft.* Berkeley: University of California Press.

Weick, K. 1976. Educational Organizations as Loosely Coupled Systems. *Administrative Science Quarterly,* 21:1–19.

Weick, K. 1979. *The Social Psychology of Organizing,* 2nd. ed. Reading, Mass.: Addison-Wesley.

Weinberg, M. W. 1977. *Managing the State.* Cambridge, Mass.: MIT Press.

Weinberger, C. W. 1978. Government Reorganization and Public Purpose. *Publius,* 8:39–48.

Weiner, S. 1976. Participation, Deadlines, and Choice. In J. G. March and

J. P. Olsen, eds., *Ambiguity and Choice in Organizations.* Bergen: Universitetsforlaget.

Weiss, C., and H. Wollman, eds. 1986. *Social Science and Governmental Institutions.* London: Sage.

Wheeler, H. 1968. *Democracy in a Revolutionary Era: The Political Order Today.* Harmondsworth, Middlesex: Penguin.

White, H. C. 1970. *Chains of Opportunity: System Models of Mobility in Organizations.* Cambridge, Mass.: Harvard University Press.

White, L. D. 1958. *The Republican Era.* New York: Macmillan.

Wildavsky, A. 1987. Choosing Preferences by Constructing Institutions: A Cultural Theory of Preference Formation. *American Political Science Review,* 81:3–22.

Williamson, O. E. 1975. *Markets and Hierarchies: Analysis and Antitrust Implications.* New York: Free Press.

Williamson, O. E. 1985. *The Economic Institutions of Capitalism.* New York: Free Press.

Willoughby, W. F. 1923. *The Reorganization of the Administrative Branch of the National Government.* Baltimore: The Johns Hopkins University Press.

Willower, D. J. 1979. Ideology and Science in Organization Theory. Presented at meetings of the American Educational Research Association, San Francisco.

Wilson, E. O. 1975. *Sociobiology: The New Synthesis.* Cambridge, Mass.: Harvard University Press.

Wilson, H. T. 1985. *Political Management: Redefining the Public Sphere.* Berlin: de Gruyter.

Wilson, J. Q., ed. 1980. *The Politics of Regulation.* New York: Basic Books.

Winston, G. C. 1985. The Reasons for Being of Two Minds. *Journal of Law, Economics, and Organization,* 1:375–379.

Winter, S. G. 1986. The Research Program of the Behavioral Theory of the Firm: Orthodox Critique and Evolutionary Perspective. In B. Gilad and S. Kaish, eds., *Handbook of Behavioral Economics.* Greenwich, Conn.: JAI Press.

Witt, U. 1985. Economic Behavior and Biological Evolution: Some Remarks on the Sociobiology Debate. *Journal of Institutional and Theoretical Economics,* 141:365–389.

Wolin, S. 1960. *Politics and Vision: Continuity and Innovation in Western Political Thought.* Boston: Little, Brown.

Woods, E. C. 1943. A Proposed Reorganization of the Executive Branch of the Federal Government. *American Political Science Review,* 37:476–490.

Wortman, C. B., and J. W. Brehm. 1975. Responses to Uncontrollable Events: An Integration of Reactance Theory and the Learned Helplessness Model. *Advances in Social Psychology,* 8:277–336.

References

WRIGHT, H. T. 1977. Recent Research on the Origin of the State. *Annual Review of Anthropology,* 6:379–397.

WRIGHT, S. 1978. *Evolution and Genetics of Populations,* Vol. 4. Chicago: University of Chicago Press.

WRIGHT, T. P. 1936. Factors Affecting the Cost of Airplanes. *Journal of Aeronautical Sciences,* 3:122–128.

YELLE, L. E. 1979. The Learning Curve: Historical Review and Comprehensive Survey. *Decision Sciences,* 10:302–328.

ZALD, M. N. 1970. *Organizational Change: The Political Economy of the YMCA.* Chicago: University of Chicago Press.

ZINK, H. 1950. Government Reform in the United States of America. *Political Science Quarterly,* 21:69–79.

ZOFFER, H. J. 1976. Introduction. In R. H. Kilman, L. R. Pondy, and D. P. Slevin. *The Management of Organizational Design.* Amsterdam: North-Holland.

ZUCKER, L. G. 1977. The Role of Institutionalization in Cultural Persistence. *American Sociological Review,* 42:726–743.

ZUCKER, L. G. 1986. Production of Trust: Institutional Sources of Economic Structure, 1840 to 1920. In B. Staw and L. L. Cummings, eds., *Research in Organizational Behavior.* Greenwich, Conn.: JAI Press.

ZUCKER, L. G. 1987. Institutional Theories of Organization. *Annual Review of Sociology,* 13:443–464.

Index

Daft, R. L., 41, 60, 62
Dahl, R. A., 9–10, 90, 93, 117, 121, 124–
    125, 130, 134, 139, 143, 147–150,
    152, 154–157
Dahrendorf, R., 3, 24, 155
Dalberg-Larsen, J., 130
Dallmayr, F. R., 118
Dan-Cohen, M., 126, 134
Day, R. H., 159
Deadlines, 29, 164
Debureaucratization, 97
Decentralization, 97, 100
Decision complexity, 14–15
Decision makers, flows of, 5
Decision theory, 160
Decisions, 5; *see also* Choice
    and intention, 50
Democracy, 100, 111; *see also* Popular
    sovereignty
    aggregative, 118–142, 146, 148, 150,
        165
    criteria for, 143
    and future citizens, 144
    geography of, 144
    integrative, 43, 100, 118–142, 144, 157
    liberal, 98, 112
    and population size, 154
Democratic centralism, 156
Dempsey, J. R., 85
Demski, J., 10
Den moderne staten, 174
Den nye staten, 174
Denmark, 99, 102–103, 131
Department of Transportation, 83
Deregulation, 97, 102, 106
Destler, A. M., 90
Deutsch, K. W., 96
Deutsch, M., 40
Diffusion, 59, 137
Dill, W., 62
DiMaggio, P., 2, 118, 128, 137
Dimock, M. E., 76–77, 92
Distance, 151
Division of labor, 26, 30–32
Dockery-Cockrell Commission, 71
Dolliver, J., 80
Downs, A., 8, 57, 120
Downs, G. W., 85, 102, 115

Due process, 101
Durham, G. H., 76
Durkheim, E., 155
Duties, 23, 59, 159, 161; *see also* Obliga-
    tion
Dyson, K., 111, 126

Easton, D., 3
Eckhoff, T., 132, 138, 164
Eckstein, H., 134
Ecologies of action, 8–16
Economic equality, 144, 150, 152; *see also*
    Political equality
Economic rights, 126; *see also* Rights
Economies, as objective of reform, 74–76,
    85
Edelman, M., 7, 48–49, 52, 90, 127
Edlefson, C. J., 49
Eduards, M., 133
Efficacy, of institutions, 129–134
Efficiency, 10
    concept of, 170
    as goal, 103, 105
    as objective of reform, 74–76
    problems of in voluntary exchange, 122
Egeberg, M., 29, 107, 112, 141, 164
Einhorn, H. J., 43
Eisenhower, D. D., 86
Eisenstadt, S. N., 10, 24, 134, 137
Elster, J., 114, 121, 129, 133, 144, 146,
    148, 155
Emmerich, H., 70–72, 74, 81–83, 86–89
Empathy, 126, 144, 147–149
    effects on equality, 149
Enactment of reality, 46–47
    effects of power, 47
Enderud, H., 29, 164
Endowments, as a problem for aggregative
    processes, 130–131
Engwall, L., 47
Enlightened understanding, 144, 154–155,
    157; *see also* Reasoned debate
Environments
    control of politics, 16, 35–36
    creation of, 46–47
Equality; *see* Economic equality; Political
    equality

217

Participation, 11–14, 104, 133, 143
Pateman, C., 48, 124, 135, 144, 147–148
Pattanaik, P. K., 119
Pelissero, J. P., 85
Pemberton, W. E., 75, 78–79, 81, 83, 85, 89–90
Perry, G., 118
Persistence, 60, 86, 108
Peters, B. G., 135, 138
Peters, T. J., 92
Petersson, O., 104, 107
Pfeffer, J., 7, 29, 49, 51–52, 59, 92, 117
Pinkett, H. T., 70–72, 87
Pitkin, H., 117, 123–124, 127–129, 132, 134, 144, 147–148
Pitz, G. F., 43
Plato, 47, 129
Pluralism, 101
Poggi, G., 111, 137
Polenberg, R., 75, 79, 81, 83, 85–86, 88–89
Political aggregation, 157; see also Aggregation
Political change, 165–166; see also Change
Political cleavages, 55
Political community, 165–166; see also Community
Political development, 97, 165
Political discontent, 168–169
Political education, 48; see also Civic education; Socialization
Political equality, 143–146, 154, 157; see also Economic equality
Political institutions; see Institutions
Political integration; see Integration
Political leadership; see Leadership
Political metaphors, 10
Political parties, 169
Political promises, 10
Political realism, 77
Political theory, 118
  institutional perspectives, 1–2, 2–8, 16–18, 118
Politics
  aggregative, 118–142, 146, 148, 150, 165
  and economics, 139–140
  evaluation of, 160

as exchange, 122–124
integrative, 43, 100, 118–142, 144, 157
as interpretation, 47–52
as managing symbols, 51–52
and petroleum, 34–37
and reorganization, 76–78
understanding of, 160
Pollitt, C., 104
Polsby, N. W., 147
Polyarchy, 156
Pondy, L. R., 29, 49, 92
Popular sovereignty, 111, 117–119; see also Democracy
  dilemmas of, 134
  and integrative processes, 140
  voting and, 120
Posner, R. A., 25
Potter, A. L., 2
Powell, W. W., 2, 29, 137
Power, 77, 120
  ambiguity of, 144
  distribution of, 143, 145
  and enactment, 47
  endogeneity, 4
  and indifference, 151–152
  institutional, 97
  and preferences, 143, 151–154
  reputations for, 153–154
  and resources, 113
  subjective, 151
Powerlessness, 152–154
Pragmatism, 108
Preferences, 146, 160; see also Interests
  and aggregative processes, 120–121, 130
  and ambiguity, 40–41, 51, 56, 65–67, 154
  of citizens, 157
  construction of, 124, 162–165
  effects on equality, 150–158
  endogeneity, 4, 6, 121, 130, 143, 154–156, 158
  heterogeneity, 150–154
  inconsistency, 6, 121, 156
  instability of, 6, 121, 146–147, 154, 163–165
  interpersonal comparison of, 143–145
  intertemporal comparison of, 143–146

Index

225

Index